Other Mexicos

Other Mexicos:
Essays on Regional Mexican History, 1876–1911

Edited by
Thomas Benjamin
William McNellie

University of New Mexico Press
Albuquerque

Library of Congress Cataloging-in-Publication Data

Other Mexicos.

   Bibliography: p.
   Includes index.
   1. Mexico—Politics and government—1867–1910—Addresses, essays, lectures. 2. Mexico—Economic conditions—Addresses, essays, lectures. 3. Mexico—Social conditions— Addresses, essays, lectures. 4. Mexico—History, Local—Addresses, essays, lectures. I. Benjamin, Thomas, 1952–   . II. McNellie, William, 1949–
F1233.5.O84 1984   972.08'1   84–5052

© 1984 by the University of New Mexico Press. All rights reserved.
Manufactured in the United States of America.
Library of Congress Catalog Card Number 84-5052.
International Standard Book Number 0-8263-0754-X (cloth).
                                          0-8263-0755-8 (paper).
First edition.

Paperbound ISBN-13: 978-0-8263-0755-2

To David C. Bailey

Contents

Illustrations	ix
Preface	xi
Political Chronology	xv

1 Introduction: Approaching the Porfiriato, *Thomas Benjamin*	3
I *Regional Politics*	27
2 Chihuahua: Family Power, Foreign Enterprise, and National Control, *Mark Wasserman*	33
3 Coahuila: Centralization against State Autonomy, *William Stanley Langston*	55
4 Puebla: Breakdown of the Old Order, *David LaFrance*	77
II *The Rural Economy*	119
5 Soconusco: The Formation of a Coffee Economy in Chiapas, *Daniela Spenser*	123
6 La Sierra de Jacala: Ranchos and Rancheros in Northern Hidalgo, *Frans J. Schryer*	145

III *And the People* 173

7 Sonora: Indians and Immigrants on a Developing
  Frontier, *Evelyn Hu-DeHart* 177
8 Yucatán: Violence and Social Control on Henequen
  Plantations, *Allen Wells* 213
9 La Comarca Lagunera: Work, Protest, and Popular
  Mobilization in North Central Mexico,
  William K. Meyers 243

10 Conclusion: Opportunities for Further Regional Study,
  William H. Beezley 275

  Suggestions for Additional Reading: Still Other
  Mexicos 301

  Editors and Contributors 311

  Index 313

Illustrations

Maps

Mexico, 1910	5
Chihuahua, 1910	35
Coahuila, 1910	57
Puebla, 1910	79
Soconusco, 1910	125
La Sierra de Jacala, 1900	147
Sonora, 1910	179
Yucatán, 1910	215
La Comarca Lagunera, 1910	245

Photographs

President Porfirio Díaz	107
The Plaza, Mexico City	108

General Bernardo Reyes	109
Porfirio Díaz and His Cabinet	110
General Mucio P. Martínez	111
Adobe Huts	112
Watching the Train	113
Indian Home in the Hot Country	114
Pisaflores, 1895	115
Yaqui Indian	116
Campesino Ploughing	117
Peasant Couple	118

Preface

Mexico is both a city and a nation. Mexicans generally refer to the capital city as *México*. The city gave its name to the country. Power, wealth, and learning have been concentrated in the capital for centuries. Its inhabitants have frequently confused their interests with the larger interests of the nation. And yet the city is not the country: there are other Mexicos. Indeed, few countries in the world have such a rich regional diversity. We cannot overlook its regions and know Mexico.

This volume examines Mexican history at the regional level during the age of Porfirio Díaz, the Porfiriato, as it is called today, from 1876 to 1911. The essays review issues of political, economic, and social change in eight regions during a crucial period in Mexican national development. Working from previously neglected vantage points and with long ignored archival materials, the contributing authors refine, deepen, and reassess widely held generalizations about the nation as a whole. Each essay can stand alone as an original contribution to Mexican historiography. The sum, however, is greater than the parts. Together they begin the process of reconstructing the history of a modernizing nation.

The essays written for this volume embody a diversity of regional perspectives on one well-defined epoch in Mexican history. There is balance, but there is not pretense of treating all regions or issues. Regional Mexico is vast; relevant topics and issues are almost inexhaustible; and regional Porfirian scholarship has only just reached its adolescence. It is precisely because of these limitations, and the challenge they evoke, that we believe this volume serves useful purposes at this time. We present these selections to expand the understanding and coverage of this era in Mexican history, to exhibit the range and nature of research done so far, to suggest the possibilities inherent in regional studies, and to spur further regional investigation.

We express our thanks to the contributors for their patient cooperation. Their team spirit is responsible for the success of this project. The good advice of David V. Holtby, editor at the University of New Mexico Press, and that of the referee, is gratefully acknowledged. We also extend our appreciation to the Faculty Research and Creative Endeavors Committee of Central Michigan University for financial assistance toward the preparation of this volume. One of the enjoyable by-products of the preparation of this book was the session entitled "Regional Perspectives on Social and Economic Change in Porfirian Mexico" at the 1982 annual meeting of the American Historical Association in Washington, D.C. The session was chaired by Professor John M. Hart of the University of Houston. Evelyn Hu-DeHart and Frans J. Schryer presented their papers on Sonora and the Sierra de Jacala, included here, and Thomas Benjamin discussed the evolution of Porfirian historiography. Mark Wasserman commented on the "triumph of the periphery" in the recent historiography.

Finally, and sadly, we dedicate this volume to our teacher, David C. Bailey, professor of Latin American history at Michigan State University, who died on 19 November 1982. Professor Bailey studied with the late Charles C. Cumberland at Michigan State University, where he received his doctorate in 1969. He completed for publication Professor Cumberland's *Mexican Revolution: The Constitutionalist Years* (1972) and authored *¡Viva Cristo Rey! The Cristero Rebellion and the Church-State Conflict in Mexico* (1974). Professor Bailey's abiding interest was the Catholic Church in Latin America, but he was also fascinated by Mexico's regional variety. He coauthored, with William H. Beezley, *A Guide to Historical Sources in Saltillo, Coahuila* (1975) to promote the "doing" of regional history. With his enthusiastic support and encouragement, Professor Bailey's three doctoral students researched topics in regional Mexican history. Dave Bailey was an exemplary teacher, a meticulous scholar, and a true professional. Those of us who knew him, however, will always remember him as an altogether decent human being. He was our good friend and we will miss him.

Thomas Benjamin
St. Mary's Lake, Michigan

William McNellie
Falls Church, Virginia

Political Chronology

1876	Porfirio Díaz's successful rebellion against President Sebastián Lerdo de Tejada
1877–1880	First presidency of Díaz
1878	Constitutional amendment prohibiting successive presidential reelection
1880–1884	Presidency of Manuel González
1884–1888	Second presidency of Díaz
1887	Constitutional amendment permitting immediate presidential reelection
1888–1892	Third presidency of Díaz
1890	Constitutional amendment permitting indefinite presidential reelection
1892–1896	Fourth presidency of Díaz
1896–1900	Fifth presidency of Díaz
1900–1904	Sixth presidency of Díaz
1904	Constitutional amendment creating a six-year presidential term and the office of vice-president
1904–1910	Seventh presidency of Díaz
1908	Creelman interview
1910	Reelection of Díaz and publication of Francisco Madero's *Plan de San Luis Potosí,* calling for Díaz's overthrow
1910–1911	Rise of anti-Díaz insurrection
1911	Resignation and exile of Díaz

Other Mexicos:
Essays on Regional Mexican History, 1876–1911

1
Introduction: Approaching the Porfiriato

Thomas Benjamin

"From the outside looking in," as Mark Wasserman describes regional history, is but one way of approaching the Porfiriato.[1] It is an approach which should broaden rather than restrict our view of late nineteenth- and early twentieth-century Mexican history. From the perspective of any one region it makes less sense to limit the field of vision to precisely those years (1876–1911) which seemingly have been carved in stone in Mexican historiography. The flow of events was somewhat different in the periphery than at the center. It also makes less sense to focus exclusively on a small group of actors who lived and exercized power in the national capital. To most Mexicans Porfirio Díaz was less real, less important than the local boss. Taking the nation apart to examine its regions, to see how they have changed over time, and to explore their interrelationships and their connections to national and international developments is ultimately a powerful way to broaden our understanding of Mexico as a nation and as a region itself within the larger global community. Regional history need not be provincial.

The regional approach also complements another approach, long-practiced and dominant, which might be characterized as the center looking out, or perhaps, the center looking at itself. The so-called national perspective, that is, the view from Mexico City, too often has been narrowly confined to purely metropolitan affairs. In studying the societal architecture of this and other periods in Mexican history both approaches are required. To understand the whole, we examine its parts; to understand those parts, and how they form one entity, we must also have an approximate understanding of the whole. The process is reciprocal and historical.

Many Mexicos

"There is more than one Mexico," observes Victor Alba. "Its history can never be spoken of in the singular."[2] Time and geography have created many Mexicos. Geographic, climatic, ethnic, cultural, and linguistic diversity, combined with a variety of economic patterns and forms of political administration, have produced a patchwork quilt of localities and regions. The *patria chica*, the immediate society of the village, *hacienda, ranchería,* or *municipio,* have long claimed the first allegiance of most Mexicans. Resilient local attachment has become a defining characteristic of Mexican nationality. The many thousands of localities blend into hundreds of regions. Many of these, of course, are artificial constructs designed for political administration (such as districts, departments, and states). Most, however, are indeterminate areas possessing some kind of unifying character. Regions achieve a certain authentic coherence through geographical or climatic distinction, cultural and economic consistency, and common historical experience. Identification with the region also characterizes Mexicans and, historically, has been much stronger than nationalism.[3]

Regionalism has always coexisted uneasily with central control, or pretensions of central control, in Mexican history. The Aztec empire was not a singular political structure but a confederation of three separate and sovereign city-states situated in the Valley of Mexico. The empire of the Three City League, as a result, was

Mexico, 1910

loosely conceived and inefficiently administered. It was never a homogeneous block of territory but a mixture of subject peoples paying tribute to one or another of the three imperial city-states, interspersed with a few independent peoples, such as the Tlascalans. The Aztec conquerors imposed tribute requirements on the subdued provincials but did not impose their language, customs, or internal political structure. The Aztecs sought booty, not loyal citizens. The Spanish invaders capitalized on the survival of strong and resentful native regionalism by attracting as allies numerous Indian states who also sought the destruction of the league's most powerful member, the city of México, Tenochtitlán.[4]

Castilian rule of New Spain was centralist and hierarchical in design but weak, loose, and flexible in operation. Regionalism, so pervasive throughout the Iberian Peninsula, survived in the Spanish immigrants to Mexico, where it found an even more receptive environment. Under the Hapsburg dynasty (1517–1700) the imperial structure yielded to local conditions and political realities, accepted regional self-interest, and tried to balance imperial and regional needs. The system worked, but that was not good enough for the Bourbon dynasty of the eighteenth century. They wanted, and instituted, an empire that was more responsive to central control by the crown and more economically beneficial to Spain. Bourbon centralization of government challenged regional authority; liberalization of trade, however, stimulated regional economies and strengthened the elite families doing business there. Regionalism, temporarily repressed, emerged even stronger when the Bourbon system collapsed, in 1808. When Mexico achieved independence, in 1821, it was a nation in name only. Sovereignty was fragmented; the nominally national government of Mexico City tried to exercize authority over numerous regional regimes which in turn attempted, with about the same lack of success, to preside over numerous municipal regimes. Many Mexicos was never a more accurate description of this land than during the first half of the nineteenth century.[5]

Perhaps, if one did not look beyond the Valley of Mexico, a nation could be imagined. Certainly the residents of Mexico City were willing to accept such an illusion. After all, they possessed the National Palace, the National Cathedral, and—most important of all—the national treasury; they wrote the national laws and drew up the maps of the national territory, which they called Mexico. Outside the Valley, however, the concept of Mexico was questionable. The country possessed only three highways, which barely extended beyond the central plateau, and they were in hopeless disrepair. At least a third of all Mexicans did not speak the national language (more than that in the South). For the vast majority of its citizens, "Mexico was an abstraction not easily fathomed, and even neighbors in the next village were not really trusted."[6] What did the presidio of Tucson have in common with the farming rancherías of the Bajío or the Tzotzil hamlets in the highlands of Chiapas? What was Mexico?

"The absurdity of this handful of men pretending to impose laws upon the whole republic," wrote Fanny Calderón de la Barca, wife of the Spanish minister to Mexico, in 1840.[7] Her reference was to a specific clique but it has much wider validity. Mexico was ungovernable. The record is legendary: thirty different individuals headed more than fifty different governments during Mexico's first fifty years of national existence. In the same period there were eight hundred revolts.[8] State governments were no more stable. There were genuinely national institutions—the Church, the army, and important commercial interests—but rarely were their partisans, the Centralists, able to secure the consent of the provinces and their bosses. Federalists, those with a vested interest in regional autonomy, fared only slightly better as national leaders. Regional *caudillos* who were elevated to the presidency by their peers discovered that the National Palace was in the center of enemy territory. Federalism, as a more informal system of triumphant regionalism maintained by constant disorder, was successful.

By the mid-1840s the fractured republic fell prey to the expansionist republic to the north. The loss of one-half of the national territory, the northern provinces, as a result of the Mexican-American War nearly destroyed what was left of the nation. "Mexico had become many Mexicos in fact," noted Lesley Byrd Simpson: "The municipal district of Cuernavaca seceded from the state of Mexico, and the district of Yautepec seceded from Cuernavaca. Mexico split into cells, and the cells into more cells, each with its cacique making and interpreting laws, and collecting taxes and import duties as he pleased."⁹ It was the beginning of a twenty-year national nightmare of dictatorship and reform, civil war and foreign intervention, and finally national regeneration.

The crisis generated by the war with the United States transformed the Centralists into monarchical Conservatives and the Federalists into centralizing Liberals. The latter party seized control of the debilitated national government in the mid-1850s and began imposing reforms which undermined the institutional power and prerogatives of the Church and the army and encouraged republicanism, capitalism, and individualism. Their model was the United States. The former party responded by going to war and, when that failed, by inviting a Hapsburg prince, backed by French troops, to rule Mexico. Their model was Bourbon New Spain. In the ensuing struggle, the War of Reform and the French Intervention (1859–61 and 1861–67), a new nationalism was forged. The war began to break down the isolation of the many Mexicos; it moved large numbers of soldiers and their hangers-on across the length and breadth of the country; it was a nationally shared experience. The process of nation building under Liberal guidance and the leadership of Benito Juárez, however, required expedient compromises. The military triumph of the Liberal party was substantially based upon alliances with powerful regional caudillos. And their interests remained the same: local autonomy. But even before the conclusion of the conflict, and with even more vigor thereafter, the Liberals began the delicate and dangerous process of bringing them to heel, one by one.¹⁰

The development of national governmental authority during the ten-year Restored Republic (1867–76) was dependent, in part, upon exploiting political fragmentation within the regions of Mexico. Presidents Juárez (1858–72) and Sebastián Lerdo de Tejada (1872–76) supported cooperative governors and regional caudillos in their local factional struggles. The rivals of uncooperative and unfriendly regional chiefs, on the other hand, readily found national government support in their own bids for power. Over time a new generation of regional leaders emerged, leaders who found it beneficial and sometimes necessary to get along with the national government. This political strategy was not without risk, however. The losers of the regional power struggles played the same game, lending their assistance to opponents of the national government. One of the most important of these opponents was Porfirio Díaz, a Liberal general during the wars and a regional caudillo with national ambitions. As the national government consolidated power in regional Mexico, many of the discontents gravitated toward Díaz. His revolt against the Juárez regime, in 1871–72, was premature and failed, but by 1876 the imposing Benemerito was dead. Díaz's revolt that year against President Lerdo de Tejada succeeded. The new caudillo of Mexico had harnessed the bronco of regional discontent; it remained to be seen whether he could ride it.[11]

Díaz's Mexico

The Mexico that Porfirio Díaz sought to control in 1876 was still very much a plural entity. It was still a land of disconnected regions, isolated pockets of distinct peoples, segregated economies, and local sovereigns; but less so than before. In the mid-1850s the Liberals had seized control of hardly anything at all. Their bequest to Díaz by the mid-1870s was at least an outline of a nation, a stronger sense of nationalism, and fewer regional strongmen. Díaz followed the strategy of Juárez and Lerdo de Tejada to extend his control over the states. There is no doubt that he was a skilled practitioner of the method. Through shrewd political alliances, electoral manipulations, liberal rewards to supporters, and the selective use of violence against opponents, Díaz was able to increase his own power, diminish regional autonomy, and establish a kind of peace. At the same time, regional Mexico was also becoming more accommodating. In the states of Sonora and Sinaloa, as Stuart F. Voss shows, political and economic elites "premised their control of state government on the determination that the realization of progress required the forging of close, working connections with those who directed the nation's politics in Mexico City. Only with such direct federal assistance could the region's security be assured, its transportation greatly improved, its politics stabilized (in their hands preferably)."[12] From the national level downward and from the regional level upward a nation was being constructed.

During his first term in office, from 1877 to 1880, President Díaz proceeded cautiously. Conciliation rather than confrontation guided his actions. Potential rivals were given well-paid but insignificant government posts, often attached to Mexican embassies abroad. Where possible Díaz eased supporters into gubernatorial posts and regional military commands, but he did not challenge the remaining powerful regional caudillos. Despite this caution, heavy military expenditures, and lucrative payoffs, Díaz still faced rebellions in Guerrero, Colima, Jalisco, Veracruz, Baja California, and Sinaloa. During his first term, writes Paul J. Vanderwood, "Díaz barely hung on."[13]

The cautious caudillo also limited himself, at first, to one term in office. Having come to power pledged to the principle of no reelection, he could continue in power only at great peril. At his request, therefore, Congress amended the constitution in 1878 and prohibited successive reelection. A number of candidates thereupon threw their hats into the ring, but Díaz supported General Manuel González, a Díaz loyalist with some political influence in his own right. With Díaz's support and intervention, González was elected president for the term from 1880 to 1884.[14]

President González, while always loyal to Díaz, was his own man, as recent research has demonstrated. The new president accomplished much with respect to political centralization and economic development that assisted Díaz's consolidation of control of the country after 1884. Unfortunately for González but fortuitously for Díaz, Mexico suffered a financial crisis caused by a recession, in 1883–84. Economic problems, combined with charges of corruption and favoritism, discredited González and led to calls for the return of Díaz to the presidency. There had been no question in González's mind, or anyone else's, that Díaz would return to power in 1884. The crisis, however, insured a successful restoration that greatly expanded Díaz's freedom of action in his succeeding terms of office.[15]

During the next eight years, Díaz maneuvered himself into a position of unassailable power. Manuel González had been discredited, in large part, by an increasingly hostile press. To forestall a similar fate for himself, President Díaz began his second term with a campaign to bridle the press by means of fines, imprisonment, and (allegedly) even the assassination of certain editors and journalists.[16] Díaz retired more than five hundred army officers, of whom twenty-five were generals, and shifted commands for the rest so that no officer could easily build a personal following.[17] He continued to place more unconditional supporters in key military posts, in Congress, in the judiciary, and in state palaces. Díaz even went to the trouble to select numerous *jefes políticos,* local political prefects, for districts around the nation. Opponents were either bought off with jobs and cash or imprisoned, exiled, or, if necessary, killed. Díaz became the hero of the peace, *el necesario,* the only man who could discipline Mexico. When he asked Congress in 1887 to approve a single reelection, there was little opposition. Once reelected in 1888, the President proceeded to the final coup. In 1890 Congress removed all restrictions on reelection and in 1892 Díaz had achieved, or so it seemed, life tenure.[18]

Don Porfirio capitalized on national exhaustion and enforced stability by inviting foreign investment into a most hospitable Mexico. The regime awarded generous concessions to foreign entrepreneurs (or their Mexican agents) and sacrificed village lands to commercial agriculture. A reorganized rural police force protected property and enforced labor discipline, while important legislative reforms established a more rational and capitalistic economic environment. As a result foreign capital built a network of railroads throughout the country, revitalized mining, expanded and modernized the textile industry, initiated petroleum exploration and recovery, began steel production, and revolutionized semitropical commercial agriculture. The increase of banking, manufacturing, and commercial endeavors, results of foreign economic penetration from the 1880s to the early 1900s, dazzled both Mexicans and foreign observers. Economic growth also created a solvent national government which further enhanced Díaz's power and prestige.[19]

"The principle of national authority," don Porfirio once said, "justifies itself more and more in Mexico."[20] The ruling elite at all levels and in all regions agreed; between 1892 and 1911 Porfirio Díaz was reelected president four times. It appears that he possessed the consent of the governed. The middle and upper classes, by and large, viewed Díaz as indispensable to the continuation of peace and progress. They measured his (and their) success with statistical tables: more railroad mileage, greater agricultural and industrial production, more pieces of mail carried by the postal service, etc.[21] Villagers, workers, ranchers, peons, and Indians also appear to have supported the president. To judge from an extensive but unscientific sampling of letters in Díaz's personal archive, Mexico's *gente ordinaria* saw the president as a man of justice and a friend who would help them, if only he understood their particular difficulties.[22] Díaz also attracted the enthusiastic backing of foreign investors, entrepreneurs, and financiers, a significant new constituency. The North American journalist James Creelman mentions in his book that when Díaz suffered a slight illness in 1901, reported as life threatening, "instantly the price of Mexican bonds fell in the markets of Europe and Porfirio from $101 to $78."[23] Porfirio Díaz became a legend in his own time—"the greatest statesman now living," said President Theodore Roosevelt.[24] The progress of Díaz's Mexico seemed spectacular to contemporary observers. There were spectacular shortcomings as well.

The burden of evidence supports the conclusion that the modernization of Mexico under Díaz, as Frank Tannenbaum put it, "was coincident with the lowering standards of life for the masses of the people."[25] Railroads enhanced production and commerce but also precipitated the seizure of village lands by *hacendados* and land speculators, aided by new land laws. Certainly fewer Mexicans owned land by the end of Díaz's tenure and more of them had less to eat. The expansion of commercial agriculture for export in southern Mexico led to an increase in indebted servitude and, in some places, de facto slavery. Industrialization created a new class of Mexicans who received a wage that often did not provide even the bare necessities of life. Industrial working conditions were unsafe, workdays and workweeks were excessively long, and workers' efforts to defend their rights and advance their collective interests were repressed. Although Mexico City possessed new street lamps, fine theaters, and imposing public buildings—the standard monuments of progress—the city for most of its residents was overcrowded, expensive, and dirty, and also a dangerous place to live because of diseases, accidents, and violent crime. For most Mexicans progress meant poverty.[26]

Success in politics, as in economic modernization, was structurally defective. Díaz's personal monopolization of power occurred at the expense of the development of political institutions and respect for law. Administration of the nation by the mid-1890s had gravitated into the hands of an elitist political clique close to the president, led by Treasury Secretary José Y. Limantour and called the *científicos*. Rigidity came to characterize the system, resulting in less turnover in officeholders and the creation of a threatening generation gap between the ins and the outs. During the last decade of his rule, Díaz increasingly lost contact with the reality of the country and often resorted to violence instead of compromise. His retention of power at an advanced age (he was seventy in 1900) led to the fracturing of his political machine and eventually to a succession crisis. The high politicians of Mexico City and the provinces—the científicos and their opponents in and out of the regime—began their devisive maneuvering for position in the early 1900s. In the midst of a severe international recession and widespread industrial unrest in 1908, Díaz announced his desire to step down and permit democracy in Mexico. Although he soon changed his mind, running for reelection and winning in 1910, it was too late. An invisible but very real breastwork protecting the regime had been breached. Mexico had begun the search for Díaz's replacement without Díaz. When the son of a northern hacendado promised political democracy and his supporters took up arms, the regime disintegrated with surprising rapidity and ease.[27]

Until the very end it seemed to nearly all observers in and out of the country that Díaz had created a nation, one Mexico, and it was his. The changes that he and his collaborators introduced and presided over were national both in scope and effect. Mexico's integration into the North Atlantic economy during the Porfiriato was felt in every region. And, more than ever before, Mexico possessed a national economy. Policies promoting political centralization and economic modernization were designed to create one nation out of many isolated and disparate parts. The task was monumental and its realization was substantial. In Díaz's time, wrote historian Daniel Cosío Villegas, "Mexico began to have the appearance, and even the essence, of a modern state and of a true nation."[28] The revolutions that engulfed Mexico after Díaz, however, were regional phenomena. Díaz's Mexico had repressed but not supplanted its many selves.

Many Porfiriatos

National policies and international capitalism during the age of Díaz percolated through the different physical, human, and historical geographies of the regions and their localities. This process, paradoxically, facilitated national consolidation and greater local and regional distinction. The disparate nature of the Porfirian experience can clearly be seen in two villages in the state of Michoacán. The Porfiriato was a time of peace and prosperity for the predominantly mestizo population of San José de Gracia. Land was not concentrated in the hands of a few, but rather was held by ranchers whose numbers increased during this period. Wages were low but oppressive peonage did not exist. For most San Joseanos, life was probably better in 1910 than it had been thirty years before. The Tarascan Indians of Naranja, on the other hand, lost most of their land to outsiders, Hispanic hacendados, during the Porfiriato. Naranjeños after 1900 were forced into sharecropping arrangements and, for part of the year, migration to lowland plantations to earn thirty-seven centavos for a ten-hour day. For these Indian villagers the Porfiriato was a prolonged nightmare. Life became harder; family life was disrupted; diet, housing, and clothing deteriorated.[29]

The Porfiriato, village by village or even region by region, was an aggregate of what would seem to be innumerable unique histories. A broader perspective is necessary to avoid the confusion of too many Porfiriatos. To this end scholars have delineated a rough arrangement of three macroregions: the central core, the southern periphery, and the northern periphery. The central core comprises the high mountain valleys of the Mesa Central, extending along a wide axis from Guadalajara to Puebla and including the port city of Veracruz. The southern periphery extends beyond Morelos and Puebla, from Guerrero in the southwest to Yucatán in the southeast. The northern periphery includes everything above a line from Tepic, on the Pacific coast, through Aguascalientes and San Luis Potosí, to Tampico, on the gulf. A brief examination of these macroregions, of change within them and differentiation between them, indicates the importance of persistent regionalism within Díaz's Mexico.[30]

When Porfirio Díaz seized power in 1876, he inherited the tradition of political hegemony on the part of central Mexico. Here was located much of Mexico's population, urban development, wealth, commerce, industry, and arable land. Control of the country was impossible without control of the larger states in the Center, particularly the states which straddled the country's economic lifeline—Puebla and Veracruz.[31] The Rurales, Mexico's rural police force, not surprisingly, were concentrated in central Mexico. Three corps, out of a total of ten, protected the Mexico City–Veracruz railway.[32]

The commercialization of agriculture and the concentration of land tenure, general trends throughout Porfirian Mexico, were particularly harmful to the numerous free Indian and mestizo villages of central Mexico. Regarding the two villages in Michoacán discussed above, the ruinous experience of Naranja was the more common. The expropriation of village lands was perhaps milder in the Bajío and in the region of Guadalajara, but was certainly more severe in lowland areas of Veracruz, Morelos, Michoacán, Colima, and Jalisco, where plantation crops were cultivated for export. The massive expropriations, coupled with population increases, created a large class of landless campesinos, some of whom became industrial workers but most of whom remained in the countryside as temporary contract laborers and sharecroppers.[33]

Central Mexico became more closely interconnected during the Porfiriato, as it developed into the hub of national rail traffic. "Frantic railroad construction under [President Manuel] González allowed Mexico City to regain a political, economic, and social prominence it had not known since colonial days."[34] The expansion of cheap, rapid transport increased the flow of foreign capital and technology into Mexican industry and agriculture and from there into the Center.[35]

The southern periphery offers a striking contrast to the Center. While the Mesa Central tended to unify the Center, geography divided regions in the South from each other and from the Center. Railroad lines further integrated the Center but contributed to regional separation in the South. Common features such as political marginality, a large Indian population, commercial agriculture for export, and forms of coerced labor made the southern periphery a distinctive macroregion during the Porfiriato.

States in the South were of marginal political importance during the Porfiriato because they offered only a slight threat to the national government. Rurales were stationed in Guerrero and Oaxaca, states where insurgent movements in the recent past had helped bring down governments in Mexico City. Beyond the Isthmus of Tehuantepec, however, there were none.[36] Although more studies are needed before any detailed political portrait of the southern periphery can be drawn, available evidence suggests that Díaz did face internal conflicts in the South, but nothing he could not handle. Opposing factions in Oaxaca "appeared almost ludicrous in their indecent haste to curry favor with the dictator."[37] In Guerrero and Chiapas, the president imposed reliable outsiders as governors. Oligario Molina possessed great political and economic power in Yucatán, yet this did not stop Don Porfirio from detaching the territory of Quintana Roo from the state, in 1902, which "represented a political defeat for the region as well as a severe economic loss."[38] The South, it would seem, was tame and harmless.

An increase in the cultivation of plantation crops, primarily henequen, sugar, rubber, chicle, coffee, and tobacco, transformed life and work in the South. The commercialization of agriculture, at the behest of foreign capital and in response to rising world prices, led to a massive transfer of sparsely settled national lands to private ownership. Nearly 50 percent of the total territorial extension of Tabasco and Chiapas, for example, passed to colonization companies.[39] In central Mexico the concentration of landholdings produced a labor surplus, but in the South a similar development led to seasonal labor scarcity, debt peonage, and, in some places, slavery. Southern plantations were generally not located in or near large population centers, so that large numbers of harvest workers had to be enticed, recruited, and forced to the plantations and kept there until the work was done. The rise of plantation agriculture, the survival of free villages in the highlands and hinterlands, increased labor scarcity and coercion, and the inadequate expansion of railroads, discouraged agricultural diversification and industrialization. In a country of unbalanced development, the southern periphery led the way.[40]

During the Porfiriato the vast, isolated, and sparsely inhabited northern periphery "experienced more definitive change than in all its previous history."[41] Railroad construction, large foreign investment, industrialization and the mining of industrial minerals, the commercialization of agriculture and the accompanying appropriation of public lands, and the development of the American Southwest all transformed the North into Mexico's most dynamic macroregion.[42]

Railroads, beginning in the 1880s, linked central Mexico with the United States. The north-south network of iron rails, in league with an influx of United States investment, turned small towns into cities, opened up new lands and pastures to commercial exploitation, increased the value of nearby land, and thereby led to the appropriation of public land and its concentration in a few hands. The creation of huge *latifundios,* however, was also accompanied by the expansion of small and medium-size landholdings. The railroads also fed U.S. industries the products of northern mines: zinc, copper, iron, and lead. The growth of mining centers, in turn, increased the demand for foodstuffs.[43]

The expansion of the economy in the North was not as injurious to villagers, campesinos, and smallholders as it was in the central core or the southern periphery. Economic growth in this sparsely populated region led to labor scarcity, competition for workers, a rising wage level, and attractive land rental and sharecropping schemes. Resident peons on northern haciendas, according to Friedrich Katz, possessed a markedly higher standard of living than their counterparts in the South.[44] Even so, there were significant exceptions to this beneficent economic transformation. Yaqui Indians, possessers of the fertile Yaqui Valley in Sonora, were brutally expelled from their lands. Frontier military colonies in Chihuahua lost much of their land and political independence. Miners, cowboys, industrial workers, and migrant farm hands, although well paid when employed, were vulnerable to the business cycle and were thrown out of work during recessions.[45]

Political control of the northern periphery assumed new importance to the national government during the Porfiriato. Díaz moved to destroy the independence of northern caudillos as much to shape and tap into the economic expansion of the region as to extend the power of the national government. Although he achieved more control in some states than in others, it was clear that state autonomy no longer was tolerated by Mexico City. One indication of the increasing importance of the North was the placement of Rurales.

In 1886 the northernmost post was located in the troublesome state of Nayarit. By 1910, however, there were Rurales in Aguascalientes, San Luis Potosí, Nuevo León, Coahuila, Chihuahua, and Sonora.[46] The political importance of the northern periphery was most dramatically underscored in 1910–11. The insurrection which toppled Díaz emerged not in the vital Center or the dismal South, but in the faraway, dynamic, and relatively prosperous North.[47]

In an age of political centralization and economic modernization, regionalism lingered and had an influence on national development that only recently has come to be more fully appreciated. National political consolidation coincided with increasing regional economic variation. Díaz's Mexico was still a complex mosaic of regions. There were many Porfiriatos. From our perspective the pattern is faint, incomplete, and, in places, confusing. There is work to be done.

Other Mexicos

The region has long attracted the attention of those who write history in Mexico and elsewhere, but until recently the other Mexicos were the literary province of amateurs and antiquarians. Regional Mexican history was written with care and pride, unearthing and recording useful information that otherwise might have been lost. This history was written for a limited, local audience, which it informed and entertained, but only rarely did it engage the central themes of national and global history.[48] Only in the past two decades have professional historians made regional Mexican history their own. Its emergence as a valid focus for investigation has been both the product and the generator of new concerns and issues. The people, the nation, and global change have become the subjects of regional history, subjects which transcend the limited and particularistic meaning of geography.[49]

The rise of the new social history in the 1960s led many historians away from national and metropolitan elites and rulers, their laws, policies, and attitudes, and into the countryside where most people lived, worked, politicked, and died. By restricting their focus to a particular geographic region (and therefore to a more manageable documentary record), historians have been able to expand their coverage and write "history that undertakes all aspects of human life in all classes of men."[50] A more discriminating, detailed, and complete portrait of "the people," of men and women, workers, immigrants, Indians, farmers, as well as elites, has resulted from regional investigation.[51]

The nation, as well as its people, can be rediscovered and reconstructed through regional analysis. A nation is more than the sum of its geographical parts, but an analysis of those parts and their interaction is essential to an understanding of the national whole. Friedrich Katz's groundbreaking essay on rural labor conditions in Porfirian Mexico demonstrates the dangers of national generalizations.[52] Regional investigation is useful in the study of political and economic change, contributing to the view of such change as a function of the center impinging on the periphery and the periphery imposing itself on policies and forces emanating from the center.

Comparative regional history can also illuminate such global themes as state formation, modernization, and formal and informal imperialism. Broad historical developments effect different changes in different regions. Foreign economic penetration in Porfirian Mexico, for example, led to direct control of the means of production in certain regions and industries, to indirect control in others.[53] Comparison of the differences refines our understanding of global historical forces.

Regional investigation, in short, has much to offer. It is useful in examining relevant topics and permits a variety of innovative approaches. Unexploited regional archives far outnumber those which have been perused. Regional study, however, does not automatically lead to historiographical progress. Regional studies have been, and continue to be, based on disparate data. They examine a wide variety of themes from a large number of methodologies and theoretical frameworks. The increase in regional history has achieved little coordination and coherence; but synthesis, the ultimate goal, is attainable. The first step, as Bernard Bailyn suggests, is to "put the story together again."[54] This volume is a beginning.

In part one, Mark Wasserman, William Stanley Langston, and David LaFrance examine the relationship between state and national leaders. Regional reaction to Porfirian centralization is one of the central questions for historians of modern Mexico. In three regional settings the erection, functioning, and breakdown of the Díaz political machine is evaluated. These three essays reveal that regional politicians resisted or invited the central government's encroachment to suit their ambitions or to protect their positions. It is clear that Díaz faced different problems in Chihuahua, Coahuila, and Puebla and achieved varying levels of success. It is also apparent that Porfirian centralization, however accomplished in the short run, fashioned the conditions for its own undoing. Regional differences survived—and perhaps flourished in some places—after thirty years of centralization and laid the basis for the disparate nature of the Revolution.

In part two, Frans J. Schryer and Daniela Spenser explore aspects of the economic transformation of Mexico during the Díaz era. Although the dual processes of urbanization and industrialization were accelerated during the final decades of the nineteenth century, the country retained a profoundly rural character. Change in Mexico's agricultural structure was pivotal. Not only were the lives of the great majority of Mexicans altered, but the commercialization of the rural economy tied Mexico closely to the North Atlantic economy and its ups and downs.

The essays in part two examine two important topics—the rise of a class of small commercial farmers in northern Hidalgo and the development of plantation production in the Soconusco region of Chiapas—that reflect a pattern found in many parts of Mexico. The formation of ranchero and plantation economies, as the authors point out, was closely related to the larger changes in national and international economic developments. That such important changes occurred in those remote regions demonstrates the magnitude of the economic forces at work during this period. The essays also discuss the unintended consequences of economic change: factional disputes in northern Hidalgo and the deterioration of living standards in Soconusco.

In part three, Evelyn Hu-DeHart, Allen Wells, and William K. Meyers examine the social consequences of political and economic change on Yaqui Indians, Chinese immigrants, and agricultural workers. The modernization process over which Díaz presided brought to light a host of problems, some of them of ancient origin, some new. The essays on Sonora, Yucatán, and the Laguna district of Coahuila and Durango reveal the social costs of Porfirian development: pauperization, discrimination, servitude, and violent repression and deportation. These essays, however, also reveal that worsening conditions produced resistance, not docility. The underside of the *pax Porfiriana*, as unveiled here, shows the great potential for disorder in Díaz's Mexico. The explosion of violence that characterized the Mexican Revolution had its origins in the conditions outlined in these three chapters.

In the concluding chapter, William H. Beezley discusses the possibilities for further regional research on Porfirian Mexico. Beezley, professor of Latin American history at North Carolina State University and the author of several regional studies, demonstrates that the topics in search of historians are nearly inexhaustible and totally engaging.

"Because Mexico is the name of one country, we customarily regard it as if it had always been a single entity."[55] This tendency has been perhaps most pronounced with regard to the Porfiriato, the only age in Mexican history which bears the name of a ruler. Díaz did dominate his time and his country; it is not, nevertheless, his story alone. In approaching the Porfiriato we must be sensitive to other Mexicos. It is there that the drama of this age began and ended.

NOTES

1. Mark Wasserman, "From the Outside Looking In: A Short Comment on the Regional History of Mexico," paper presented at the 1982 meeting of the American Historical Association, Washington, D.C.

2. Victor Alba, *The Mexicans: The Making of a Nation* (New York, 1970), 8.

3. Luis González y González, "Microhistoria para multimexico," *Historia Mexicana* 21 (octubre–diciembre 1971): 227.

4. R. C. Padden, *The Hummingbird and the Hawk: Conquest and Sovereignty in the Valley of Mexico, 1503–1541* (New York, 1970).

5. Colin M. MacLachlan and Jaime E. Rodríguez O., *The Forging of*

the Cosmic Race: A Reinterpretation of Colonial Mexico (Berkeley, 1980); and Bradley Benedict, "El estado en México en la época de los Habsburgo," Historia Mexicana 23 (1974): 551–610.

6. Michael C. Meyer and William L. Sherman, The Course of Mexican History (New York, 1979), 360.

7. Mme. Calderón de la Barca, Life in Mexico During a Residence of Two Years in that Country (New York, 1931), 245.

8. Charles C. Cumberland, Mexico: The Struggle for Modernity (New York, 1968), 141–42; Paul J. Vanderwood, Disorder and Progress: Bandits, Police, and Mexican Development (Lincoln, 1981), 26.

9. Lesley Byrd Simpson, Many Mexicos, 4th ed. (Berkeley, 1974), 253–54.

10. Richard N. Sinkin, The Mexican Reform, 1855–1876: A Study in Liberal Nation-Building (Austin, 1979), chapters 2 and 6. An excellent regional study of this period is Charles R. Berry's The Reform in Oaxaca, 1856–1876: A Microhistory of the Liberal Revolution (Lincoln, 1981).

11. The best study of the Restored Republic is Laurens Ballard Perry's Juárez and Díaz: Machine Politics in Mexico (De Kalb, 1978).

12. Stuart F. Voss, On the Periphery of Nineteenth-Century Mexico: Sonora and Sinaloa, 1810–1877 (Tucson, 1982), xv.

13. Vanderwood, Disorder and Progress, 68.

14. David Hannay, Díaz (New York, 1917), 210–16.

15. Don M. Coerver, The Porfirian Interregnum: The Presidency of Manuel González of Mexico, 1880–1884 (Fort Worth, 1979), chapter 6.

16. Ernest Gruening, Mexico and Its Heritage (New York, 1928), 57.

17. Edwin Lieuwen, Mexican Militarism: The Political Rise and Fall of the Revolutionary Army (Albuquerque, 1968), 2.

18. Daniel Cosío Villegas, El Porfiriato: Vida política interior, segunda parte, vol. 9 of Historia moderna de México (México, 1972), part 1, "El último toque."

19. Francisco I. Madero, La sucesión presidencial en 1910 (México, 1963), 233–43; José C. Valadés, El Porfirismo: Historia de un régimen. El crecimiento, vol. 1 (México, 1977), chapter 5, "Deber y haber."

20. James Creelman, Díaz: Master of Mexico (New York, 1911), p. 401.

21. Anuario estadístico de la república mexicana (México, 1894–1912).

22. Donald Fithian Stevens, "Agrarian Policy and Instability in Porfirian Mexico," The Americas 39 (October 1982): 166, suggests that perhaps their trust was not misplaced: "Díaz seems to have lacked not the will but the strength to defend Indian lands. . . . Díaz was unable to prevent local pressures from gradually eroding away village lands; there were other

groups, including foreign and Mexican capitalists and powerful politicians, who could also threaten the fragile 'stability' of Porfirian Mexico."

23. Creelman, *Díaz,* 410–11.

24. Thomas B. Davis, "Porfirio Díaz in the Opinion of his North American Contemporaries," *Revista de Historia de América* (diciembre–enero 1967/68): 79–93.

25. Frank Tannenbaum, *The Mexican Agrarian Revolution* (New York, 1929), 154.

26. John H. Coatsworth, "Railroads, Landholding, and Agrarian Protest in the Early Porfiriato," *Hispanic American Historical Review* 54 (February 1974): 48–71; Valadés, *El Porfirismo . . . El crecimiento* 1, chapter 6, "Paraiso y desierto"; Rodney D. Anderson, *Outcasts in Their Own Land: Mexican Industrial Workers, 1906–1911* (De Kalb, 1976), chapter 2.

27. The best contemporary analysis of the last decade of the Porfiriato is Rafael de Zayas Enríquez's *Porfirio Díaz* (New York, 1908). See also Ramón Eduardo Ruiz, *The Great Rebellion: Mexico, 1905–1924* (New York, 1980), part 1, "The Whys and Whereofs of Rebellion."

28. Daniel Cosío Villegas, *Memorias* (México, 1976), 209.

29. Luis González, *San José de Gracia: Mexican Village in Transition,* trans. by John Upton (Austin, 1974), 106–12; Paul Friedrich, *Agrarian Revolt in a Mexican Village* (Englewood Cliffs, 1970), 43–49.

30. This division is taken from Howard F. Cline, *The United States and Mexico* (New York, 1963), 90–97.

31. Ibid.

32. Vanderwood, *Disorder and Progress,* 120.

33. Friedrich Katz, "Labor Conditions on Haciendas in Porfirian Mexico: Some Trends and Tendencies," *Hispanic American Historical Review* 54 (February 1974), 30; D. A. Brading, *Haciendas and Ranchos in the Mexican Bajío: Leon, 1700–1860* (Cambridge, Eng., 1978), 205; Heather Fowler Salamini, *Agrarian Radicalism in Veracruz, 1920–1938* (Lincoln, 1978); Arturo Warman, *"We Come to Object": The Peasants of Morelos and the National State* (Baltimore, 1980), 65–67; Friedrich, *Agrarian Revolt,* 46.

34. Vanderwood, *Disorder and Progress,* 72.

35. John H. Coatsworth, *Growth against Development: The Economic Impact of Railroads in Porfirian Mexico* (De Kalb, 1981), 119.

36. Vanderwood, *Disorder and Progress,* 121–23.

37. Peter V. N. Henderson, *Felix Díaz, the Porfirians, and the Mexican Revolution* (Lincoln, 1981), 8.

38. G. M. Joseph, *Revolution from Without: Yucatan, Mexico, and the United States, 1880–1924* (Cambridge, Eng., 1982), 67; for Guerrero see

Ian Jacobs, "Rancheros of Guerrero: The Figueroa Brothers and the Revolution," in *Caudillo and Peasant in the Mexican Revolution*, ed. D. A. Brading (Cambridge, Eng., 1980), 80; for Chiapas see Thomas Benjamin, "Passages to Leviathan: Chiapas and the Mexican State, 1891–1947" (Ph.D. diss., Michigan State University, 1981), 60–92.

39. Marco Bellingeri and Isabel Gil Sánchez, "Las estructuras agrarias bajo el Porfiriato," in *México en el siglo XIX (1821–1910): Historia económica y de la estructura social*, coord. Ciro Cardoso (México, 1980), 316.

40. Ricardo Pozas A., "El trabajo en las plantaciones de café y el cambio socio-cultural del indio," *Revista Mexicana de Estudios Antropológicos* 13 (1952): 34–38; Thomas Benjamin, "El trabajo en las monterías de Chiapas y Tabasco, 1870–1946," *Historia Mexicana* 30 (abril–junio 1981): 506–29; and Ciro Cardoso and Carmen Reyna, "Las industrias de transformación (1880–1910)," in *México en el siglo XIX*, 400–404.

41. Héctor Aguilar Camín, "The Relevant Tradition: Sonoran Leaders in the Revolution," in *Caudillo and Peasant*, 93.

42. Barry Carr, "Las peculiaridades del norte mexicano, 1880–1927: Ensayo de interpretación," *Historia Mexicana* 22 (enero–marzo 1973): 320–29; Aguilar Camín, "The Relevant Tradition," 93–94.

43. Katz, "Labor Conditions on Haciendas," 32–37; Guadalupe Nava Oteo, "La minería bajo el Porfiriato," in *México en el siglo XIX*, 339–62.

44. Friedrich Katz, *The Secret War in Mexico: Europe, the United States and the Mexican Revolution* (Chicago, 1981), 11.

45. Ibid., 8–13, 20.

46. Vanderwood, *Disorder and Progress*, 121–23.

47. Walter Goldfrank, "World System, State Structure, and the Onset of the Mexican Revolution," *Politics and Society* 5 (1975): 417–39.

48. Luis González, *Invitación a la microhistoria* (México, 1973), 77–97.

49. G. M. Joseph's *Revolution from Without* is an excellent example of the breadth possible in regional investigation.

50. Pierre Goubert, "Local History," in *Historical Studies Today*, ed. Felix Gilbert and Stephen R. Graubard (New York, 1972), 304.

51. H. J. Perkin, "Social History," in *Approaches to History*, ed. H. P. R. Finberg (Toronto, 1962), 51–82; Lawrence Stone, "History and the Social Sciences in the Twentieth Century," in *The Past and the Present* (Boston, 1981), 28.

52. Katz, "Labor Conditions on Haciendas." See also Joseph L. Love, "An Approach to Regionalism," in *New Approaches to Latin American History*, ed. Richard Graham and Peter H. Smith (Austin, 1974), 137–55.

53. Mark Wasserman, "Oligarquía e intereses extranjeros en Chihuahua durante el Porfiriato," *Historia Mexicana* 22 (enero-marzo 1973): 279–319;

Gilbert M. Joseph and Allen Wells, "Corporate Control of a Monocrop Economy: International Harvester and Yucatan's Henequen Industry during the Porfiriato," *Latin American Research Review* 17, no. 1 (1982): 69–99.

54. Bernard Bailyn, "The Challenge of Modern Historiography," *American Historical Review* 87 (February 1982): 7.

55. Alba, *The Mexicans*, 4.

I
Regional Politics

Porfirio Díaz was a master politician, as the longevity of his regime demonstrates. Díaz's power was never absolute, however, even when he reached the point of indefinite reelection, after 1890. Although he outlived the major political rivals of his generation, Díaz was never free of discontents, independent politicians, and struggles for power among subordinates at the national and regional level. From necessity and perhaps enjoyment, Díaz played the political game with consummate skill. He was always extending *pan o palo* ("bread or the club"), rewarding loyalty or punishing insubordination. He set potential rivals against each other and proved to be an able practitioner of the classic strategy of divide and rule. Díaz never relaxed his efforts to subordinate the other Mexicos and their bosses to his political machine.

Certainly all state governors and regional caudillos eventually recognized Díaz's authority and respected his power, but all were not subservient. Some governors possessed greater latitude than others regarding the affairs of their region. Beyond a point, tight centralization was not an end in itself. If strong regional bosses maintained political stability and promoted economic development they were of greater use to Díaz than weak governors who could do neither. Díaz wanted peace but was constantly confronted with disorder. Politics in the states was very volatile; governors frequently faced electoral opposition and rebellion. These troubles had their origin in local rivalries and were often designed to discredit the current governor in the eyes of the president and to force his intervention. And he usually did intervene, with great success. But it was only a limited success, a stability imposed from above that eventually blocked too many careers, alienated too many groups and towns, and provided too few avenues of redress. It was a political structure that became too rigid at all levels and because it could not change it was shattered from below.[1]

Mark Wasserman examines how Luis Terrazas erected an economic empire in Chihuahua and achieved political preeminence. By coopting his enemies and utilizing a foreign willingness to invest developmental capital in Chihuahua, Terrazas was able to withstand challenges (including those sponsored by Díaz) to his authority and power. Wasserman emphasizes the close interrelationship of Terrazas's economic control and his ability to minimize the threat of rival factions. At the same time, Wasserman is quick to point out that Terrazas's dominance contributed to an increasingly unstable situation in Chihuahua. An emerging middle class lacked sufficient opportunity for political and economic advancement and oppressive working conditions, or periods of unemployment, fueled discontent and rebellion within the lower class. The Terrazas monopolization of governmental and police functions contributed to growing criticism of political abuse, corruption, unfair taxation, and the loss of local autonomy.

Terrazas's ability to avoid Díaz's attempts to limit his power and authority made him, not Díaz, the target of regional discontent. In an ironic turn of events, the overwhelming power Terrazas wielded in Chihuahua was the key to his ultimate demise. Monopolization of political and economic power in Chihuahua, as in Mexico in general, proved ultimately fatal.

William Stanley Langston's essay on the neighboring state of Coahuila provides an interesting contrast to Wasserman's essay on Chihuahua. The divide-and-rule strategy Díaz employed more successfully in Coahuila enabled him to maintain an impressive degree of control while at the same time ensuring the tranquility needed for economic development. Díaz's manipulations of elite factions in 1893 and 1897 offer classic examples of his understanding of *realpolitik* at the regional level. As Langston suggests, however, Díaz's ability to play one faction off the other contributed to his eventual failure in Coahuila. His essentially personalistic and elitist view of politics prevented him from effectively responding to the vigorous and broadly based reform movement, headed by Francisco I. Madero, that emerged in Coahuila in 1905. Centralized political control in Chihuahua and Coahuila, although achieved in different ways, had similar results: growing disaffection, leading to revolt.

David LaFrance offers a thorough postmortem of the Díaz regime in the pivotal state of Puebla. The disintegration of the Díaz political machine began before and continued after Porfirio Díaz resigned the presidency on 25 May 1911. The resignation and exile of Díaz was an extremely important step but, as LaFrance demonstrates for Puebla, it was part of an ongoing process in the breakdown of centralized political authority and of the Díaz system from top to bottom.

In Puebla Díaz achieved the kind of political control which he sought in every state. Layers of Porfirista officialdom built up over decades to monopolize power and opportunities for enrichment and to deal harshly with opponents provoked little open discontent until 1909. The possibility of political change that appeared as a result of Díaz's announced retirement in 1908 and the rise of national political campaigns, however, found an enthusiastic reception in Puebla. LaFrance shows that Díaz, in response to increasing disaffection and rebellion, offered first repression and then conciliation by purging unpopular state officials. This crack in the regime's facade encouraged opposition; even Porfiristas in Puebla began to put some distance between themselves and Díaz. The fall of the Díaz government only eliminated the top half of the Porfirian political structure in Puebla. Conflict between the remaining state and local Porfiristas and revolutionary factions prevented the erection of a new political order and further facilitated the breakdown of the old one. It is a simple fact, but one not sufficiently examined, that the Díaz political system briefly survived its creator. Its final demise, as LaFrance suggests, removed the last obstacle to social revolution.

The Revolution did not negate the political pattern of centralized control which characterized Porfirian Mexico. The personalistic nature of Díaz's rule prevented the institutionalization and peaceful transmission of power. The methods were flawed but the goal—a strong, centralized state—was not rejected by Díaz's successors. As Gilbert M. Joseph argues, "the epic revolution would ultimately have the effect of creating a 'modern leviathan,' of consolidating the increasingly centralized, increasingly capitalistic modern state which had already been emerging during the Díaz period."[2] It can be argued that the Revolution modernized the old order and that the Partido Revolucionario Institucional (Revolutionary Institutional Party) in fact institutionalized the essence of the Porfiriato.[3]

Mark Wasserman is assistant professor of History at Douglass College, Rutgers University. He received his Ph.D. at the University of Chicago in 1975 and has published articles on Mexican history in several journals. Professor Wasserman is coauthor with Benjamin Keen of *A Short History of Latin America* (1980) and author of *Capitalists, Caciques, and Revolution: Elite and Foreign Enterprise in Chihuahua, 1854–1911* (1984). William Stanley Langston received his Ph.D. in Latin American history in 1980 from Tulane University. Dr. Langston, the author of articles on Mexican history, currently resides in Washington, D.C. David LaFrance is research professor at the Centro de Investigaciones Históricas y Sociales, Instituto de Ciencias of the Universidad Autónoma de Puebla. He received his Ph.D. from Indiana University in 1984 and has published articles in *Inter-American Economic Affairs*, *The Americas*, and *Historia Mexicana*.

NOTES

1. Daniel Cosío Villegas, *El Porfiriato: Vida política interior, segunda parte*, vol. 9 of *Historia moderna de México* (México, 1972), chapter 3, "Y ahora los gobernadores," and chapter 8, "Los Porfiritos."

2. Gilbert M. Joseph, "Mexico's 'Popular Revolution': Mobilization

and Myth in Yucatan, 1910–1940," *Latin American Perspectives* 6 (Summer 1979): 47.

3. Lorenzo Meyer, "Historical Roots of the Authoritarian State in Mexico," in *Authoritarianism in Mexico,* ed. José Luis Reyna and Richard S. Weinert (Philadelphia: Institute for the Study of Human Issues, 1977), 4; Peter H. Smith, *Labyrinths of Power: Political Recruitment in Twentieth-Century Mexico* (Princeton, 1979), 187.

2
Chihuahua: Family Power, Foreign Enterprise, and National Control

Mark Wasserman

The political history of Chihuahua from 1854 to 1911 is a chronicle of the rise and fall of the Terrazas family. Coming of age during the Liberal revolt of 1854 and the War of the Reform (1858–61), the patriarch Luis Terrazas was the only regional cacique who retained his political base through the French Intervention, the purges of Juárez, and the Díaz dictatorship. The family survived repeated challenges to its power through adept political maneuvering, the astute choice of allies, the shrewd use of its enormous economic resources, and a measure of good luck. The Terrazas fell from power in 1911, the victims of the excesses of their own awesome authority and the severe economic dislocations engendered by the state's cyclical export economy, based on mining.

The Rise of Luis Terrazas

The family's rise took place against a backdrop of endemic violence, political turmoil, and economic depression. From the sixteenth century, when the first brave friars ventured north through the Sierra Madre, vicious warfare between whites and Indians had torn Chihuahuan society. After independence the terror progressively worsened, until by the early 1850s the region was in ruins. Although the major Indian threat ended in 1880, with the defeat of the Apache chief Victorio, raids continued on a lesser scale into the 1890s.[1]

Intense political competition, first between Conservatives and Liberals and later among Liberal factions, added another dimension to the violence. The twenty-five years after the Liberal Plan de Ayutla revolt overthrew Emperor Antonio López de Santa Anna, in 1855, witnessed successively the War of the Reform, the French Intervention, and two insurrections by Porfirio Díaz. Each produced a related upheaval in Chihuahua.

All of this took its toll. By the end of the 1870s, most of the region's rich mines were flooded or caved in. The grasslands which once had fed thousands of cattle and other livestock were virtually empty. Incessant disorder and poor or nonexistent transportation facilities discouraged investors who might have attempted to reconstruct the mines. Periodic, prolonged droughts multiplied the misery.[2]

In the midst of this turmoil Luis Terrazas's rise was meteoric.[3] He won his first elected office in 1854, at age twenty-five, as a member of the *ayuntamiento* (city council) of Ciudad Chihuahua, the state's capital and largest city. As such, he swore his allegiance to the Conservative Santa Anna when the Plan de Ayutla revolt broke out at the end of that year. Once the Liberal victory was apparent, however, young Luis quickly joined the winners. In 1859 he won election to both the ayuntamiento and the state legislature (as an alternate). Governor Angel Trías, Sr., the leader of the Liberals in Chihuahua, then appointed Terrazas *jefe político* of Iturbide District, which included the capital. The following year Trías named him to the state's Junta de Guerra (war council) against the Apaches.

In September 1860, the state legislature installed Terrazas as governor, although, according to the state's constitution, he was at thirty too young for the office. He was elected to a full, four-year term, beginning in 1861. Terrazas was a compromise choice. The state's leading soldier and statesman, Angel Trías, Sr., was fighting in the south and Chihuahuan Liberals were badly split. Luis Terrazas

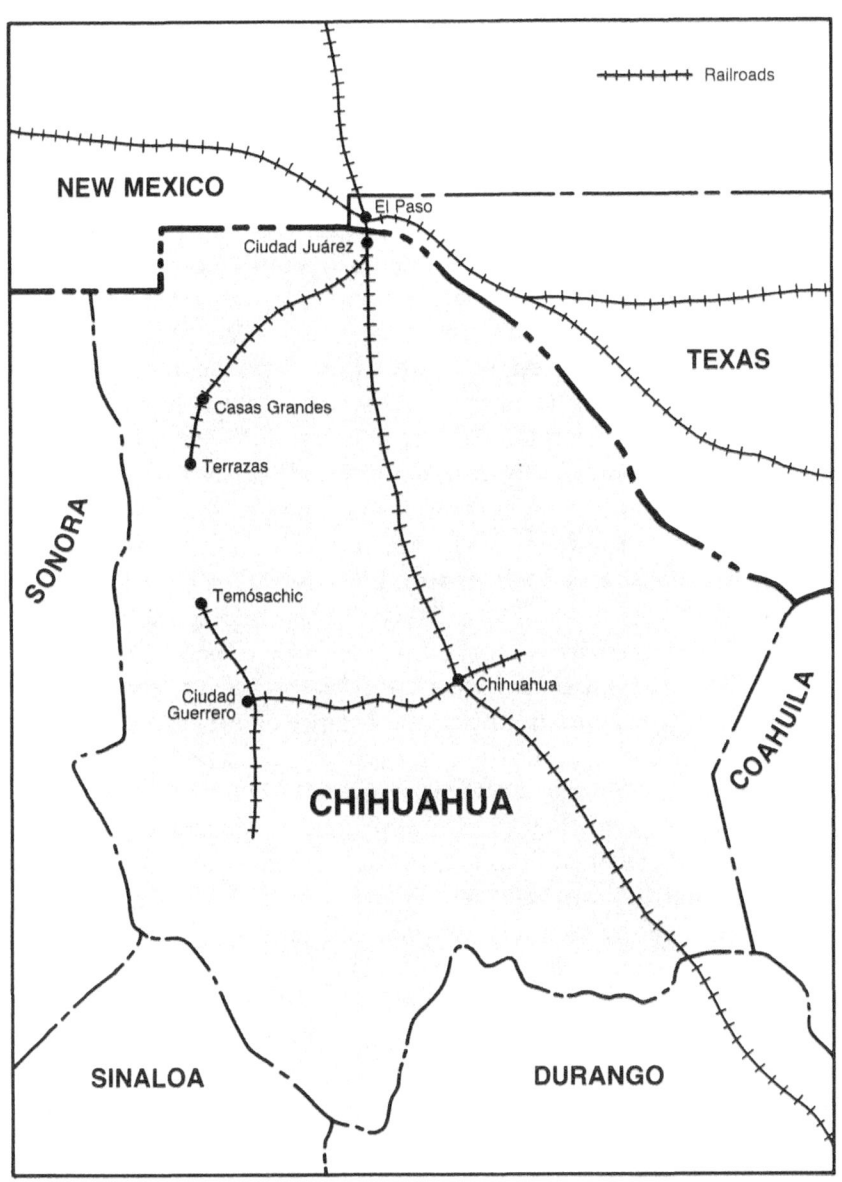

Chihuahua, 1910

was acceptable to all factions of a squabbling legislature, many members of which were part governors or had aspirations for the post. Moreover, Terrazas had close family ties to the discredited but still influential Conservatives in the state. If some Liberals thought that young Luis was to remain a stopgap, they were mistaken.

The next four decades of Chihuahuan politics can be seen as a series of challenges to the Terrazas family's power from local rivals acting alone and in conjunction with national regimes seeking to consolidate their hold on the state. Luis Terrazas and his family won out in this long struggle because they chose their allies well and because they mastered the use of economic power in politics.

The Terrazas family acquired two vital allies: the state's Conservative faction and foreign entrepreneurs. Luis Terrazas had extensive ties to the most prominent old Conservative families, such as the Zuloagas, Irigoyens, and Bustamentes, by virtue of his marriage to Carolina Cuilty Bustamente. The marriages of his children increased these bonds.[4] The Conservatives, discredited by their support of the French, furnished silent political and financial support for Luis, enabling him to gain the upper hand in the delicate balance of forces among Liberal factions in Chihuahua. The young cacique established his first links with foreign entrepreneurs during the 1860s when, in partnership with German immigrant Enrique Müller, he purchased the enormous Hacienda de Encinillas, in northern Chihuahua. Foreigners, some of whom married into the family, were involved as managers or stockholders in almost every business and industrial enterprise subsequently undertaken by the Terrazas family.[5]

The family used its financial resources and widespread business interests to purchase the cooperation of even its most bitter opponents. Some were made partners in family enterprises, some were permitted to acquire valuable government concessions, contracts, and favors, while others married into the family. By 1910 most of the leading families in Chihuahua were related by blood, marriage, or money to the Terrazas.

Terrazas and Juárez

Luis Terrazas soon encountered opposition during his first term as governor, when he had only just begun accumulating his fortune and Chihuahuan politics were still badly fragmented. His critics, led by former governor José Eligio Muñoz, claimed that he had obtained his office illegally and sought the assistance of President Benito Juárez in deposing him. The president complied, when Terrazas refused to transfer to the Juárez government revenues to which it was entitled from customs collections at Paso del Norte and from the sale of church and public lands in the state. Terrazas was reluctant to release these funds to the shaky Juárez regime at a time when they were desperately needed to help prosecute the war against the Apaches and to defend Chihuahua from French invasion.[6]

Juárez ordered his partisan General José María Patoni to Chihuahua to proclaim martial law and to replace the uncooperative Terrazas with a new governor, Jesús José Casavantes, a respected Indian fighter from the western district of Guerrero. Casavantes, however, lacked widespread popular support outside his home region and disliked the intrigues that went with the office. In addition, the state legislature refused to recognize Juárez's actions. The president was forced to compromise, recalling Angel Trías, Sr., to Chihuahua to become governor once again. Trías was easily the match of Luis Terrazas in popularity and political acumen, but by then he was tired and sick; and after years of campaigning he was out of touch with local conditions. He was to die two years later.[7]

In desperate need of strong allies and faced with tough opposition from Terrazas, Juárez backed down. By the end of 1865, Terrazas had returned as governor with the added honor of a commission as general in the Republican army. In exchange, Terrazas pledged his support to Juárez.[8] The newly minted general led Chihuahuan forces in liberating the state from French rule in 1866. He won a second term as governor in 1865 and a third in 1869.

In the aftermath of the French defeat, Terrazas moved shrewdly to conciliate the warring factions. He obtained amnesty for Conservatives who had collaborated with the French and allowed other Conservatives to acquire substantial tracts of public and confiscated church lands.[9]

Terrazas and Díaz

Terrazas's political base was by no means secure. The most serious challenge to his power came from Porfirio Díaz. A military hero of the war against the French, Díaz had seen his ambitions frustrated by Juárez's reelection as president in 1871. He revolted against his old chief, proclaiming the Plan de Noria. In Chihuahua Terrazas remained loyal to Juárez. Porfirista forces invaded the state and defeated Terrazas in June 1872. The rebellion sputtered, however, when Juárez died in October. Because Díaz was in Chihuahua when the revolt ended, Luis Terrazas assumed a key role in negotiations that arranged amnesty for him from the newly installed government of Sebastián Lerdo de Tejada. The future dictator never forgave Terrazas for the humiliation he suffered on this occasion.[10] Terrazas maintained cordial relations with Lerdo, but the latter was considerably less popular in Chihuahua than Juárez had been.

The uncertainty of the Terrazas family's political base was underlined by the defeat of the family's candidate, Dr. Mariano Samaniego of Paso del Norte, in the gubernatorial election of 1873. Luis had not dared to run for a fourth term in view of the protests that had arisen against Juárez's reelection. Antonio Ochoa, a rich mineowner from southwestern Chihuahua, relying on support mainly from western mining districts and Hidalgo de Parral, won by a slim margin of 105 votes.[11]

When Lerdo sought a second term in 1876, Porfirio Díaz revolted again, under the banner of the Plan de Tuxtepec. The *tuxtepecanos* in Chihuahua, under General Angel Trías, Jr., the son of the deceased Liberal hero, took over the state, jailing Governor Ochoa. Luis Terrazas, in alliance with the Casavantes family and other ranchers from western Chihuahua, defeated the tuxtepecanos in August 1876. The rebels, however, were victorious throughout the rest of the nation. In early 1877 Díaz sent a large contingent of troops to Chihuahua to install Angel Trías, Jr., as governor.[12]

Despite the advantages of his name, his own fine military record, and the backing of the Díaz regime, Trías soon dissipated his support in Chihuahua. He alienated many of the state's wealthy citizens when he imposed forced loans, raised taxes, and proposed the abolition of the *tiendas de raya* (company stores). In addition his personal habits became the object of scandal, for he was allegedly a drunkard. With none of the financial resources of the Terrazas family and unable to break their alliance with the western ranchers, Trías could not solidify his rule. Proclaiming the Plan de Guerrero, the Terrazas-Casavantes alliance ousted Trías in 1879. Porfirio Díaz, occupied in pacifying the South, was unable to send reinforcements until it was too late. Luis Terrazas returned as governor in 1879, resigned the office so as to be eligible for the 1880 election, and won that election for a new term.[13]

Terrazas governed Chihuahua until 1884. During that time Díaz and his successor as president, Manuel González, consolidated their hold on Mexico, deposing regional caciques in Sinaloa, Jalisco, Nuevo León, Guerrero, and Coahuila.[14] Simultaneously the completion of the Mexican Central Railway, which connected Ciudad Chihuahua with Mexico City and the United States border, ended the state's isolation and removed the military and communications obstacles to reasserting the national government's control over Chihuahua.

Díaz, however, did not move against the Terrazas family until he had made reliable local allies, the Guerrero group, headed by the Casavantes family. The *guerrerenses* had split with the Terrazas during the Juárez era, but had rejoined them against Angel Trías, Jr. Now the younger generation of the family, Manuel de Herrera and Celso González, sought to extend its influence beyond the foothills of the Sierra Madre. In the early 1880s they became convinced that Luis Terrazas would not share power with them; as a result they joined with Porfirio Díaz. At the same time, the guerrerenses broadened their support, adding to their group Félix Francisco Maceyra of Ciudad Chihuahua, a former business partner of the Terrazas, and Lauro Carrillo of Rayón district, in southwestern Chihuahua.[15]

As he did in Nuevo León with General Bernardo Reyes and in Coahuila with Julio Cervantes, Díaz interjected a trusted general to act as governor and intermediary with local allies. The Chihuahua-born General Carlos Pacheco, a long-time Díaz aide, became governor in 1884.[16] He held the post until 1888, but spent little time in the state, instead fulfilling his duties as minister of development in the national cabinet. He left the day-to-day administration of state affairs to porfirista bureaucrats or guerrerenses such as Mauro Candano, Carlos Fuero, Rafael Pimentel, Herrera, Maceyra, and González.

The Terrazas family retired to their estates and tended to their growing fortunes, aided to a great extent by the dictator's policy of allowing deposed political factions in the states to prosper economically as long as they cooperated with the regime. Family members augmented their landholdings considerably and began an important banking business.

The Guerrero group controlled the state government from 1884 to 1892, but was never able to subjugate the Terrazas family. The latter, after twenty-five years in power, were too firmly entrenched. Moreover, during the 1880s the family received a crucial infusion of new blood when Enrique C. Creel, the son of a former United States consul in Chihuahua and General Terrazas's sister-in-law, married one of Luis's daughters. Creel was a brilliant administrator, businessman, and financier. He moved the family into banking and engineered its diversification into manufacturing and transportation. In addition, Creel was an adept negotiator who won friends among the inner circle around Porfirio Díaz. He also became the family's main intermediary with foreign investors.[17]

Unlike many of the other regional groups Díaz unseated, the Terrazas family was unwilling to settle for wealth without political power. Eventually the enormity of their economic resources and the persistence of their opposition overwhelmed the Guerrero group.

Through incompetence or bad luck, the guerrerenses failed to take advantage of the major economic opportunities in Chihuahua during the years they held the reins of state government, while the Terrazas family built a great empire of land, cattle, and banks. The Guerrero group did not benefit from the cattle boom of the 1880s. Although members of this faction acquired two million acres of public lands in the state, they obtained virtually none in the main cattle regions. The Terrazas family, on the other hand, accumulated enormous profits from cattle exports to the United States, which they used to expand and diversify their economic interests and to finance their opposition to the guerrerenses and Porfirio Díaz. With these revenues the family withstood the severe depression during the 1890s that ruined the Guerrero group.[18]

The guerrerenses also did not successfully establish an independent source of credit. They founded at least two banks, but one fell victim to the financial crisis of the late 1870s and the other to the depression of the 1890s. During the hard times of the 1890s, the leader of the guerrerenses, Celso González, went deeply into debt with Enrique Creel in order to sustain his merchant house. He died bankrupt, and his estate had to turn over to Creel several large tracts of land held as collateral for the loan.[19]

The Guerrero group never tapped the enormous potential of foreign investors. It was hampered in establishing contacts with foreigners by the fact that no one of the group was a lawyer. Nor did the group have a counterpart to Enrique Creel, a highly successful go-between for the Terrazas family in their dealings with foreigners.[20]

In the face of these financial setbacks, the guerrerenses' political base crumbled. They had shifted their business and political operations to Ciudad Chihuahua in order to take advantage of the opportunities there, but in so doing they had lost touch with their home base. The treacherous politics of western Chihuahua required constant attention. An active group of Terrazas loyalists, or *terracistas,* appeared in the region while the guerrerenses conducted state affairs in the capital.

The Terrazas family cautiously waited two years before they embarked on a two-pronged strategy to regain control of Chihuahua. The first part involved increased pressure on both the guerrerenses and Díaz. The family clandestinely encouraged a series of rebellions in western Chihuahua. Luis Terrazas also helped finance a revolt in Tamaulipas, led by Catarino E. Garza, in 1891.[21]

The family provoked a bitter split in the state legislature in 1887 that so upset the region that Pacheco had to hurry back from Mexico City. As a result, Pacheco and Creel hastily arranged a deal whereby Lauro Carrillo became governor, in 1888. The arrangement broke down in 1892, when Carrillo sought reelection. In the intervening four years the position of the Guerrero group deteriorated badly. Creel ingratiated himself into the innner circle in Mexico City, while the guerrerenses' contact in the capital, Pacheco, fell from grace in 1891 and died the same year, leaving them without a patron of commensurate influence. Moreover, Carrillo proved unable to maintain order in Chihuahua. His mishandling of a minor disturbance in Tomochic, in the western part of the state, led to a massacre of the entire population of this *pueblo* by federal troops. Nor could Carrillo quell the violence that accompanied the gubernatorial campaign of 1892. Pressured by these events, Díaz jettisoned his alliance with the guerrerenses and appointed Colonel Miguel Ahumada, a bureaucrat who for several years had served in Chihuahua, as governor. Ahumada was acceptable to the Terrazas, who found him cooperative. The state enjoyed a decade of Ahumada's efficient administration from 1892 to 1903.[22]

Creel continued to work for total reconciliation. He became a stalwart of the *científicos,* headed by José Yves Limantour, the minister of finance, one of the two major competing factions around Díaz. Partly because of Limantour's influence and partly because Díaz seemed to detect growing ambition in Ahumada, the dictator arranged to restore Luis Terrazas as governor in 1903. In return, Terrazas reportedly agreed to furnish a specified number of recruits for the federal army.[23] Satisfied with his victory, Luis Terrazas shortly thereafter retired from office in favor of Enrique Creel. Creel subsequently won election in his own right in 1907. He was succeeded by Alberto Terrazas, the general's youngest son, in 1910.

The Economic Empire of the Terrazas

While the Terrazas successfully fought Juárez and Díaz to a standstill, they also built a vast economic empire. Many men, such as Olegario Molina of Yucatán, and families, such as the Maderos of Coahuila, constructed great fortunes during the Porfiriato, but none rivalled that of the Terrazas.[24] Luis Terrazas and his immediate family owned more than ten million acres of land in Chihuahua. Over a half million head of livestock grazed their pastures. The family either owned or managed all the major banks in the state. Nationwide, family members controlled or were principals in banks with assets of more than two hundred million pesos in 1910. Terrazas enterprises included the largest meat packers and flour millers in Chihuahua. Family members owned the state's only brewery, four textile and clothing factories, and numerous other industrial companies, including an iron foundry and broom and brick factories. They were also major shareholders in several important industrial ventures outside Chihuahua. Several of these enterprises were undertaken in partnership with the Madero family and other important businesspeople from the Laguna region of Durango and Coahuila. The family owned the urban transit lines in the state's three largest cities. Its members were stockholders or officers in all the railroads that went through the state. Terrazas companies supplied electricity and telephone service to Ciudad Chihuahua.[25]

Luis Terrazas used his political influence to enrich himself and his family. In turn, great riches enabled them to buy the cooperation of even their most recalcitrant enemies. During his early years as governor, Luis Terrazas took advantage of his position to acquire several large haciendas. He saw to it that his estates were lightly taxed and heavily defended (to the extent feasible) from Indian attack. As governor during the 1880s, he fought off the efforts of the central government to cancel his valuable banking concessions. Every enterprise in which the family invested was exempted from taxation for at least ten years by the state government. Their railroads received generous state subsidies. The Terrazas banks were the state government's major creditors and managed the bulk of state funds as well.[26]

A partnership or a position in a family-owned business often served to win over long-time opponents. The Arellano family, for example, were opponents of the Terrazas as allies of Porfirio Díaz and the guerrerenses. But by 1902 members of the family were business associates of the Terrazas. One brother managed a Terrazas-owned insurance company and two brothers were members of the board of directors of one of the Terrazas family banks. In addition there were numerous instances of old foes whom the Terrazas saved from bankruptcy with timely loans from the Banco Minero, the clan's largest bank.[27]

Although the Terrazas family forged a kingdom of cattle, banks, commerce, and industry from a desolate, isolated land ruined by years of war and disorder, the sum of their achievement was not positive. The family's permeation of virtually every sector of the economy, and its privileged position, stymied the development of a middle rank of entrepreneurs. The proliferation of relatives and cronies preempted many opportunities. The family's control of banking shut off the middle class from available capital resources. Furthermore, as the state's largest employers (more than ten thousand people depended on the family for their living) the Terrazas family set the standard for the oppressive working conditions that existed in Chihuahua. The peons, seamstresses, and laborers who worked for them toiled long hours in unsafe and uncomfortable environments at low pay, often harassed and cheated by arbitrary and capricious overseers, with no rights of protest or grievance.[28]

Foreign Enterprise

At the same time that the Terrazas built their political and economic empire, a massive influx of foreign investment, primarily from the United States, into Chihuahua's mining industry profoundly altered the state's economy and society. Foreign investment and entrepreneurs poured into Chihuahua during the 1880s, after the defeat of the Apaches and the completion of the Mexican Central Railway had restored peace and ended the region's centuries-old isolation. Lured by the prospect of cheap, docile labor and tax exemptions, foreign companies had by 1907 invested more than fifty million dollars in the state's mines, ranches, and commerce.[29]

New investment in mining attracted thousands of workers and their families to the region, where they earned relatively high wages and enjoyed relatively good working conditions. The expanding mining industry combined with the economic boom in the southwestern United States, which created a demand for thousands more Mexican workers, to produce a huge migration north from the central plateau. In the view of at least one observer, this situation engendered nothing less than a "social revolution."[30] Workers in Chihuahua (and Sonora as well) became accustomed to high wages, improved working conditions, payment in cash, and impersonal relations with employers. In the United States many were exposed to union organization and radical political ideologies. The Chihuahuan work force (and that of the North in general) was in great part divorced from traditional ties to land and village and was highly mobile.[31]

The expansion of the mining economy also created an emergent middle class composed of artisans, tradesmen, foremen, small mineowners, small merchants, shopkeepers, and white-collar employees. These, especially in the cities, objected to the lack of political opportunity under the Terrazas regime. They protested unfair taxation, government abuses, and the loss of local autonomy.[32]

Despite the generally upward trend of the mining economy, it was subject to severe downturns, depending on the world market demand for silver and other metals. Demand very often depended on decisions made by foreign governments on tariffs and monetary policy. Chihuahua was hard hit by the imposition of high tariffs in the United States in 1890 and the world financial crisis that lasted from 1892 to 1897.[33] The period from 1897 to 1907 was, however, one of unprecedented boom. Severe shortages of labor in the mining industry pushed up wages and increased the flow of workers northward. The Creel administration's vast public works program stimulated employment further. The ranks of the middle class swelled from this prosperity. The state experienced record crops of corn and wheat in 1905 and 1906, which decreased the cost of living and therefore increased real wages and living standards.[34] In 1907 the boom turned to bust. Financial crisis in the United States dried up investment in Chihuahuan mines as the price for metals plunged on the world market. Thousands of miners were laid off. Unemployed workers roamed the state, their numbers multiplied by laborers returning from the United States. Harvest failures in 1907, 1908, and 1909 pushed up the cost of living, adding immeasurably to the misery of the lower classes.[35] Some turned to violence. Along the border with Durango bandit gangs raided haciendas and mines. Others joined the Partido Liberal Mexicano (PLM), led by the Flores Magón brothers, which staged an uprising in Chihuahua in 1908. Later unemployed workers joined the Revolution.[36]

The depression devastated the middle class. While their businesses failed they saw foreign companies and the Terrazas family and its cronies protected by tax exemptions and access to credit, all of which was denied to them. Moreover, because they had no representation in state and local governments, there was no legitimate way for them to protest within the system. Some of the middle class joined the Flores Magón. More joined the Anti-Reelectionist clubs that sprang up in Chihuahua in support of the presidential candidacy of Francisco I. Madero in 1909.[37]

The depression also struck hard at small landholders who were simultaneously losing their property to speculators under the provisions of the Municipal Land Law of 1905. During the boom many *rancheros* worked seasonally in the mines and lumber mills and across the border in the United States, to augment their incomes. The economic crisis shut off this employment.[38] As in Morelos and other areas, returning migrants added to the pressure on diminishing land resources.[39] The same drought that drove up the price of staples for the working and middle classes ruined the smallholder's crops and killed their livestock.[40]

After a decade of unprecedented prosperity and rising expectations, the depression of 1907 struck especially hard. When combined with the political crisis engendered by the restoration of the Terrazas family to power after 1903, it produced the crucial ingredients for revolution in 1910.[41]

The Restoration

The restoration of the Terrazas family upset the balance of politics in Chihuahua by removing all constraints on the family's activities. By 1903 there was no rival faction left in the state. The guerrerenses had long fallen from favor and had suffered irremediable financial reverses. The Terrazas family's lack of touch with day-to-day affairs, their unending efforts to centralize power in a region that fiercely guarded local autonomy, and their unwillingness to control the excesses of their subordinates led to an increasingly unstable situation in Chihuahua between 1903 and 1910.

The transfer of leadership of the family from Luis Terrazas to Enrique C. Creel brought a change of both style and substance. The general had been an exceptional nineteenth-century cacique, as much at home in the milieu of western ranchers as in the society and business world of Ciudad Chihuahua. He was a hero of the Indian wars and the French Intervention. Creel, on the other hand, was half-American, a científico, concerned less with ex-Indian fighters than with the intrigue of Mexico City and the intricacies of international finance. Luis Terrazas rarely left Chihuahua. Creel as governor was away from the state as often as he was at home, serving on international commissions, as Ambassador to the United States, and as Minister of Foreign Relations in the Díaz cabinet; but governing Chihuahua was not a part-time job.

Creel's policies to centralize the family's authority, streamline state government, and modernize the local economy alienated the newly emergent middle class, disaffected the residents of small towns and villages, oppressed the working class, and induced small landholders to rebellion. The Terrazas family monopolized public office. Virtually every member of the state legislature was a family member or close associate. The state Supreme Court was similarly staffed. Before 1903 other factions had obtained at least token representation in these institutions. When Luis Terrazas returned as governor, however, he replaced nine of the eleven jefes políticos, thereby denying further district representation.[42] The growing middle class, as a result, saw its political ambitions stymied.

Local government was a major source of dissatisfaction. The Law for the Reorganization of the Districts, promulgated in 1904, replaced the most important locally elected officials, *presidentes municipales*, with *jefes municipales* appointed by the governor. These officials, who presided over municipal councils and exercised far-ranging legislative and judicial powers in addition to their executive functions, were the objects of numerous and increasing complaints. Often coming from outside the municipality, they proved abusive and unresponsive to local needs. Protests against their violations of political rights, physical abuse of citizens, and corruption filled the pages of the state's major newspaper, *El Correo de Chihuahua*.[43] It was in areas where these abuses were chronic and severe that support for opposition to the Terrazas family drew its earliest and strongest support. Initially protesters were attracted to the PLM. Later dissidents joined the Anti-Reelectionist party in 1909.[44]

The courts and police, too, were objects of bitter resentment. In 1908 Silvestre Terrazas, the editor of *El Correo* and a critic of the regime (he was a distant cousin of Luis Terrazas), proclaimed that "justice was a fiasco and liberty was dead in Chihuahua."[45] The police acted as agents of repression, guards on large estates, and engaged in the abuse of citizens.

There were also loud protests against unfair taxation. To pay for his ambitious program of public works, Creel raised taxes. These placed the major burden on the middle and working classes. Large landowners, large merchants, and foreign entrepreneurs paid at best only minimal taxes and usually enjoyed total exemption. Chihuahuans often took violent exception to these impositions. The residents of San Andrés rioted against levies on their livestock and work in 1909. The taxes were particularly galling because the tax collector managed the undertaxed holdings of Governor Creel in the region. San Andrés thus proved fertile ground for the Revolution in 1910. The village supplied three of its early leaders: Pancho Villa, Ceferino Pérez, and Cástulo Herrera.[46]

As widespread as were the protests against political abuses, loss of local autonomy, corruption, and unfair taxes, the greatest outcry erupted against the Municipal Land Law of 1905. After 1898 a railroad construction boom spread an east-west transportation network across Chihuahua. This substantially increased the value of land along the new lines and prompted a massive attack on small landholders and municipal landholdings similar to that which took place during the 1880s in Chihuahua and elsewhere in Mexico. The villages that once formed *presidios,* the main line of defense against the raiding Apaches in the nineteenth century, were especially hard hit. These communities had fought for decades to protect their land. The Spanish and Mexican governments had rewarded their bravery with land grants. After 1905 these villages were cheated out of their land by hacendados, slick lawyers, and speculators applying the provisions of the new land law. The villages protested. When their protests fell on deaf ears both in Ciudad Chihuahua and Mexico City, they joined the Revolution. Cuchillo Parado, San Carlos, Janos, and Namiquipa provided many of the troops that won the Revolution's first great victories and furnished many of the movement's best military leaders, such as Toribio Ortega and Porfirio Talamantes.[47] Guerrero District, which suffered from a combination of all these complaints (tyrannical jefes, oppressive taxation, usurpation of lands), became a hotbed of revolutionary activity. Pascual Orozco, Jr., the most important military leader of the *maderista* revolution, came from San Isidro in Guerrero District.[48]

Revolution

By the time Madero appeared to lead the opposition nationally, discontent had spread widely in Chihuahua. The PLM and the Anti-Reelectionists received considerable support in the state from the middle and working classes. Small landowners, armed and with horses, some well schooled in warfare from the Indian campaigns, formed the leadership and made up the best troops of the maderista army. The middle class provided political leadership through such men as Abraham González, Chihuahua's first revolutionary governor, and Silvestre Terrazas. Disaffected workers, though less numerous than the peasants, also joined the ranks and some, like Cástulo Herrera, played key roles in the revolt.

The Terrazas family, alone at the top, were the obvious target of the revolutionaries' wrath; in Chihuahua the protest was aimed at them. Their very achievement of unchallenged power served to unite the various groups with grievances against them and the Porfirian regime.

Chihuahuans throughout the state responded to Francisco Madero's call to revolt in November 1910. In Cuchillo Parado, in far eastern Chihuahua, Toribio Ortega led a band of peasants against the local jefe. Pancho Villa headed another group of rebels in the San Andrés region, just west of Ciudad Chihuahua. The major uprising took place in Guerrero District, under the leadership of Pascual Orozco, Jr. Orozco scored several victories over government troops during the last week in November and succeeded in capturing Ciudad Guerrero during the first week in December. A few days later federal troops forced Orozco from the city, but the rebellion persisted. In January 1911, Díaz tried to stem the tide by returning Miguel Ahumada as governor, but the gesture was futile. Madero crossed over the border into Mexico on 14 February and joined Orozco. The rebels suffered a major defeat at Casas Grandes in early March, when Madero insisted on personally taking command of military operations. Thereafter the maderistas reorganized under Orozco and began the road to victory. They laid seige to Ciudad Juárez in early April. The Díaz regime entered into negotiations with the rebels, but the talks soon broke down. The maderistas captured the city in May. This victory precipitated the final negotiations that led to the resignation and exile of Porfirio Díaz. The maderista revolution had won by force of Chihuahuan leadership and arms.[49]

NOTES

1. The best secondary works for the colonial era and the first half of the nineteenth century are Francisco R. Almada, *Resumen de la historia de Chihuahua* (México, 1955) and Fernándo Jordán, *Crónica de un país bárbaro* (Chihuahua, 1975). For the Indian wars see Ralph A. Smith, "Apache Plunder Trails Southward, 1831–1940," *New Mexico Historical· Review*

(*NMHR*) 37 (January 1962): 20–42; "The Scalphunt in Chihuahua," *NMHR* 40 (April 1965): 117–40; and "Indians in Mexican-American Relations before the War of 1846," *Hispanic American Historical Review* (*HAHR*) 48 (February 1963): 34–64; *El Mensajero*, 15 Feb. 1856, 3–4; *El Eco de la Frontera*, 22 Feb. 1856, 3; Pedro García Conde, "Ensayo estadístico sobre el estado de Chihuahua," *Boletín de la Sociedad Mexicana de Geografía y Estadística* 5 (1857): 253.

2. *La República*, 9 Oct. 1868, 12 April 1874; *Semanario Oficial*, 20 Feb. 1876; *El Periódico Oficial del Estado de Chihuahua* (hereafter *POC*), 26 May 1878, 4; L. H. Scott, U.S. Consul, Chihuahua City, to William H. Seward, secretary of state, 19 Sept. 1879; Scott to Assistant Secretary of State, 13 Nov. 1879; George L. McManus to Secretary of State Lewis Cass, 3 Feb. 1860; Scott to Assistant Secretary of State, 22 Oct. 1880; all United States of America, National Archives, Record Group 59, General Records of the Department of State, Consular Dispatches, Paso del Norte (after 1897 Ciudad Juárez) and Chihuahua City, 1850–1906 (hereafter NARG 59); Joaquín Terrazas, *Memorias del Sr. Coronel D. Joaquín Terrazas* (Chihuahua, 1905), 71–82; *POC*, 25 March 1882, 3; 25 Nov. 1882, 3; 24 Feb. 1883, 3; 5 June 1886, 3; *El Paso Daily Times*, 24 Sept. 1892, 1.

3. Francisco R. Almada, *Gobernadores del estado de Chihuahua* (México: Imprenta de la Cámara de Diputados, 1950), 219–89; José Fuentes Mares, . . . *Y México se refugió en el desierto: Luis Terrazas, historia y destino* (México, 1954), 5–9, 168–69.

4. I am indebted to Ing. Miguel Márquez for furnishing an extensive family tree of the Terrazas. The extended family included Cuilty, Bustamente, Ramírez, Molinar, Moye, Zuloaga, Muñoz, Luján, Guerrero, Márquez, Bobadilla, Creel, Horcasitas, Urueta, Falomir, Laguette, Sisniega, Madero, Picard, Cortázar, Robinson, and Irigoyen.

5. For a complete discussion of the relations between the Terrazas family and foreigners see Mark Wasserman, "Foreign Investment in Mexico, 1876–1910: A Case Study of the Role of Regional Elites," *The Americas* 36 (July 1979): 3–21.

6. Francisco R. Almada, *Juárez y Terrazas: Aclaraciones historicas* (México, 1958), 72–73; Reuben W. Creel to Secretary of State, 10 Dec. 1863, 2 March 1864, 4 May 1864, 7 June 1864, and 17 June 1864; all NARG 59; *Alianza de la Frontera*, 3 May 1864.

7. The relationship between Juárez and Terrazas, and the latter's dealings with the French, are a matter of hot controversy between Almada and Fuentes Mares. See Almada, *Juárez y Terrazas*, 222–25 and Fuentes Mares, *Luis Terrazas*, 103–10.

8. Emperor Maximillian appointed Terrazas to the post of Imperial Prefect in Chihuahua. Terrazas ignored the offer, but Juárez had to move to protect his last bastion in Chihuahua.

9. Reuben Creel to Brigadier General James H. Carleton, 18 Sept. 1864; Creel to Secretary of State, 20 July 1865; Creel to Seward, 30 March 1866, 2 March 1866, 28 Feb. 1866, 7 June 1864; Cuniffe to Seward, 2 Feb. 1866, 12 Jan. 1866, 17 June 1864; all NARG 59; Francisco R. Almada, *Gobernantes de Chihuahua* (Chihuahua, 1929), 60–63; Almada, *Juárez y Terrazas*, 143–62; T. H. Smith to McManus, 30 Oct. 1863, NARG 59.

10. Daniel Cosío Villegas, *La república restaurada: La vida política,* vol. 1 of *Historia Moderna de México* (México, 1955), 735–36; A. M. Carreño, ed., *Archivo del General Porfirio Díaz: Memorias y documentos* (hereafter *AGPD*), 30 vols. (México, 1947–61), 10: 112; J. R. Robinson to William H. Brown, 31 Jan. 1872; William H. Brown to Second Assistant Secretary of State, 10 Feb. 1872, 14 Feb. 1872, 10 June 1872, 27 June 1872, 16, 18, and 31 July 1872, 31 August 1872; Pierson, U.S. Consul, Paso del Norte, to Second Ass't Sec'y of State, 15 March 1872 and 2 Sept. 1872; all NARG 59. Porfirio Díaz to Luis Terrazas, 12 Oct. 1872, *AGPD*, 10: 162; Díaz to Terrazas, 21 Oct. 1872, *AGPD*, 10: 174–75; Pierson to Second Ass't Sec'y of State, 2, 24, and 28 Sept. 1872; Brown to Second Ass't Sec'y of State, 14 Sept. 1872; all NARG 59.

11. Almada, *Gobernadores,* 200.

12. J. C. Huston, U.S. Consul, Chihuahua City, to Second Ass't Sec'y of State, 2 June 1876; F. McManus and Son and H. Nordwald to John Foster, U.S. Minister to Mexico, 5 March 1871; L. H. Scott to Foster, 8 March 1871; all NARG 59; POC, 9 Feb. 1879, 2; L. H. Scott to Second Ass't Sec'y of State, 12 and 18 Sept. 1879; NARG 59.

13. L. H. Scott to Seward, 31 Oct. 1879, Scott to Newton, 28 Nov. 1879; NARG 59.

14. Don M. Coerver, *The Porfirian Interregnum: The Presidency of Manuel González of Mexico, 1880–1884* (Fort Worth, 1979), 75–94; Robert T. Haden, "The Federalist: Porfirio Díaz and Coahuila, 1884–1886 and Porfirio Díaz and Nuevo Leon, 1885–1887," Unpub. ms., Cholula, [Mexico], 1973; Ian Jacobs, "The Rancheros of Guerrero," in *Caudillo and Peasant in the Mexican Revolution,* ed. D. A. Brading (London, 1980), 79–81.

15. Francisco R. Almada, *Diccionario de historia, geografía, y biografía chihuahuenses,* 2nd ed. (Chihuahua, n.d.), 90–91, 94–95; Almada, *Gobernadores,* 290–95, 333–37, 381–84, 408–15; *Engineering and Mining Journal* 88 (13 Nov. 1909): 1002; POC, 26 Sept. 1909, 28; 11 Nov. 1882,

1; 23 Dec. 1882, 3; 20 Jan. 1883, 2; 6 Jan. 1883, 2; 20 April 1887, 4; 19 July 1884, 3; 29 Oct. 1892, 1. Chihuahua, México, Gobernador, *Mensaje del gobernador, 1888* (Chihuahua, 1888); Chihuahua, México, Secretaría del Gobierno, Sección Estadística, *Anuario estadístico del estado de Chihuahua, 1905, 1906, 1907, 1908, 1909* (Chihuahua, 1906–13).

16. Coerver, *Interregnum*, 75–94; Haden, "The Federalist." See also Anthony T. Bryan, "Mexican Politics in Transition, 1900–1913: The Role of General Bernardo Reyes" (Ph.D. diss., University of Nebraska, 1970).

17. Almada, *Gobernadores*, 437–47; Alejandro Creel Cobián, *Enrique Creel: Apuntes para su biografía* (México: Edición Familiar, 1974); Alvaro de la Helguera, *Enrique Creel, Apuntes biográficos* (Madrid, 1910).

18. I estimate that the Terrazas family earned $US 700,000 in the cattle trade during the 1883–89 boom. See Mark Wasserman, "Oligarchy and Foreign Enterprise in Porfirian Chihuahua, Mexico, 1876–1911," (Ph.D. diss., University of Chicago, 1975), 93–95.

19. *El Correo de Chihuahua*, 24 May 1903, 2.

20. Chihuahua, Gobernador, *Memoria de la administración pública del estado de Chihuahua, 1892–1896* (Chihuahua, 1896), 175–81.

21. William H. Beezley, "Opportunity in Porfirian Mexico," *North Dakota Quarterly* 40 (Spring 1972): 36–37.

22. Daniel Cosio Villegas, *El Porfiriato: La vida política interior*, vol. 9 of *Historia moderna de México* (México, 1970), 2: 58–64; Almada, *Resumen*, 350–51, 356; *POC*, 21 Feb. 1887, 2; 2 July 1887, 3; 30 July 1887, 2; 2 Sept. and 26 Nov. 1892. Francisco R. Almada, *La Rebelión de Tomochi* (Chihuahua, 1938).

23. Cosío Villegas, *La vida política interior*, 2: 458–60; "Mexican Revolution from Publication of the Plan de Potosí, February 6, 1910 to Maderos' Entry into Mexico City, June 7, 1911," Mono. no. 4 to be found in the U.S. National Archives, Record Group 76, Records of the United States and Mexican Claims Commission, Suitland, Maryland, 37–38; Beezley, "Opportunity," 38.

24. Wasserman, "Oligarchy," 90–153; Allen Wells, "Henequen and Yucatan: An Analysis of Regional Economic Development, 1876–1915," Ph.D. diss. (State University of New York, Stonybrook, 1979); Stanley R. Ross, *Francisco I. Madero: Apostle of Mexican Democracy* (New York, 1965).

25. Mark Wasserman, "Oligarquía e intereses extranjeros en Chihuahua durante el Porfiriato," *Historia Mexicana* 22 (1973): 279–319. I am indebted to Harold D. Sims and Eduardo Creel of Mexico City for two

documents—"Negocios de Enrique C. Creel" and "The General Terrazas Estate"—from the private papers of the Creel family.

26. Almada, *Juárez y Terrazas*, 332, 323–27, 343–58, 649–90; *POC*, 18 Oct. 1906, 13; Chihuahua, Gobernador, *Memorias, 1892–1896*, 55; Chihuahua, *Anuario*, 1908, 167; *1909*, 205.

27. Almada, *Diccionario*, 43–44; *El Correo de Chihuahua*, 3 Nov. 1904, 1; 7 March 1904, 1; 17 March 1905, 1. *La Nueva Era*, 16 March 1885 and 19 June 1885; enclosure in letter of Martín Falomir to Enrique Creel, 22 Dec. 1910, Silvestre Terrazas Papers, Silvestre Terrazas Collection, Bancroft Library, Berkeley, California.

28. Chihuahua, *Anuario, 1909*, 12–22; Friedrich Katz, "Labor Conditions on Haciendas in Porfirian Mexico: Some Trends and Tendencies," *HAHR* 54 (February 1964): 31–35; *Mexican Financier*, 18 Jan. 1896, 415–16; 19 Jan. 1889, 399; 11 Jan. 1896, 399. *POC*, 10 March 1878, 1; *Bankers Magazine* 80 (Jan.–June 1910): 793; *Mexican Herald*, 5 Jan. 1909, 9; 28 June 1908, 5; 16 April 1906, 10. México, Ministerio de Fomento, Dirección General de Estadística, *Anuario estadístico de la república mexicana, 1893–1907* (México, 1894–1908). Federico Sisniega to Central Administration of the Banco Nacional de México, 21 Nov. 1909, Part II, reel 11, Silvestre Terrazas Papers.

29. Fuentes Mares, *Luis Terrazas*, 168; Almada, *Juárez y Terrazas*, 346; Harold D. Sims, "Espejo de caciques: los Terrazas de Chihuahua," *Historia Mexicana* 18 (enero 1969): 395; New York *Times*, 19 Feb. 1901, 10; 26 Feb. 1901, 1.

30. Victor S. Clark, "Mexican Labor in the United States," *Bulletin of the Bureau of Labor* 17 (Sept. 1908): 466 passim.

31. Katz, "Labor Conditions," 1–47.

32. Chihuahua, *Anuario, 1905*, 38; *1906*, 139, 144–60; *1907*, 129; *1908*, 171; *1909*, 210. México, Secretaría de Economía, Dirección General de Estadística, *Estadísticas sociales del Porfiriato* (México, 1956), 16–19; Mark Wasserman, "Social Origins of the 1910 Revolution in Chihuahua," *Latin American Research Review* 15 (1980): 25–28.

33. *POC*, 4 June 1892, 2.

34. Wasserman, "Social Origins," 28–30.

35. Chihuahua, *Anuarios*, provide crop figures for these years.

36. *Engineering and Mining Journal* 86 (August 1908): 350; Richard M. Estrada, "Border Revolution: The Mexican Revolution in the Ciudad Juárez–El Paso Area, 1906–1911," M.A. thesis (University of Texas at El Paso, 1975), 78–79.

37. Wasserman, "Social Origins," 25–33.

38. Informe de José Muñoz, Jefe Político del Distrito de Benito Juárez, in *POC*, 17 May 1908, 11–12; Letter to General Ignacio C. Enríquez, Governor of Chihuahua, 24 Jan. 1922, Box 11, Mexico North Western Railway Papers, John McNeely Collection, University of Texas at El Paso.

39. Alan Knight, "Nationalism, Xenophobia, and Revolution: the Place of Foreigners and Foreign Interests in Mexico, 1910–1915," Ph.D. diss. (Oxford University, 1974), 162–64, claims that the so-called Morelos model was applicable for the entire central plateau. John Womack, *Zapata and the Mexican Revolution* (New York, 1968), 37–66.

40. Edgar Pinchon, *Viva Villa* (New York, 1933), 100.

41. James C. Davis, "Toward a Theory of Revolution," *American Sociological Review* 27 (February 1962): 5–18 describes the "j-curve," where a prolonged period of economic growth is followed by a sharp downturn. Rising expectations are crushed, leading to potentially revolutionary discontent. For the effect on political expectations especially, see G. E. Lenski, "Status Crystallization: A Non-Vertical Dimension of Social Status," *American Sociological Review* 19 (1956): 405–13.

42. Francisco R. Almada, *La revolución en el estado de Chihuahua*, 2 vols. (Chihuahua, 1964), 1: 23–24, 27–36; Chihuahua, *Anuario, 1907*, 181; *POC*, 3 March 1894, 1.

43. *El Correo de Chihuahua*, 20 May 1908, 1; 10 April 1908, 1; 25 Nov. 1905, 1; 4 Feb. 1907, 1.

44. *El Correo*, 3 Aug. 1909, 1; 28 Jan. 1908, 1; 29 Jan. 1908, 2; 19 Feb. 1909, 1; 26 Feb. 1909, 2; 7 April 1909, 1; 19 April 1909, 1; 19 May 1909, 1; 1 Oct. 1909, 1; 2 Dec. 1909, 1; 19 May 1910, 1; 23 Nov. 1910, 1; 5 Feb. 1909, 1; 1 July 1910, 4. These affected areas were Bachíniva, Bocoyna, Ciudad Camargo, Nonoava, Namiquipa, Temósachic, and Valle de Zaragoza.

45. *El Correo*, 19 Oct. 1908, 1.

46. *POC*, 4 April 1909, 2–3; *El Correo*, 30 March 1909, 1; 31 March 1909, 1; 2 April 1909, 1; El Paso *Times*, 1 April 1909, 1.

47. Wasserman, "Social Origins," 30–33; Friedrich Katz, "Peasants in the Mexican Revolution of 1910," in *Forging Nations: A Comparative View of Rural Ferment and Revolt*, ed. Joseph Spielburg and Scott Whiteford (East Lansing, 1976), 89–120.

48. Michael C. Meyer, *Mexican Rebel: Pascual Orozco and the Mexican Revolution* (Lincoln, 1967); William H. Beezley, *Insurgent Governor: Abraham González and the Mexican Revolution in Chihuahua* (Lincoln, 1973).

49. Almada, *La Revolución*, 1: 189–250; Meyer, *Orozco*, 19–37.

3
Coahuila:
Centralization against State Autonomy

William Stanley Langston

For more than sixty-five years after independence from Spain, Mexico suffered almost continuous political anarchy coupled with economic stagnation. This tumultuous situation ended in 1876, when General Porfirio Díaz fought his way into the presidency. During the next thirty-four years, Díaz forged an authoritarian regime beneath a democratic veneer which brought peace, stability, and economic growth.

Yet the *pax Porfiriana* concealed considerable political conflict. The nature of this conflict was characteristic of that which occurs in authoritarian regimes: political mobilization was restricted to an elite composed of elements with autonomous power bases which struggled to secure the limited available political and economic opportunities. This essay examines intraelite political competition in Coahuila during the Porfiriato by focusing on gubernatorial elections in 1893, 1897, and 1905. More importantly, it analysizes the dynamic interplay between the national government, committed to centralized control, and regional elite groupings, equally committed to local autonomy.¹

The Coahuilan Elite

Coahuilan intraelite political conflict took the form of competition among collective groupings, or *camarillas,* comprised of individuals bound by loyalty to a leader (*gallo*) who served as a political patron. The camarillas resulted from the juxtaposition of a static agrarian sector and a modernizing industrial sector that coexisted in Porfirian Coahuila. While caramilla members occupied multiple positions in the modernizing social structure, the ties were not contractual or formal, as would befit an industrial society, but feudalistic (personalistic and kin-based), as in a traditional agrarian-dominated society.² Through their members, camarillas were cliques providing mutual protection and insulation from the law. At the same time, these groups offered an excellent means for the promotion of members' political fortunes.³

From 1893 to 1911 three camarillas—Maderista, Garza Galanista, Cárdenista—dominated politics in Coahuila. The Madero camarilla, headed by Evaristo Madero, was the oldest. Madero had been a major contender for political hegemony in the state along with other veteran caudillos of the struggle against the French: Victoriano Cepeda, Francisco Naranjo, and Hipólito Charles. The basis of Madero's camarilla was the strong economic and kinship ties that Madero forged with several major families in the state. Although most of Madero's followers resided in the Parras and Río Grande districts, he also had contacts with prominent Saltillo *políticos*. Madero's camarilla was ousted from power after Díaz returned to the presidency in 1884, due to the long-standing enmity between the president and Madero. Throughout the period, however, Madero maintained good relations with José Limantour, a *científico* and secretary of the treasury, while remaining a force in Coahuilan politics.⁴

Colonel José María Garza Galán headed a second camarilla. As in the case of the Maderistas, the Garza Galanistas were primarily composed of the colonel's friends and relatives. His staunchest supporters were the Elguezabal, Múzquiz, and Galán families, who lived near the colonel's hometown of Múzquiz. Garza Galán and

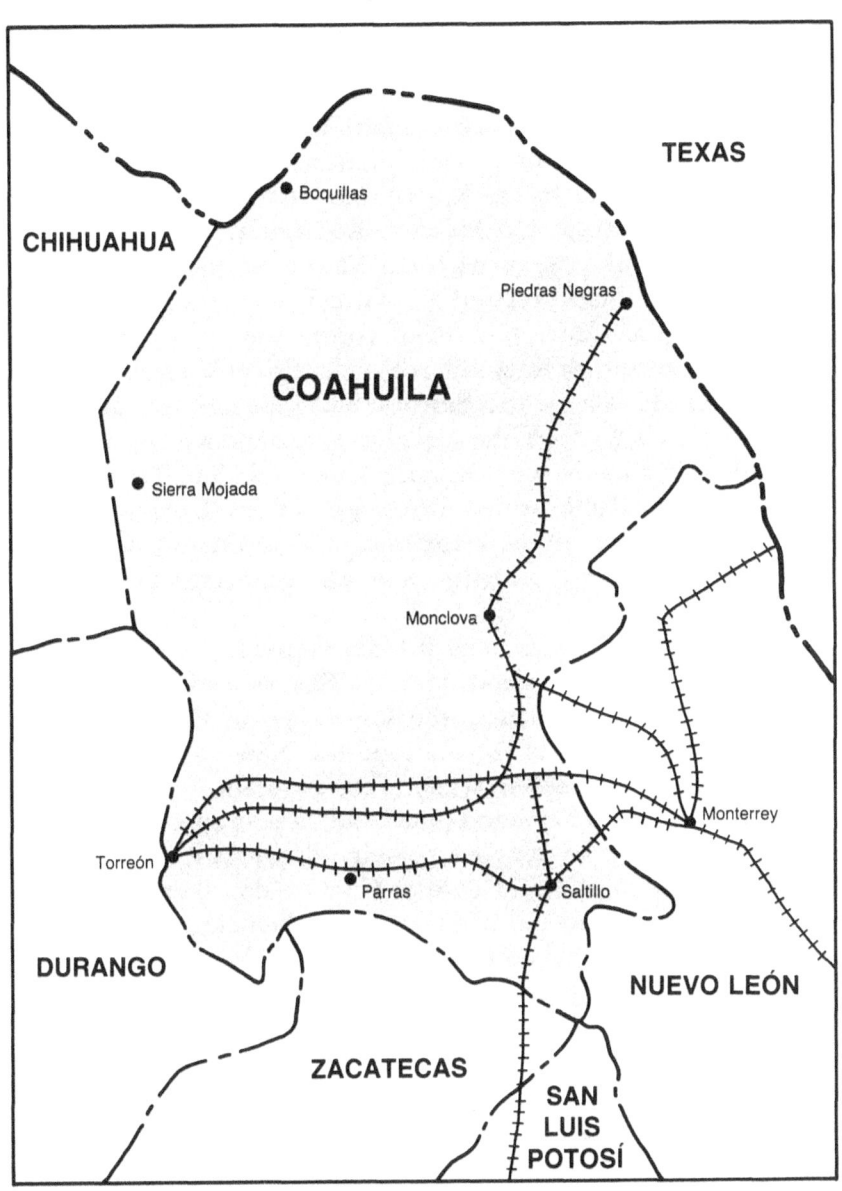

Coahuila, 1910

his relatives also formed an important economic bloc in the Monclova district. Although the core of his camarilla was centered in Múzquiz, the colonel forged alliances with prominent individuals in other sections of the state. In the Río Grande district, he relied on two cousins, Manuel Rosas and Mauricio Rodríguez.[5] Garza Galán also fashioned a useful alliance with the Valdés family, influential hacendados in the Monclova and Río Grande districts.

In the Laguna district, a major cotton producing area, Garza Galán was aligned with three influential planter-entrepreneurs; Colonel Carlos González, Frumencio Fuentes, and Luis Lajous. Early in his career, Garza Galán made the acquaintance of and formed a political and economic alliance with Manuel Romero Rubio, Díaz's father-in-law. Romero Rubio served as secretary of development (*fomento*) and was a founder of the científicos. Garza Galán's adversaries, especially the Madero camarilla, were also connected to that influential group.[6]

The state's third major camarilla was dominated by Miguel Cárdenas, a lawyer and hacendado from San Buenaventura, in the Monclova district. Cárdenas, the son-in-law of Cayetano Ramos Falcón, a political ally of the old caudillo, Naranjo, and an enemy of Garza Galán, had been secretary of the government under Madero (1880–84) and Julio Cervantes (1884–86), a post which often served as a stepping stone to the governorship. Cárdenas forged a broader based camarilla than did Madero or Garza Galán. He relied on his kinsmen, friends, and businessmen in the Monclova district, such as the Carranza brothers—Emilio, Sebastian, Venustiano, and Jesús—and their friends and relatives, the Salinas, Castro, and Arredondo families.[7] He was also allied with a number of Saltillo *políticos* and entrepreneurs. In addition, Cárdenas's progressive views attracted a number of young, aggressive, well-educated professionals, who viewed him as a development-orientated administrator. As Cárdenas and his partisans rose in the political structure, they increasingly identified with General Bernardo Reyes, the governor of neighboring Nuevo León and an archenemy of the científicos.[8]

The Revolt of 1893

The factional tensions ever present in Coahuilan politics intensified during gubernatorial elections, at times erupting into violence. Such an eruption occurred in 1893 when Governor José María

Garza Galán's attempt at reelection provoked significant elements of the elite to take up arms. Garza Galán had governed Coahuila since 1886, when Díaz decided to return the state to local civilian control after the two-year military governorship of General Julio Cervantes, imposed in the wake of an 1884 revolt. In exchange for federal support, Garza Galán was to curb the influence of two tuxtepecano caudillos, Francisco Naranjo and Hipólito Charles, as well as that of the Madero camarilla. Backed by Díaz, Garza Galán effectively eliminated Naranjo, Charles, and Madero from the political scene.[9]

While he subordinated other camarillas, Garza Galán strengthened his own hold on the state. He dominated municipal governments by reinstating the *jefe político* system and by promulgating a decree which allowed the governor to remove and replace municipal officials. The governor's supporters and relatives monopolized government posts, particularly such political plums as the *jefatura política* of the Sierra Mojada, a rich mining district in western Coahuila.[10]

Supported by Díaz and Romero Rubio, Garza Galán enriched himself and his camarilla, while attempting to convert the state into a personal fief. In 1889 he persuaded the unicameral state legislature to pass an amendment which partially abrogated the state constitution's no-reelection clause by allowing the governor to seek reelection for one term. Near the end of his second term, however, Garza Galán faced serious opposition. In 1892 two of his partisans introduced a second amendment to the state constitution, which would have permitted the perpetual reelection of the governor as well as other ranking state officials.[11] This amendment, passed on 7 February 1893, furnished the growing opposition to Garza Galán with a viable constitutional basis for their campaign against his reelection. In a letter to Díaz, one wealthy Saltillo businessman, Encarnación Dávila, warned that the new amendment "opened a parenthesis in the quietude of the Coahuilans."[12]

Three groups, the Maderistas, the Cardenistas, and Cárdenas's allies, the Saltillo elite, joined in an attempt to prevent the reelection of Garza Galán. All three groups resented the Garza Galanistas' monopolization of political and economic power and charged that the governor's nepotistic distribution of industrial concessions, tax exemptions, and public-works contracts hindered the state's development. The railroad concession from Sierra Mojada to Barroterán, which the governor granted to his friend Enrique Baz, a federal senator, was a sore point. Garza Galán's opponents believed the railroad would benefit not only the Sierra Mojada but the entire state as well, and they were especially angry when Baz could not complete it.[13]

Saltillo's elite was also angry over Garza Galán's refusal to grant a tax concession to the Guggenheims, who sought to erect a foundry and smelter to serve northern Mexico, in Saltillo. Exactly why the governor refused the exemption is not clear. Perhaps he feared that the Guggenheims would dominate mining in Coahuila, a sector in which he had substantial investments. Whatever the reasons, the Guggenheims found Bernardo Reyes, the governor of Nuevo León, more receptive to their needs and they constructed a huge operation in Monterrey, which began production in 1892.[14]

In addition, a significant number of Garza Galán's opposition, particularly the Madero camarilla, held large cotton properties in the Laguna district. For many years Coahuilan planters had complained bitterly about the land and water concessions which the foreign-owned Tlahualilo Company obtained from the federal government. Both the company and the local planters depended on water from the Nazas River to irrigate their crops. The river's limited flow could not provide adequate water for both, and bitter disputes resulted. A severe drought between 1891 and 1893 exacerbated the problem. The local planters had become disgusted with Garza Galán's unwillingness, or inability, to resolve the matter in their favor.[15] In general, by 1893 a majority of the Coahuilan entrepreneurial elite had become convinced that Garza Galán was unreceptive to programs which were beneficial to their economic interests.

The opposition constituted a formidable force. The Madero camarilla's vast investments in every sector of the economy made it an especially impressive bloc. Sixteen of the most prominent Saltillans opposing the governor possessed nearly seventeen percent of the total taxable capital in the Saltillo area, the state's industrial heartland.[16] Miguel Cárdenas and a number of the young entrepreneurs who followed him also had considerable economic influence. These men could also count on the support of influential foreign entrepreneurs such as William Purcell, an Irishman. Indeed, the foreign-dominated Chamber of Commerce publicly opposed Garza Galán.[17]

Garza Galán's opponents possessed significant investment capital and were reluctant to engage in developmental projects as long as they perceived Garza Galán's political power as retarding the state's development. The Saltillo opposition and the Madero camarilla represented an older generation of entrepreneurs and professionals, who had controlled the state since the end of the French Intervention. Garza Galán's policies alienated these men from the power structure at a stage in their lives which the Spanish philosopher José Ortega y Gasset referred to as "the age of dominance," from forty-five to sixty, when a generation of men generally dominate their society. Their opposition to Garza Galán helped them find allies among a younger generation of entrepreneurs and professionals in their twenties and thirties, who found their access to political and economic power blocked at a time when their careers should have been blossoming. None of them were likely to suffer this alienation in silence.[18]

Even though his base of support in Coahuila was tenuous, Garza Galán was confident that Díaz would ensure his reelection. Nevertheless, he unleashed a vigorous campaign of harassment against his opponents: hired thugs intimidated them; postal officials opened their mail; police officials collected signatures on petitions supporting the governor.[19] In the spring of 1893, state judges issued arrest warrants for leaders of the Saltillo opposition, charging them with sedition. Many fled to Tamaulipas and to Mexico City, where they joined a Coahuilan commission (opposed to Garza Galán) that was pressuring the president for an interview.[20]

Díaz forced the commission to wait through June and July. A majority of the opposition in Coahuila had thrown its support for a successor to Garza Galán behind General Julio Cervantes, a former military governor of Coahuila, who was then serving as military zone commander in Oaxaca. By the end of June, however, the opposition realized that Díaz intended to continue to support Garza Galán and to leave Cervantes in Oaxaca.

With the demise of the Cervantes candidacy, Miguel Cárdenas and his partisans took the initiative. On 7 July, in Mexico City, the exiled opposition established the Club Juan Antonio de la Fuente, which proceeded to nominate Miguel Cárdenas for governor.[21] Two days later, Cárdenas wrote Díaz, explaining that he had accepted the candidacy only to prevent the violence which appeared inevitable if the opposition movement could not channel its energies into peaceful activities. Cárdenas assured the president that he would remain at the head of the movement only until Díaz had decided what action to take.[22] In Coahuila Cárdenas's adherents established clubs supporting his candidacy.[23]

By August Díaz's intransigence moved the Carranza brothers (supporters of Cárdenas) to declare a revolt. Almost simultaneously, near Allende in the Río Grande district, two Intervention veterans and friends of the Carranzas, General Francisco Treviño and Colonel Jesús Herrera, seconded the call to arms. In a carefully worded telegram to Díaz, the rebels asserted that they were not rebelling against the federal government, but were resorting to violence only because there was no alternative.[24] The Carranzas and their supporters removed Galanista municipal officials and skirmished with state troops in the Río Grande and Monclova districts.[25]

Fortunately for Garza Galán, the hostilities ended almost as quickly as they began. The armed revolt had forced Díaz's hand. Reluctantly, and very coldly, the old autocrat received the commission which he had kept waiting for months. Obviously angered, Díaz lectured the commission members: "First you point carbines at me, and then come to ask for a better government for your state."[26] In spite of his anger, Díaz acted quickly and sent General Reyes to end the hostilities and negotiate a settlement.[27]

The outcome of Reyes's intervention was a trade-off, in which Garza Galán's opposition accepted continued federal domination in exchange for increased access to political and economic power. Once Reyes (backed by a large contingent of federal troops) convinced the rebels to desist, he set to work reconciling the various interests. From the outset, it was evident that Garza Galán had to resign, but the matter of his replacement, for a while at least, was hotly contested.[28]

Garza Galán resigned on 3 September, but attempted to retain his influence by supporting his friend Frumencio Fuentes, a Parras de la Fuente attorney, who, despite his connections with the colonel, was well liked by the Maderos and many prominent Saltillo businessmen. The Cardenistas objected strongly. They wanted nothing that smacked of a continuation of the Garza Galán administration, which they described as a "gangrenous member which it is necessary to amputate so that the social organism can save itself."[29]

The Garza Galanistas, likewise, completely rejected the imposition of Cárdenas, fearing reprisals if he became governor.[30] Reyes first inclined toward the Cardenistas, but then reconsidered and decided to instruct the rebels in the virtues of obedience to the center. The Madero clan, which did not back Cárdenas's move to become governor, agreed to back Reyes's selection, after he had impressed upon them the dire consequences (economic devastation) of taking an opposite tack. Taking advantage of the Madero camarilla's enforced backing, and reminding the Cardenistas that he could use federal troops to eliminate them if necessary, Reyes was able to exact approval from all parties for José María Múzquiz, a politically neutral lawyer from Saltillo, to assume the governor's post. Múzquiz appealed to Reyes as well because of his willingness to be manipulated by the federal government.[31]

The 1893 revolt increased Díaz's determination to impose greater federal control in Coahuila. General Bernardo Reyes became the president's instrument for both intimidating and conciliating the camarillas. Reyes, an astute judge of character and a clever politician, was as brutal, direct, subtle, or conciliatory as the situation demanded. Although personally ambitious, he protected the interests of the federal government and President Díaz. He attended to the interests of camarillas or individuals with close connections to Díaz, although he often mistrusted and disliked them. Such was the case with the Garza Galanistas, whom he protected from their adversaries when Garza Galán was ousted from office, in 1893. At the same time, he did not allow camarillas or individuals he favored, such as the Cardenistas, to become too independent. He dispensed favors and punishments to maintain a balance of power conducive to continued federal control.

The Election of 1892

From 1893 to 1897, political tensions continued to grow beneath the federally imposed tranquility. At the core of the conflict was the governorship. The various camarillas vied for the post, while the regime sought a governor it could manipulate. Governor Múzquiz, the compromise candidate in 1893, proved to be a disappointment. He was a respected lawyer and scion of the prominent Múzquiz family, and was not a member of any major camarilla; in addition, he was malleable and listened obediently to Reyes. Unfortunately, however, the governor did have one insurmountable problem: alcoholism. Múzquiz was an able and conscientious bureaucrat when sober, but sobriety became less and less his normal state. Periodically the governor embarked on drinking binges which he tried to combat by using morphine. As his ability to govern deteriorated, the state legislature threatened to remove him.[32]

Presented with the problem of Múzquiz's drunkenness, Díaz and Reyes decided to remove the governor and grant him the post of federal senator from Coahuila.[33] Múzquiz suggested for interim governor either Miguel Cárdenas or Francisco Arizpe y Ramos, a prominent, middle-aged entrepreneur from Saltillo. The two men had cooperated in the anti–Garza Galán movement, but the regime used the governorship to drive a wedge between them. Because Reyes and Díaz disapproved of Cárdenas's close connection with the rebels, they selected Arizpe y Ramos, who assumed the post in February 1894. To avoid alienating Cárdenas, as well as to ensure Arizpe y Ramos's loyalty, the regime appointed Cárdenas secretary of the government.[34]

In spite of Díaz's and Reyes's careful plans, Cárdenas moved quickly into the governor's palace. The governorship proved too exacting for Arizpe y Ramos, who insisted on resigning in August 1894, after less than six months in office. Although Arizpe y Ramos balked at the suggestion, Reyes favored Cárdenas as his replacement. Reyes convinced Díaz that Cárdenas's political ambition would cause him to sacrifice his own and his camarilla's independence. When Cárdenas addressed an effusive loyalty letter to Díaz, the president agreed to his appointment as interim governor, in mid-August 1894.[35]

The loyalty Cárdenas demonstrated in two years as interim governor led Díaz to permit him to seek the constitutional governorship in 1896. The Garza Galán camarilla, anxious to regain its former influence, immediately launched a campaign against Cárdenas's candidacy. They found an ally in Arizpe y Ramos. The rift between

Cárdenas and Arizpe y Ramos had widened after the former became interim governor; by 1897 Arizpe y Ramos had decided that the pressures of the govenror's office were preferable to allowing Cárdenas to remain in office. Backed by his old enemies, the Garza Galanistas, Arizpe y Ramos announced his opposition. His decision proved to be a foolish one. Well respected in the community, his alliance with the Garza Galanistas discredited him in the eyes of the Saltillo elite and the Madero camarilla. Moreover, his refusal to continue as interim governor in 1894, coupled with his temerity in opposing the official candidate, alienated Díaz and Reyes.

Besides the Garza Galanistas, Arizpe y Ramos could count only on his friends and relatives for support. Allied with an unpopular, minority camarilla, and bereft of federal backing, he stood no real chance of winning.[36] Cárdenas, on the other hand, had skillfully forged a strong base. Although subservient to the federal administration, he was nonetheless an adroit politician. He formed the core of his camarilla from the young professionals and entrepreneurs who had spearheaded the movement against Garza Galán. In addition, as interim governor Cárdenas was attentive to the interests of the Saltillo elite and the Madero camarilla. His judicious use of federal support ensured the backing of the most important elements of Coahuilan society.[37]

Determined to impose Cárdenas, Díaz ordered Reyes to stifle the brewing factional conflict. Reyes organized an intensive campaign against Arizpe y Ramos and the Garza Galanistas. The general first concentrated on Arizpe y Ramos, whom he judged to be a weak, vacillating man. After a series of letters in which Reyes accused him of disloyalty, Arizpe y Ramos buckled under the pressure and withdrew from the race.[38] Left in the lurch by Arizpe y Ramos, the Garza Galanistas quickly selected another, even less viable candidate, Leonardo de los Santos, a Saltillo hacendado and, ironically, an uncle of Miguel Cárdenas.[39]

With Arizpe y Ramos removed from the race, Reyes was free to intensify the pressure on the Garza Galanistas. He orchestrated a campaign in a Nuevo León newspaper against the Garza Galanistas and resorted to outright physical intimidation by sending periodic cavalry patrols through the Múzquiz region, a Galánista stronghold.[40] The pressure took its toll. After a pro-Santos commission received a strong rebuke from Díaz, the campaign against Cárdenas withered. On 15 December 1897, Cárdenas assumed office as constitutional governor.[41]

The Election of 1905

From 1897 to 1904, Coahuila remained calm under the aegis of Bernardo Reyes and the governorship of Miguel Cárdenas. The governor's skillful formation of a broad-based camarilla, his accommodation of the Madero camarilla, and the state's impressive economic development prevented the alienation of the elite which had occurred in 1893. In 1901 Cárdenas easily won reelection. By 1905, however, when he sought reelection for a second time, the governor faced serious opposition. The científico-backed Garza Galán and Madero camarillas sought to use the election to institute limited, but significant, reforms in the Porfirian political system. The confluence of Porfirian factional politics and a reform movement gave the 1905 election national importance.

The intensification of the struggle between General Reyes and the científicos was crucial to the course of Coahuilan politics. The general's capable management of northeastern affairs led Díaz to appoint him minister of war, in 1900. Reyes was an exemplary minister, but the científicos, led by Limantour, cut short his tenure by successfully portraying him as a rival to Díaz. Frustrated by the científicos' machinations, Reyes resigned his post in 1902 and returned to his hacienda, Galeana, in Nuevo León.[42]

The general's resignation was a personal setback, but it did not signify the end of his political career. In 1903 Reyes asked, and received, permission to run for governor of Nuevo León. Assured of Díaz's support, Reyes formed anew his old political organization, the Club Unión y Progreso, which immediately nominated him for governor. In a move that has puzzled historians, Reyes promised a free and public gubernatorial campaign. Reyes might have done so to prove his popularity to his enemies or to lure the opposition into the open where he could combat it. Whatever his reasons, the populace took him seriously and opposition groups formed rapidly.[43]

Reyes was taken aback by the intensity of the opposition and reacted, initially with harassment and later with repression. Increasing tensions sparked violence. In early April 1903, police and oppositionists engaged in a shoot-out in which at least five died. Although most of the victims were police officers, the opposition screamed massacre.[44] The científico-dominated National Congress conducted an investigation, but under pressure from the president—and in the absence of concrete evidence—acquitted Reyes.[45]

Reyes emerged the victor in the Nuevo León gubernatorial race, but his struggle with the científicos continued and spread into Coahuila. The científicos tried to use the 1904 presidential election to subdue Reyes. Contrary to past practice, Díaz allowed the científicos to sponsor him for reelection. In March 1903, the científicos reformed the old Union Liberal Party and asked state governments to send delegates to a national convention.[46] They hoped to force Reyes to send delegates to the Union Liberal convention or, if he refused, to risk appearing disloyal to Díaz. In Monterrey the Club Unión Liberal was composed of men antagonistic to Reyes. Among the club's officers were Lázaro Garza Ayala and members of the Madero and Zambrano families. The Maderos, closely linked to the científicos, had decided to dissolve the alliance they had made with Reyes in 1893 and began to oppose him. The Zambranos were powerful entrepreneurs and in-laws of Reyes's enemy Gerónimo Treviño.[47] In Coahuila, members of the Madero and Garza Galán camarillas formed branches of the Club Unión Liberal.[48]

Científico efforts to thwart Reyes proved fruitless. Reyes promised the national Unión Liberal that regional clubs in Nuevo León and Coahuila would assist in the campaign efforts, but "without entering into the rest of the formalities" conducted by the científico organization.[49] In Nuevo León he allowed the Unión Liberal to operate, but supported his own Club Unión y Progreso as the official Porfirian party. In Coahuila, adherents of Reyes's protégé, Governor Cárdenas, organized a Club Unión y Progreso to counter the Unión Liberal. In addition, Cárdenas accused the Club Unión Liberal of conducting proceedings which were neither "sane nor legal."[50] Under pressure from Cárdenas and Reyes, the Unión Liberal merged with the Reyista club. The incident was a victory for Reyes, since no delegation from Coahuila or Nuevo León attended the Unión Liberal convention in Mexico City.[51]

Outmaneuvered by Reyes in both the Nuevo León gubernatorial

race and the 1904 presidential campaign, the científicos persisted in their efforts to destroy Reyes politically. The 1905 gubernatorial election in Coahuila afforded them the opportunity to reduce Reyes's political base in the state by eliminating his protégé, Miguel Cárdenas. Two camarillas, the Maderistas and the Garza Galanistas, joined their attempt. While the Madero camarilla had participated in Garza Galán's ouster in 1893, they found common cause with them by 1905. Evaristo Madero and his partisans felt increasingly isolated by Reyes's influence in Coahuila. They believed that Reyes's instrument, Cárdenas, was indifferent to their interests. The Garza Galanistas, led by the colonel's son, Andrés, sought to settle the score with Cárdenas.[52]

A new group's entrance into the anti-Cárdenas campaign made the upcoming election more than a factional struggle. Composed primarily of young professionals isolated from the Coahuilan power structure, they viewed the election as an opportunity to effect reform. This group had its origin in 1904, when two young men, Francisco I. Madero, Evaristo Madero's grandson, and Gabriel Calzada, a schoolteacher, established the Club Democratico Benito Juárez, in San Pedro. The club's first involvement in politics came in 1904, when it decided to oppose the official candidate for municipal president of San Pedro. Francisco Rivas, a respected hacendado, was the club's candidate for the post. He ran on a platform calling for improved educational facilities, municipal improvements, free suffrage, and antialcoholism. On election day, club members stood outside the polls counseling voters to exercise their rights without fear. Although he won the popular vote, Rivas did not take office. When the *junta de escrutinio* (election board) met, Mariano Viesca y Arizpe, the official candidate, was declared the winner.[53]

The 1905 gubernatorial election spurred the growth of the movement initiated by the Benito Juárez club. Calzada and Madero were joined by others, especially a group of young professionals from Torreón, headed by a physician, José María Rodríguez, and a schoolteacher, José Gálvez. Rodríguez had supported Cárdenas in 1893 and 1897, but had become dissatisfied with the Cardenistas' monopoly of power. The *continuismo, personalismo,* and fradulent elections that Rodríguez and others had combated in 1893 still existed. They were not totally disaffected with the regime at this point, but merely desired more autonomy for their state and region within the Porfirian system.⁵⁴

Faced with serious opposition, Cárdenas reacted swiftly. He requested and received federal support. Díaz instructed military officers, federal officials, and prominent professionals and entrepreneurs whom he considered bulwarks of his regime in the state to use their influence to ensure Cárdenas's reelection. Assured of federal support, the governor then set out to rally his own forces. In spite of the opposition's strength, Cárdenas's backing was considerable. He had strong economic and personal ties with the Saltillo entrepreneurial elite. The alliance he had made with prominent families in the Monclova district remained in effect. In the Río Grande district, where the Maderos and Garza Galanistas were strong, he could rely on Reyes's adherent, Colonel Fructuoso García, the unchallenged authority there.

Political expediency dictated that the two camarillas and the young professionals that opposed Cárdenas present a united front. Nevertheless, the three groups bickered constantly. The young men from the Club Benito Juárez proposed a convention (scheduled for February) to choose a gubernatorial candidate. The Garza Galanistas, however, opposed a convention at that time. The young reformers and the Garza Galanistas finally reached an agreement with the others to postpone the convention until May. But further disputes occurred over the convention site. The Garza Galanistas and the Maderos wanted the convention to be held in Mexico City, close to one of their major científico supporters, Ramón Corral. The Club Benito Juárez's members feared the influence of Corral, and wished to hold the convention in Coahuila. The Garza Galanistas, better organized and more numerous, prevailed.⁵⁵

The convention was held in May in Mexico City, amid considerable dissension. Madero clan members wanted to nominate one of their own, Ernesto Madero, for governor.⁵⁶ The young reformers supported a Saltillo physician, Dionisio García Fuentes. Andrés Garza Galán had spread money liberally around Coahuila to ensure the presence of a large Garza Galanista delegation at the convention. As a result, the Garza Galanistas ensured the nomination of their candidate, Frumencio Fuentes.⁵⁷

Francisco Madero and his colleagues were dissatisfied with the convention's outcome. In their estimation, Fuentes's election would result in an even more repressive and corrupt administration. To offset the influence of Fuentes in a future administration, the club worked to capture the state legislature and the municipal governments.[58]

The election was set for September, and both the opposition and the government established political clubs throughout the state. Authorities harassed the opposition clubs constantly. In Múzquiz, the jefe político, Alberto Guarardo, used the election to intensify his attacks on the Garza Galán clan.[59] Rumors of revolt circulated in the Monclova and Río Grande districts, and the authorities reacted with arrests of opposition leaders.[60] Cárdenas increased the public security forces in the districts, and ordered frequent patrols in the area.[61]

Constant pressure by the federal government wore away the resolve of the opposition candidate. In late August, Díaz summoned Fuentes to Mexico City for an interview. There is no record of their conversation, but Fuentes returned to Coahuila obviously chastened. He informed his supporters, in a meeting in Torreón on 3 September, that he was withdrawing from the race. Fuentes's followers asked him to reconsider, but Fuentes countered that the cause was hopeless without Díaz's support. Although the Garza Galanistas vacillated, the young reformers prevailed and Fuentes reluctantly agreed to continue the campaign.[62]

Election day, 17 September, passed without incident. Municipal authorities went to ridiculous lengths to prevent the opposition from voting. In Matamoros de la Laguna, a voter asked the location of the voting booth and was told that it had been moved to Ireland.[63] In spite of such tactics the opposition won in a number of municipalities. Election officials, however, ensured victory for official candidates by manipulating the juntas de escrutinio.[64]

Conclusions

Porfirian rule rested on a delicate and volatile balance of forces. The Coahuilan elite was divided into collective groupings which engaged in rough and tumble, and, at times, violent political competition. The general consensus on economic development and the personalistic character of the camarillas meant that economic factors played a role in factional politics generally on the level of crass personal interest. In a broader sense, monopolization of political power by one camarilla, coincidental with an economic recession (such as occurred in 1893), could spell the demise of the camarilla in power. Personalism also meant that alliances among camarillas formed and dissolved rapidly.

Díaz encouraged competition among the camarillas as a control mechanism. He always attempted to tie camarilla leaders to the regime, to prevent the development of independent political groups. The camarillas' linkage to warring factions in the national administration accentuated the impartial pose which Díaz assumed, and facilitated his divide-and-conquer strategy. In dealing with elite conflict and revolts, the Porfirian regime proved capable of exercising the restraint which the delicate equilibrium of forces required. Díaz and his políticos, like Reyes, analyzed a situation and acted in a manner most conducive to continued federal control.

In 1893 the regime found itself facing a majority of the elite intent on removing a federally imposed governor. The regime offered limited concessions, while at the same time reasserting federal control. In 1897 the Díaz administration backed a candidate who was less popular, but who still had impressive support among significant elements of the elite. It appears that a camarilla with a broader base obtained federal support more readily and governed more easily than a camarilla with a narrow base. Above all, Díaz took pains to protect a minority camarilla and to cushion a camarilla's fall from power.

Díaz's manipulation of Coahuila's camarillas was impressive. With the aid of capable lieutenants like Reyes, Díaz kept them dependent, divided, relatively content, and docile. However, his personalistic approach to politics gave him a stagnant view of the political system. For Díaz, political movements represented little more than the base ambitions of individuals. In 1893 and 1897, his perceptions of Coahuilan political reality were, for the most part, accurate. By 1905, however, the situation had altered. The emergence of a reform group in the 1905 gubernatorial campaign signified an increase in the scope of political mobilization with which the regime would have to contend, at the risk, as ultimately developed, of facing serious consequences.

NOTES

1. Juan Linz, "An Authoritarian Regime: Spain," in *Mass Politics: Studies in Political Sociology,* ed. Erik Allardt and Stein Rokkan (New York, 1970), 261.

2. Peter Smith, in his study of contemporary Mexican politics, states that political struggle takes place not between the three components of the PRI, but rather among factional camarillas. Smith's definition of camarillas is used here, with one difference: Smith notes that businessmen do not belong to modern Mexican camarillas, since the political and economic elites are separate. In Porfirian Coahuila, the two were interlocked and camarillas did contain entrepreneurs. See Peter H. Smith, *The Labyrinth of Power: Political Recruitment in Twentieth Century Mexico* (Princeton, 1979), 55, 277.

3. In a study of the *panelinhas* of Brazil, Anthony Leeds has hypothesized that such groups are products of a stage of socioeconomic development such as occurred in Mexico and Brazil. See Anthony Leeds, "Brazilian Careers and Social Structures: A Case History and a Model," in *Contemporary Cultures and Societies of Latin America,* ed. Dwight P. Heath and Richard N. Adams (New York, 1965), 379–404.

4. Bernardo Reyes to Porfirio Díaz, 18 April 1903, *Colección General Porfirio Díaz* (hereafter cited as *CPD*), legajo 28, nos. 4378–79.

5. Mauricio Rodríguez to Porfirio Díaz, 5 May 1907, *CPD,* leg. 32, no. 5458; E. Guerrero, *La cuestión electoral del estado de Coahuila: Reminiscencia histórica de los acontecimientos más notables ocurridos en el estado de Coahuila con motivo de la reelección del C. Coronel J. M. Garza Galán* (Saltillo, 1894), 144.

6. Colonel José María Garza Galán and don Manuel Romero Rubio were partners in the former's Sierra Mojada mining company, the Sociedad Minera La Exploradora. *Registro de Propiedades del Estado de Coahuila* (hereafter cited as *RPC*), partido 2, folio 3, tomo 1, libro 1.

7. Bernardo Reyes to Porfirio Díaz, 24 June 1894, *CPD,* leg. 19, no. 11270; *El Pendón Coahuilense,* 16 July 1893; *Periódico Oficial del Estado de Coahuila de Zaragoza,* 25 November 1896; José María Garza Galán to Porfirio Díaz, 19 Aug. 1893, *CPD,* leg. 18, no. 11666.

8. Ildefonso Villarello Vélez, *Historia de la revolución mexicana en Coahuila* (Saltillo, 1970), 140.

9. José María Garza Galán to Porfirio Díaz, 29 June 1893, *CPD*, leg. 18, no. 9872; Archivo General del Estado de Coahuila (hereafter cited as *AGEC*), leg. 106, expediente 4035 and 4037, 1886–87; *El Coahuilense*, 24 April 1889.

10. Guerrero, *La cuestión electoral*, 15. Interview with Pablo Cuellar Valdés, 7 Sept. 1978.

11. *Informe del Comité Puntos Constitutionales del Congreso del Estado de Coahuila de Zaragoza*, 7 Feb. 1893, Archivo del Poder Legislativo del Estado de Coahuila (hereafter cited as *APLC*), leg. 6, exp. 75.

12. Encarnación Dávila to Porfirio Díaz, 28 Feb. 1893, *CPD*, leg. 18, no. 3224.

13. Guerrero, *La cuestión electoral*, 149.

14. Anthony Bryan, "Mexican Politics in Transition: The Career of General Bernardo Reyes," Ph.D. diss. (University of Nebraska, 1969), 122.

15. Amador Cárdenas to Julio Cervantes, 2 May 1893, *CPD*, leg. 18, no. 5958; Amador Cárdenas to Julio Cervantes, 18 April 1893, *CPD*, leg. 18, no. 5957; William K. Meyers, "Politics, Vested Rights, and Economic Growth in Porfirian Mexico: The Company Tlahualilo in the Comarca Lagunera, 1885–1911," *Hispanic American Historical Review* 57 (Aug. 1977): 442.

16. In the catastral survey of 1890 for the Saltillo district the total listed capital was 3,121,289 pesos. For the sixteen men referred to, the total listed capital was as follows: Dámaso Rodríguez 43,397; Francisco Arizpe y Ramos 65,306; Marcelino Garza 17,866; Clemente Cabello 49,866; Valeriano Ancira 92,133; Jesús María Martínez Ancira 12,099; Gabriel Flores 39,399; William Purcell 40,000; Bernardo Sota 43,166; John Carothers 18,266; Hipólito Charles 24,572; Guadalupe Dávila 11,733; Desiderio Dávila Valle 45,667; Melchor Lobo Rodríguez 17,466; David Zamora 8,000; Thomás Dávila 8,000. Catastro Municipalidad de Saltillo, Comunicaciones al Jefe Político, 1892, Archivo Municipal de Saltillo.

17. Guerrero, *La cuestión electroal*, 19–21; *El Pendón Coahuilense*, 30 July 1893.

18. Alan B. Spitzer, "The Historical Problem of Generations," *American Historical Review* (Dec. 1973): 1353–85. This article offers an excellent discussion of generational theory in history.

19. Miguel Cárdenas to Julio Cervantes, 12 May 1893, *CPD*, leg. 18, no. 5981.

20. Miguel Cárdenas to Julio Cervantes, 12 May 1893, *CPD, leg. 18, no. 5929*.

21. *El Pendón Coahuilense*, 9 July 1893; José María Garza Galán to Porfirio Díaz, 9 July 1893, *CPD*, leg. 18, no. 9942.

22. Miguel Cárdenas to Porfirio Díaz, 7 July 1893, *CPD*, leg. 18, no. 9335.

23. *El Pendón Coahuilense*, 9 July 1893; José María Garza Galán to Porfirio Díaz, 9 July 1893, *CPD*, leg. 18, no. 9942.

24. Emilio Carranza et al. to Porfirio Díaz, 13 Aug. 1893, *CPD*, leg. 18, no. 11685; Alfonso Taracena, *Venustiano Carranza* (Mexico, 1963), 11–13.

25. *El Pendón Coahuilense*, 10 Sept. 1893; *La Raza Latina*, 29 Aug. 1893; *El Monitor Republicano*, 26 Aug. 1893; Villarello Vélez, *Historia*, 29.

26. José de la Luz Valdés, *José García Rodríguez* (Saltillo, 1969), 18–19; Pablo C. Moreno, *Galería de coahuilenses distinguidos* (Torreón, 1951), 182.

27. Third Army Zone Commander to Governor of Coahuila, 17 Aug. 1893, *AGEC*, leg. 148, nos. 1189, 1191.

28. Bernardo Reyes to Porfirio Díaz, 31 Aug. 1893, *CPD*, leg. 18, no. 10742.

29. José María Garza Galán to Porfirio Díaz, 3 Sept. 1893, *CPD*, leg. 18, no. 13653; Francisco García de Letona to Coahuilan People, August 1893, *CPD*, leg. 18, no. 12325.

30. José María Garza Galán to Porfirio Díaz, 3 Sept. 1893, *CPD*, leg. 18, no. 13533.

31. Bernardo Reyes to Porfirio Díaz, 21 Sept. 1893, *CPD*, leg. 18, no. 12542.

32. Arnulfo García to Porfirio Díaz, 28 Jan. 1894, *CPD*, leg. 19, no. 132.

33. Bernardo Reyes to Porfirio Díaz, 10 Jan. 1894, *CPD*, leg. 19, no. 3097.

34. Miguel Cárdenas to Porfirio Díaz, 18 Feb. 1894, *CPD*, leg. 19, no. 2577.

35. Bernardo Reyes to Porfirio Díaz, 5 Aug. 1894, *CPD*, leg. 19, no. 12622; Bernardo Reyes to Porfirio Díaz, 13 Aug. 1894, *CPD*, leg. 19, no. 2663.

36. Bernardo Reyes to Porfirio Díaz, 25 July 1897, *CPD*, leg. 22, no. 9802; Bernardo Reyes to Porfirio Díaz, 9 Aug. 1897, *CPD*, leg. 22, no. 11305.

37. Bernardo Reyes to Porfirio Díaz, 20 May 1897, *CPD*, leg. 22, no. 6400; Villarello Vélez, *Historia*, 42.
38. Bernardo Reyes to Porfirio Díaz, 17 July 1897, *CPD*, leg. 22, no. 1176; Bernardo Reyes to Porfirio Díaz, 9 Aug. 1897, *CPD*, leg. 22, no. 11319.
39. *Periódico Oficial*, 6 Sept. 1905; Bernardo Reyes to Porfirio Díaz, 11 Aug. 1897, *CPD*, leg. 22, no. 11320.
40. Porfirio Díaz to Bernardo Reyes, 16 Aug. 1897, *CPD*, leg. 22, no. 11323.
41. Pablo Cuellar Valdés, *Historia de la ciudad de Saltillo* (Saltillo, 1975), 256.
42. Bryan, "Mexican Politics," 186.
43. Ibid.; Francisco Naranjo to Porfirio Díaz, 25 March 1903, *CPD*, leg. 28, no. 2438; Porfirio Díaz to Francisco Naranjo, 30 March 1903, *CPD*, leg. 28, no. 2442.
44. Bryan, "Mexican Politics," 189.
45. Ibid., 191.
46. Ibid., 194.
47. Bernardo Reyes to Porfirio Díaz, 18 April 1903, *CPD*, leg. 28, nos. 4378–79.
48. Miguel Cárdenas to Porfirio Díaz, 10 May 1903, *CPD*, leg. 28, no. 6441; Miguel Cárdenas to Pragedis de la Peña, 10 May 1903, *CPD*, leg. 28, no. 6448.
49. Bryan, "Mexican Politics," 195.
50. Miguel Cárdenas to Porfirio Díaz, 10 May 1903, *CPD*, leg. 28, no. 6441; Miguel Cárdenas to Pragedis de la Peña, 10 May 1903, *CPD*, leg. 28, no. 6448.
51. Bryan, "Mexican Politics," 197.
52. Miguel Cárdenas to Porfirio Díaz, 19 Jan. 1905, *CPD*, leg. 30, no. 1559; Citizens of Múzquiz to Porfirio Díaz, 16 Jan. 1905, *CPD*, leg. 30, no. 248.
53. Stanley Ross, *Madero* (Mexico, 1955), 44; Villarello Vélez, *Historia*, 59; *Periódico Oficial*, 24 Dec. 1904.
54. Gabriel Calzada to Porfirio Díaz, 22 May 1950, *CPD*, leg. 30, no. 6787.
55. Ross, *Madero*, 44–45; Villarello Vélez, *Historia*, 59.
56. Miguel Cárdenas to Porfirio Díaz, 16 May 1905, *CPD*, leg. 30, no. 6430.
57. Miguel Cárdenas to Porfirio Díaz, 20 May 1905, *CPD*, leg. 30, no. 5459; Villarello Vélez, *Historia*, 50–60; Ross, *Madero*, 45.

58. Ross, *Madero*, 46.
59. *AGEC*, leg. 241, exp. 223, Municipal President, Múzquiz, 2–6 June 1905.
60. Eduardo Elizondo to Frumencio Fuentes, 2 July 1905, *CPD*, leg. 30, no. 8692; Miguel Múzquiz Dávila to Porfirio Díaz, 3 July 1905, *CPD*, leg. 30, no. 9018; Juan José Galán to Porfirio Díaz, 12 July 1905, *CPD*, leg. 30, no. 8828.
61. Miguel Cárdenas to Porfirio Díaz, 3 July 1905, *CPD*, leg. 30, no. 9490.
62. Torreón Municipal President to Miguel Cárdenas, 10 Sept. 1905, *CPD*, leg. 30, no. 11920.
63. Mariano López de Lara to Frumencio Fuentes, 20 Sept. 1905, *CPD*, leg. 30, no. 12984.
64. Bernardo Reyes to Porfirio Díaz, 19 Sept. 1905, *CPD*, leg. 30, no. 11763.

4
Puebla:
Breakdown of the Old Order

David LaFrance

The highly centralized political machine that long-time Mexican dictator Porfirio Díaz created and controlled was one of the principal factors contributing to the stability of his regime. Nevertheless, this system planted the seeds of its own destruction, as its personalistic and increasingly rigid nature could no longer contend effectively with the ever-growing numbers of outsiders attempting to participate in national life. The Maderista movement attracted large numbers of these outsiders, eventually overwhelming the military capability of the regime. With Díaz's defeat, the linchpin of this mechanism was removed, and the power source of government officials throughout the nation, their links to the dictator, disappeared. With their connection to the top disrupted, these Porfirian officials faced relentless attacks by all varieties of the discontented, who wanted the privilege, power, and gain they surely thought would come by personally attaching themselves to the new leader,

Francisco I. Madero. Madero, however, failed to support fully his followers' desire to eliminate the officials of the old regime, thereby alienating many of his more radical adherents and breathing new life into the Porfiristas. Both groups sought out alternative leaders, leaving Madero isolated and with increasingly less political control at the state and local levels. By late 1912 and early 1913, chaos reigned in many sections of the country as the Porfirian structures finally toppled. The February 1913 coup d'état, led by Victoriano Huerta, was a desperate and vain attempt to restore the Porfirian order through the use of arms. The brittle system based solely on the person of Díaz had crumbled, exposing the hollow nature of the political institutions he had created.

Events in the state of Puebla during this period clearly manifest the process of disintegration of the Díaz political machine. An agriculturally and industrially important state with a large population, Puebla lies on the strategic route between the capital and the main port of Veracruz. A tight rein on its government officials was a key factor in Díaz's control of the central region of the republic. By examining the evolution of the relationship between the governorship and the presidency from Mucio P. Martínez's term through that of Juan B. Carrasco, ending in 1913, this chapter illustrates the breakdown of Díaz's carefully crafted, yet faulty, system.

Mucio P. Martínez

Mucio P. Martínez, governor of Puebla from 1892 to 1911, was the archetypical Porfirian state executive. Described by contemporaries and historians alike as, among other things, arbitrary, corrupt, harsh, and unpopular, Martínez remained in power and loyally served Díaz for nearly two decades.[1] Martínez equated service to the dictator with maintaining strict control over his state. By 1909–10, however, this policy proved counterproductive, and disaffected elements from the lower and middle classes joined the Maderista movement, seriously threatening the regime. In early 1911 Díaz, in an effort to save his government, sacrificed his long-time servant.

Díaz was familiar with his subordinate's heavy hand and kept a close watch over Martínez. Complaints to Díaz from Poblanos required detailed written explanations from Martínez. The president

Puebla, 1910

also relied on reports from other officials, especially Governor Próspero Cahuantzi of the neighboring state of Tlaxcala and the federal zone commander, General Luis G. Valle. On more than one occasion, Díaz had to stop Martínez from taking unnecessarily harsh action against his opponents. Nevertheless, the governor remained faithful; for example, he formed some six hundred pro-Díaz-Corral Reelectionist political clubs in the state, in preparation for the 1910 election. Even after having been ousted from his post as the state's chief executive, Martínez emphasized his continued loyalty and respect for Díaz and his belief that he had always cooperated with him to the best of his ability.[2]

Martínez, in turn, had his own coterie of subordinates, upon whom he relied to maintain control over the 1.1 million Poblanos (a tenth of whom resided in Puebla City, the nation's third largest).[3] Among the most important of these officials were the heads of the state's regular and rural forces, the Puebla City police chief and municipal president, the secretary to the governor, several state deputies, and the all-important *jefes políticos*.

The governor gained the unquestioning loyalty and support of these officials through his ability to hand out lucrative concessions. In return for his fealty to Díaz, Martínez received not only the power and prestige of office, but also the opportunity to enrich himself. Martínez, in turn, provided the same benefits to those loyal to him. The hierarchical chain of command from Díaz through Martínez to lesser officials in the state was thus reinforced by the possibility of material gain, legal or otherwise. Martínez's yearly salary of twelve thousand pesos accounted for only a very small percentage of his annual income. The governor owned a number of illegal gambling houses and several haciendas. He controlled the meat and *pulque* monopolies as well, which he awarded to concessionaires, including his son, for a price. Martínez and his cohorts also made large sums on kickbacks in conjunction with the construction of public works in the state and, upon leaving office, he reportedly took some 890,000 pesos from the state coffers. The Martinistas prospered handsomely at the expense of the city and state treasuries.[4]

Besides his network of state and local officials, Martínez could also call on a multitiered military organization to ensure control and stifle opponents. The state forces consisted of the three-hundred-man Zaragoza Batallion and a small contingent of rural troops. These could be augmented by indigenous militia from the northern sierra, called volunteers, but actually under the control of such powerful *caciques* as Juan Francisco Lucas. The federal army fielded some three hundred soldiers in the seventh military zone (the states of Guerrero, Puebla, and Tlaxcala), and parts of the first and ninth federal rural corps were scattered throughout the state. The total number of troops, excluding the militia, was about seven hundred in 1910. Considering the size, population, and varied topography of the state, this total was small; the Martínez regime was able to maintain law and order with a minimum of overt coercion.[5]

Aiding the government and the military's ability to keep watch so effectively over the state's 21 districts and 183 municipalities was a fairly well developed transportation and communication system. By 1910 five railroad lines served the state, while the telegraph network linked most towns. Many *pueblos* even had telephone connections with their respective *cabeceras* and district capitals, while Puebla City was linked by phone to several of the district seats. One could contact Mexico City from the state capital by telegram or mail, or make the approximately ten-hour trip on either the Interoceánico or Mexicano railroad.[6]

Martínez used several means to silence adversaries. Press critics were jailed or banned from the state or even murdered, as in the case of José Olmos y Contreras, the daring director of *La Voz de la Verdad,* who was stabbed to death by unknown assailants in a Puebla street. Recalcitrant labor leaders found themselves serving involuntary stints in the army; commercial competitors, such as the Cuetzalán coffee merchant Agustín Azpiróz, was thrown in jail by local Martinista officials. Those of Martínez's intimates who were repelled by his heavy-handed actions and who consequently resigned their posts, such as his personal secretary, Armando Llevera, were eliminated (in Llevera's case by poisoning) to protect the regime.[7]

Individual opponents of the state government posed little serious threat and could generally be silenced in a number of ways without provoking dangerous repercussions. Martínez, however, had no tolerance for organized political opposition, especially in the volatile rural areas, where long-standing grievances over *caciquismo,* local officials, land, and taxes provided ready tinder. In his handling of a rural disturbance in early 1909, the governor drew national attention to his harshness and provided fuel for his enemies, just as opposition political movements were organizing to challenge Díaz in the following year's election. In the southwesten community of Tehuitzingo (which would later become the heart of Zapatista country in the state), a rigged municipal election provoked a rebellion against the town fathers that resulted in several dead and wounded on the rioters' side. Afterwards troops, under the command of the jefe político, summarily shot several suspected ringleaders, while others were jailed and/or inducted into the army. Martínez asked Díaz to ensure that the supreme court would not grant reprieves (*amparo*) to any of those jailed and commented that by sending them to the coasts (i.e., to the prison of San Juan de Ulúa in Veracruz harbor and to the Yucatán), "no matter what may befall them, they will be purged of their errors."[8]

In retrospect, the Tehuitzingo rebellion was the opening scene of a four-year drama that would result in Martínez's fall from power and that would finally destroy the carefully crafted political structure that he and Díaz had constructed. Even Martínez noticed the increasing dissatisfaction in the state during the first half of 1909, and he moved to destroy its visible manifestation, the Reyista and Maderista political movements that sprang up during the year.[9] He fired the public employees who made up the majority of members in a pro-Reyes democratic club in the northern city of Huauchinango; when Bernardo Reyes failed to support his adherents, the movement folded and many of his backers joined the Maderistas.[10]

The Maderistas, however, were not so easily contained as the Reyistas.[11] Aquiles Serdán, the dynamic, even fanatical leader of the state's Maderistas, managed to overcome severe internal dissension and financial problems, as well as government repression, in his successful bid to create a viable opposition political movement in Puebla. Soon after founding a number of political clubs in Puebla and Tlaxcala, he was jailed on trumped-up charges of having stolen a pistol from a police agent.[12] State authorities took advantage of Serdán's forced absence during the autumn of 1909 to attack the movement. Despite the setback, other members carried on the work; Díaz, not yet having taken Madero and his movement seriously and worried over the image Martínez was creating with his hard-line tactics in Puebla, apparently ordered his governor to ease up.[13] From the time Serdán was released from jail, in December, until Madero's visit in May 1910, the Anti-Reelectionists faced only halfhearted persecution in the form of scattered harassment from officials at the local level, opened mail, and infiltration by police spies.[14]

The overwhelming response to Madero's mid-May visit to Puebla shocked state officials as well as Díaz. The multitude that greeted Madero was estimated at between twenty-five and thirty thousand people. All elements of society, including a large number of government employees, attended. The state government's perfunctory attempt to disperse the crowd was prompted both by the size and the makeup of the gathering and Díaz's order to allow Madero free movement and complete liberty during the visit.[15]

Sensing the mood of enthusiasm for Madero that enveloped the city during his visit and heeding Díaz's cautionary order, Martínez wisely created no martyrs. Once the Anti-Reelectionist leader had departed, however, and national attention was no longer focused on Puebla, the wave of reprisals began. In an obvious attempt to break the back of the movement before the June election, the authorities arrested dozens of Madero's sympathizers throughout the state. Groups of prisoners passed daily through Puebla on their way to Mexico City, where they were inducted into the army or sent to an almost certain death by laboring in Quintana Roo. Others languished in jail, where they were subject to torture and assassination. As the election neared, many became virtual prisoners in their own homes as police agents awaited their appearance in order to arrest them. Some fled the state. Houses and offices were systematically searched.[16]

Instead of dealing a death blow to the movement, however, these repressive tactics further served to polarize the already tense state as Martínez's base of support began to erode. One Maderista claimed that after Madero's visit, some of the police began to show signs of sympathy toward the cause. Puebla's jefe político noticed increasing difficulty in collecting taxes on wares in the market, which he blamed on Madero's promise to abolish the tax. Observers also noted increasing unrest in the northern districts of Tetela de Ocampo and Zacatlán, where the movement was gaining followers among government employees.[17]

When the fraudulent June election had passed and the repression continued unabated, the Serdán-led faction of the movement prepared for revolution. Rumors of an impending armed revolt prompted Martínez to use even harsher, almost paranoid measures. In August, for example, the police arrested a Puebla stationer and confiscated his stock merely for selling pictures of Madero.[18] In September, following an antigovernment disturbance during independence day celebrations, the police arrested nearly one hundred. Of these people, thirty-six were inducted into the army, while fifty-six others, unfit for military service, were surreptitiously loaded on a train in Puebla at 3:30 A.M., in order to avoid a scandal, and sent off to Quintana Roo.[19] These and other prisoners, held incommunicado, were denied the formality of legal sentencing before a court of justice. Martínez informed Díaz that he was unwilling to send the prisoners before the judge because, given the judge's earlier actions, he would again free them. Martínez continued, "I have wanted those troublemakers to be punished with the greatest severity. . . ." Therefore, he added, "the only exemplary lesson and punishment would be to consign them to the army or to Yucatán where they will be filled with terror."[20] Such crudely repressive tactics only made the preparations for revolution by Serdán and his followers easier, since many citizens who in other times at least tolerated the regime, for lack of alternatives, now cast their lot with the revolutionaries.

The resulting revolt severely shook the state government. Serdán, named by Madero head of revolutionary forces in Puebla with the authority to establish a government, hoped to overthrow the regime by initiating a rebellion from his house, to be joined simultaneously by worker and peasant forces throughout the state. But state authorities feared an imminent outbreak of violence and raided Serdán's house two days before the scheduled uprising, on 20 November 1910, forcing Serdán to initiate his plan then and there. The sudden change in timing caught his supporters off guard; they failed to come to Serdán's aid. He and his followers in Puebla City were quickly defeated, with about twenty, including Serdán himself, dying in the fight.[21]

In the aftermath of the battle, a serious rift emerged between Martínez on the one hand, and Díaz and the zone commander, General Valle, on the other. Díaz upbraided Martínez for his failure to prevent the revolt and for his handling of it once it had begun. In addition, he chastized the governor for not taking Serdán alive. Díaz then openly humiliated Martínez and undermined his position by sending a special investigator to Puebla. Martínez, naturally enough, became incensed at this encroachment on his jurisdiction and the questioning of his actions and loyalty.[22]

Martínez in turn tried to place the blame for the shootout on Valle, who, Martínez claimed, had always insisted on defending the forts overlooking the city rather than concentrating upon such tall buildings as the churches and the hospital. When the battle with Serdán began, Valle, the governor charged, even failed to send troops to aid in the fight. Consequently, Martínez asked Díaz, in vain, to dismiss the zone commander.[23]

The failure of the Serdán revolt and additional government security measures kept the revolutionary movement at a low ebb until February. That month began auspiciously, however, when the Tlaxcalan rebel leader, Juan Cuamatzi, operating in cooperation with the Poblanos, led a daring attack on the Los Molinos factory, near Atlixco. His ranks swelled by sympathizers from the area, including the municipal president of San Pedro Cuaco, Cuamatzi sacked two towns before returning to his sanctuary on the volcano Malinche.[24]

Governor Cahuantzi also indicated the degree to which the Maderistas had gained adherents among the state's citizenry, including its local officialdom, when he informed Díaz that everyone in the northern town of Otlatlán was a sympathizer or family member of the rebels. He also urged Díaz to replace the jefe político of the district of Alatriste because he was unable to ensure order; he also recommended firing the district judge, the entire town council, and especially the municipal president of Chignahuapan, because they were all Maderista sympathizers.[25]

Díaz was disturbed by the reports of increasing revolutionary activity, the animosity between Martínez and Valle, and the lack of enthusiasm on the part of the state's upper classes for the hardline policy of his governor. In view of the worsening situation both in Puebla and nationally, the president, in an attempt to bolster his rapidly weakening position, ordered Martínez to resign. General Valle, in turn, gladly assumed the responsibility of helping to choose a successor and arranging the transition under Díaz's guidance. Once Valle had ensured that the legislature was disposed to cooperate, Martínez stepped down on 4 March.[26] In an interview he claimed that his resignation was voluntary and necessary for reasons of fatigue and ill health. When asked about allegations of abuse on the part of jefes políticos under his administration, he denied that he had ever kept anyone in office against the peoples' wishes except where it was imperative, as in Atlixco where, he claimed, a firm hand was needed.[27] In an effort to save the state, Díaz abandoned the hard line that Martínez represented for a more conciliatory posture at the political level. This tactic, however, remained secondary in importance to military considerations, as indicated by General Valle's now dominant position in the state's hierarchy.

José Rafael Isunza

Díaz chose an independent, José Rafael Isunza, to replace Martínez. A talented lawyer, he directed the Colegio del Estado from 1894 to 1910, when he resigned in protest over the government's treatment of students involved in the Maderista movement. In agreeing to accept the governorship, Isunza informed Díaz that it was his understanding, based on conversations with Valle, that he was to "re-establish order and public confidence via a rigorously honest and methodical administration by calling for the collaboration of all honest and able Poblanos irrespective of party." However, to ensure that Isunza did not become too independent, Díaz instructed Valle to oversee Isunza's selection of personnel.[28]

At this point Díaz felt that the appointment of an independent such as Isunza would be sufficient to pacify the restless middle class. Other Martinista officials would be removed from office, but the naming of their replacements would ultimately be under the control of Díaz and Valle, not Isunza. Thus the hoped-for appearance of substantive change would in reality be nothing more than the substitution of one loyal Porfirista for another. With the call for political change muted, Valle could carry on his program of militarily defeating the rebels.

Even before Isunza assumed his duties as interim governor, Díaz and Valle began purging the state's officialdom. Among those forced to resign were several of the more unpopular state officials, including the secretary general, the jefes políticos of Puebla and Atlixco, the municipal president of Puebla, and the heads of the state rural and regular forces.[29] The rapidity with which Díaz and Valle made the changes demonstrates their urgency to initiate the plan both in the face of continued rebellion and before Isunza took office. In this manner Isunza would be faced with a fait accompli when he became governor.

Changes in personnel continued throughout March and April 1911. The Puebla police chief resigned near the end of March, and the press reported the removal of jefes políticos in the districts of Alatriste, Cholula, Huauchinango, and Tepeaca.[30] Isunza's role in these changes is not clear, but if evidence from other instances is any indication, it may have been greater than Díaz or Valle had anticipated.

For example, three citizens from the district of Tetela wrote to Díaz complaining of the excessive power of the Bonilla and Méndez families. The trio claimed that the families traded the jefe político position and other posts in order to gain control of land solely as a means to manipulate the *campesinos,* whom they forced to work on endless projects at low pay and under poor conditions. Consequently, the economy of the district had deteriorated and many people had migrated. Díaz instructed Isunza to investigate the situation, adding that the jefe político, Pomposo M. Bonilla, was allegedly taking advantage of the present social confusion to extort money by illegally jailing people. Isunza discovered not only that Bonilla was arresting people, but also that he was embezzling money from the Tetela City treasury and from monies earmarked for use against the rebels. When Isunza indicated his desire to oust Bonilla, Díaz defended the jefe político, claiming that he was an honorable man and had served well. He ordered Isunza to give Bonilla time to correct his financial accounts. Nevertheless, a week later the president finally gave way and agreed to have Bonilla replaced.[31] The new interim governor, then, played an important role in ousting and selecting new personnel, and even successfully countered the wishes of Díaz. His expanded latitude in relation to Díaz and Valle's original intention to keep him under tighter control was prompted by the steadily deteriorating military situation both in Puebla and throughout the nation. As circumstances worsened, Díaz showed more willingness to give his governor greater autonomy and to oust Martinista officials.

Simultaneous with the changeover in personnel came the task of preparing for the election of a new constitutional governor. Isunza sought the president's permission to campaign for the post, and Díaz consented, adding that he supported Isunza's candidacy and hoped that he won. In early April he formally accepted the nomination and promised to support the principle of "no reelection," as well as to improve the condition of the workers by promulgating new labor regulations, including an employers' liability law. The candidate, with Díaz's blessing, was maneuvering for the support of moderate Maderistas.[32]

In early March, with the plan under way to change the state's Martinista officials, the task of militarily subduing the rebellious elements again took priority. Díaz, in an effort to stem the rising rebel tide in the sierra, invited the powerful cacique and long-time regime supporter, Juan Francisco Lucas, to Mexico City, apparently to arrange a military accord. The astute Lucas, however, sensing the shifting political winds, refused to go, claiming poor health. Díaz then questioned the loyalty of Lucas-controlled militia stationed in Puebla City and ordered them disarmed and sent home. State officials, however, claimed that they were needed for guard duty, and in the coming weeks, as the military situation deteriorated, their presence in the capital was increased, not reduced.[33]

Rebel advances during the months of March and April radically changed the political equation in the state, as it became increasingly apparent that the state government would soon fall. Citizens who feared the possibility of destruction and bloodshed protested the fortification of the state capital. Maderista sympathizers held unauthorized rallies in the city, while every night small groups ran through the streets shouting *vivas* to Madero and *mueras* to Díaz.[34]

By the end of April, Isunza had abandoned all efforts to support the regime. He realized the cause was lost and hence took a compromising position toward the Maderistas, hoping to gather behind him the state's uneasy middle class. Such a maneuver was designed to protect middle-class lives and property and to enable them to fill the power vacuum which would inevitably be created when the disorganized rebels defeated the government.

Reports reached Díaz from regime supporters complaining of conditions in the state. Government forces were not bothering to chase the rebels and even allowed them to enter Puebla City with impunity. Seven of the state's twenty-one districts were under insurgent control, and they held parts of twelve others. Díaz backers accused Isunza and Valle of being Maderistas and of collaborating with the revolutionaries. Isunza reportedly sent personal representatives to rebel-held districts to negotiate an understanding whereby he would be named governor once the Maderistas won the war. The governor allegedly was also placing Maderista sympathizers in police and government positions and promoting the nightly disturbances in the city. Díaz, preoccupied with rebel advances throughout the nation and especially in the Ciudad Juárez area, was never able to deal with matters in Puebla by checking his increasingly insubordinate governor.[35]

The rebels continued to make impressive gains during the month of May. Indeed, when Atlixco fell on 22 May, the only important communities still under government control were Cholula and Puebla. These successes were aided by the policies of Isunza and Valle. The two, under pressure from business and other wealthier elements, who claimed that it would be better to negotiate a surrender than to defend a hopeless cause and thus ensure a sacking by the rebels, ordered local officials to hand over several towns after obtaining guarantees for lives and property.[36] Also, since early in the month, the government had been withdrawing most of its fifteen hundred troops from the rural areas to Puebla City and its immediate vicinity, in order to better protect the state capital. This strategic move proved to be a key factor in limiting rebel influence in the post-Díaz state government. While the insurgents struggled in the countryside, the moderate reformers maneuvered in the heavily garrisoned city to ensure their ascension to power when the regime fell.[37]

Despite their failure to capture the state capital before the signing of the Treaty of Ciudad Juárez, the rebels' success in Puebla, as well as in neighboring states, was a major factor in forcing the resignation of President Díaz on 25 May 1911. Preoccupied with consolidating their gains throughout the state and with the capture of the state capital, the rebels never initiated their planned drive on Mexico City. Nevertheless, the inevitability of such a drive, had the war continued, played an important role in the government's decision to capitulate.[38]

In the turbulent days following the signing of the treaty on 21 May, Isunza came under heavy pressure to resign. Despite his attempt to compromise with the rebels during the last weeks of fighting, in order to carve out a place for himself in the new political order, he was too closely identified with the discredited Porfirian system, and consequently stepped down on 29 May.[39]

The finely crafted political system so carefully built up over a period of years by Díaz and Martínez was now at risk of complete collapse. Isunza, taking advantage of his reputation as an independent and of the unusual political and military circumstances during the spring's fighting, attempted to form a new coalition of political forces, made up of disillusioned Porfiristas and moderate Maderistas. He failed, mainly because of resistance to such an accommodation from the insurgent forces, whose actions in turn convinced the moderate Maderistas to drop such a plan. This decision eliminated the top half of the Porfirian system—Díaz and his governor. The bottom half of the hierarchy, the state and local personnel, although heavily buffeted by the Maderista challenge, remained mostly intact, although under severe pressure from outsiders wishing to take advantage of their weakened position, now that the Martinistas' basis of legitimacy, Díaz and Martínez, had disappeared.

Nor was Madero, through his governors, Rafael P. Cañete, Nicolás Meléndez, and Juan B. Carrasco, able or willing to use the Díaz system to his own advantage. His ideological commitment to free elections and his inability to control the many factions of his movement opened the door to a chaotic struggle to seize the state's political posts not only by the Maderistas, but also by old regime supporters. These bitter and often violent contests further undermined Madero's already weakened authority in the state and, by the end of his presidency, had destroyed any remnant of the Porfirian structure.

Rafael P. Cañete

Madero, as revolutionary leader during the interim presidency of Francisco León de la Barra, and following the advice of the moderate wing of his movement in the state, which now controlled the governmental apparatus in Puebla City, named Rafael Cañete to be the new interim governor.[40] The choice of the fifty-five-year-old lawyer and native of Puebla City was greeted with controversy. Cañete had served for a time as president of one of the Maderista political clubs during 1910, but many thought him too conservative, too inflexible, and too weak an adminstrator. Others disliked him because he had refused to act as Serdán's defending lawyer in September 1909, and because he had taken little active part in the overthrow of the government. Also, Cañete's appointment blocked the aspirations of Camerino Z. Mendoza, an influential and popular rebel leader whom Madero had temporarily named head of the revolutionary forces and provisional governor during the fighting in May.[41]

From the beginning Cañete distrusted the Maderista insurgents; they controlled the countryside and were demanding sweeping socioeconomic reforms from the new government. The governor, however, took the position that law and order should prevail before any significant reforms were implemented. His first objective toward establishing law and order was to gain control of state and local governmental positions. From the outset the rebels were at a disadvantage in determining who filled posts at the state level, since the middle- and upper-class moderates took immediate control of the state government apparatus. Cañete rejected the radicals' calls for wholesale purges of Porfiristas. Even the complaints of revolutionaries to Madero over the governor's inaction had little effect.[42]

Unable to exert any significant influence over who occupied state-level positions, the revolutionaries struggled fiercely to retain and to expand their control of local political posts in the face of government opposition. Taking advantage of their successes in the countryside, the rebel troops commonly replaced Martinista officials with their own sympathizers. This practice at times received official approbation from high Maderista officials in Mexico City, and became so routine that to many people it seemed that the rebels hardly recognized the Cañete government.⁴³

Fearful of losing all control over the countryside, Cañete obtained additional authority from the legislature that empowered him to remove and appoint local officials at will. Armed with this far-reaching legal authority, he sent personal delegates to the countryside to replace revolutionary appointees with his own men.⁴⁴

Bolstered by legal and moral support from the state government, sympathizers of the old order defended their role in the local political structure as tenaciously as the rebels attempted to secure their ouster. This bitter conflict produced numerous complaints and instances of violence throughout the summer and autumn of 1911, as each side maneuvered to achieve control of district and town posts.⁴⁵ This refusal to accommodate the rebels' demands for control of political offices even at the local level undermined the legitimacy of the state government in the eyes of a large share of the populace; instead of creating a climate of law and order, as the government wished, this approach engendered even greater dissatisfaction among an already restless people.

The conflict in the state was a direct reflection of the contradictory policies of the interim government in Mexico City. The president, Francisco León de la Barra, a former high Porfirista official, maintained a hard line toward the insurgents, thereby backing Cañete while his cabinet, made up of several Maderistas, directly supported many of the rebels' demands. Madero, unwilling to take either side in the dispute for fear of rupturing his shaky coalition, ended up losing the confidence of both factions and seriously jeopardizing his political control in the state.

The Cañete government's effort to dominate political positions in Puebla was only one part of its program to reestablish centralized political authority; the other involved the control of the rebel armed forces. So long as the insurgents fielded troops, they could back up their demands with force. The government viewed this situation as a threat to its desired monopoly over military as well as political power.

The task, however, proved impossible, since a series of errors made the revolutionaries even more intractable. Madero named as commander of all insurgent forces in the state the upper-class Agustín del Pozo, who had weak revolutionary credentials and who refused to recognize the rebel juntas supported by many of the state's chieftains.[46] Once fighting officially ended, in late May, the government failed to provide the insurgent troops with adequate pay and provisions, thus forcing them to resort to extortion and robbery to survive. This situation exacerbated the turmoil in the countryside, alienated many erstwhile Maderista supporters, and turned soldiers into bandits.[47] Instead of disbanding the defeated Porfirian army, the authorities tried to do just the opposite; the rebels refused to cooperate. As a compromise, some of the defeated soldiers were inducted into newly created rural units. This solution, however, divided the rebel army against itself, resulting in several bloody clashes between insurgents, on one side, and newly formed rural contingents and old regime federal troops, on the other.[48]

Faced with government intransigence at both the political and military levels, and pressured by their laborer-campesino followers for reform, many rebel leaders opted to return to the field against the government. Consequently, several insurrectionary bands appeared throughout the state, the most serious being those allied with Emiliano Zapata, in the south. As these groups rampaged over varying areas of the state, Cañete lost even more control over the political system.[49]

Madero, too, seriously undermined his legitimacy as revolutionary leader and future president, perhaps fatally, by his unswerving public support for Cañete and his administration's policies in the state. Madero made other mistakes as well. He appointed del Pozo and took an active part in helping to demobilize insurgent troops. Publicly applauding the role of the federal army in the wake of its July killing of rebel troops and their families in Puebla, he refused to authorize an investigation into the massacre and into a right-wing plot to kill him. He fired Emilio Vázquez Gómez as secretary of *gobernación,* over the protests of his rebel officers. And he removed Francisco Vázquez Gómez as his vice-presidential running mate. All these moves and others alienated large numbers of his supporters in the state.[50]

Bolstered by the division within the Maderista ranks and by the government's preoccupation with containing the revolutionaries, the Porfiristas took advantage of the situation to avenge their earlier defeat. Antigovernment plots abounded, and the former governor, Martínez, and his sons were deeply involved in many of them. One, the provocation of federal and insurgent forces that ended in the massacre at the Puebla City bullring in July, seriously weakened the Cañete administration. Other Porfiristas and right-wing military elements backed Bernardo Reyes's bid for the presidency and then fled to the northern sierra in December, to combat the government under the banners of the Reyista and Vazquista rebellions.[51]

The breakdown of political order advanced yet another step as the state staggered through a highly controversial gubernatorial election prompted by Madero's inability to keep his movement unified. Cañete, in defiance of Madero, backed the conservative Catholic Luis García Armora and tried to block the official Maderista candidate, Nicolás Meléndez, on a technicality. To many Puebla Maderistas, the selection of Meléndez smacked of imposition from Mexico City; they chose a third candidate, Dr. Daniel Gúzman. After a disputed election, the decision went to the state legislature, where Meléndez was declared the winner and belatedly replaced Cañete on Christmas Day 1911.[52]

Nicolás Meléndez

When Meléndez, a fifty-eight-year-old lawyer, took over the reins of the governorship in Puebla, he faced the difficult job of reestablishing a viable political system in the state.[53] Ultimately he proved incapable of carrying out this task. Already weakened by the controversy surrounding his election and the declining prestige of the Madero regime in general, he also had to work under the burden of a less than ideal relationship with Madero, now officially the president. Meléndez's efforts to bolster the military and to combat the ever-increasing left- and right-wing rebels met with little success. In the midst of the continuing violence that disrupted the transportation and communication systems, he also attempted to oversee three different sets of elections, which had the effect of further exacerbating the already violently contested struggle for control of local and state political offices.

Almost from the outset of his governorship, Meléndez had a strained relationship with Madero; the problem only worsened as the months passed.⁵⁴ Madero, despite his pledges to give the states greater political autonomy, attempted to resort to a Díaz-style centralized control in a vain effort to save his regime. He increasingly intervened in areas that Meléndez considered his official domain as governor. Most illustrative of this situation were differences between the two over the handling of elections.

In both the elections for federal deputies and those for state representatives and a new governor, Meléndez intervened, following tradition and attempting to guarantee his and his closest cohorts' political survival, using principally the jefes políticos to influence the results. Madero, committed publicly to free elections, sent mixed signals to his governor by condemning Meléndez for his interference, while naming special agents to arrange candidates and elections.⁵⁵

Faced with a continually deteriorating security situation, Meléndez and Madero tried to bolster the state's military forces, but many of the same problems that had hindered their predecessors in the face of a determined rebel insurgency continued to plague them. Like Díaz and Isunza before them, the pair boosted the numbers of federal and state troops and rurales, created a militia, encouraged the formation of volunteer security squads by merchants and *hacendados*, and raised soldiers' pay. The effectiveness of these measures, however, was reduced by such basic problems as an inadequate supply of men and material and a lack of money to finance the troop increases. The government continued to impress recruits, which resulted in a high desertion rate, poorly motivated soldiers, and the alienation of the populace. Jurisdictional disputes among political entities and government ministries hindered coordinated action, while the charged political atmosphere proved tempting to many officers, who used their troops to further their own ambitions rather than the welfare of the state government.⁵⁶

While the problem-plagued military forces in the state struggled to contain the increasing number of antigovernment rebels, the latter operated almost at will, successfully challenging Meléndez's political control. Most numerous and of the greatest threat to the state government were the Zapatistas, who continued their insurgency following their break with Cañete and Madero, the previous year. Throughout Meléndez's term they virtually controlled the southern and western regions of the state and regularly made incursions into the central and sierra districts. They continually threatened to attack the state capital and at one point briefly held the town of Cholula, less than ten kilometers from Puebla. Twice during the year the federal government suspended constitutional guarantees in several Zapatista-held districts of the state, but to little avail.[57]

In areas under their control, the insurgents usurped Puebla's political authority by taxing hacendados and merchants and placing their own sympathizers in local offices. In March Zapata set up his headquarters in Petlalcingo (district of Acatlán) and named it the state capital. He then selected a full slate of state officials, including Jesús "Tuerto" Morales, a one-eyed Zapatista general and a native of Petlalcingo, as governor.[58]

Other rebellions, principally in the northern sierra, erupted during the year. Most were connected, at least nominally, with the call to arms against the government by Emilio Vázquez Gómez and Pascual Orozco, early in the year, and then by Felix Díaz, in October 1912. These revolts attracted disillusioned Maderistas and Porfiristas; although they did not seriously threaten the state government as did the Zapatista incursions, they too contributed to the sapping of the strength of the regime and the undermining of its effective political control over many areas.[59]

Due to continuing violence in the state, the already badly disrupted communication and transportation systems suffered further deterioration, making the state officials' efforts to restore political control even more difficult. Insurgent attacks on the railroads virtually stopped all traffic for days and weeks at a time leaving most areas (including the state capital) in isolation and hindering the transport of troops and supplies. Telephone and telegraph lines were easily cut and slow to be repaired, while telegraph operators, sympathetic to the rebels, used their positions to aid the insurgents. Telephone, telegraph, and postal offices were also favorite targets for robberies by revolutionaries needing cash.[60]

As during the Cañete interim, elections in the state gave rise to additional political conflict, since the Maderistas were unable to unify around a single candidate even in the face of right-wing challenges from the Porfiristas and Church-backed candidates. The three sets of elections held in the state between July and December

1912 (federal deputies, governor and local deputies, and *ayuntamientos*) destroyed any remaining control by the central authorities over who occupied the posts. Perhaps most divisive was the struggle over the selection of a new constitutional governor to replace Meléndez, but this clash was mirrored in the bitter encounters taking place over nearly every post at the district and local levels.

Madero, with the grudging cooperation of Meléndez, attempted to find a gubernatorial candidate acceptable to all the factions of the movement. Once the idea of extending Meléndez's term was discarded, the convention to choose a single candidate turned into a debacle, due to lack of cooperation on the part of those already declared as aspirants. Consequently, Madero and Meléndez pushed through the candidacy of Juan B. Carrasco. Observers felt that he was acceptable to Madero and Meléndez because both men thought they could control the aging ex-lawyer and bureaucrat. Carrasco, however, faced several other candidates, including the now ex-head of revolutionary forces in the state, Agustín del Pozo, who was backed by Porfirista elements in Puebla. When no one received a majority in the balloting, the decision went to the holdover Porfirian state legislature, which selected del Pozo. Meléndez refused to recognize the legislature's decision, claiming that it had illegally called itself into special session to select the governor and that the newly elected congress, which was to take office in January 1913, should choose the state's chief executive. The impasse was broken by the federal senate, which ruled in favor of Meléndez; consequently, the legislature appointed Carrasco.[61] Madero, then, experienced great difficulty controlling the state; only through manipulation could he impose his choice as governor.

Juan B. Carrasco

The selection of Carrasco irrevocably split the state's Maderistas. Upon Carrasco's inauguration on 1 February, del Pozo revolted and established a second state government, with himself as its head, in the sierra town of Xochiapulco (district of Tetela). Within the week Carrasco fell seriously ill with uremia and had to turn the reins of government over to a substitute. The confusion and breakdown of political order in the state served as an appropriate backdrop to the coup d'état led by Victoriano Huerta that ousted Madero from the presidency and led to his assassination that same month. Although Carrasco remained in the governorship until June, he merely served as a figurehead while Huerta desperately attempted to restore some degree of political order in the state by appealing for cooperation from the Maderistas. By May, however, this policy had clearly failed and Huerta, turning to a military solution to the continued resistance to his government, replaced Carrasco with the military commander and most powerful figure in Puebla since Madero's fall, General Joaquín Maas.[62]

Conclusions

As has been demonstrated, the Maderista period in Puebla marked the final collapse of the Porfirian political system. Madero, hampered by less than ideal relations with his governor, an inadequate military, the breakdown of communications and transportation, bitter and divisive elections, and, finally, armed rebellion against the state government, was unable to control his movement or to contain the Porfiristas. Consequently, his tenure witnessed the disintegration of the political structure in the state.

The breakdown and collapse of the long-time Porfirian political system in Puebla was both rapid and complete. Some of its basic weaknesses could first be discerned as early as 1909–10, when the Reyistas and then the Maderistas offered a potentially viable alternative, especially to those outside the structure. The spring rebellion of 1911 severely crippled it by eliminating Martínez and then Díaz and Isunza. Their absence created a vacuum, and no universally accepted institutional mechanism existed to fill it. Upon their fall, all other Porfirista-Martinista officials at the state and local levels, without their all-important personal connections to the centers of power, lost their legitimacy, creating a scramble among outsiders for their positions. Madero, immediately after his military victory over Díaz, might have been able to build up his own personalized and centralized system, but his ambiguity toward exercising tight, Díaz-style political control, together with the alienation of his left while encouraging the right with such appointments as Cañete and del Pozo, nullified this chance.

Consequently, no official at any level was able to recreate the hierarchically structured stability of the Díaz-Martínez system. The result was a chaotic and bloody struggle for political control at all levels in the state. The end of the Díaz system signaled the beginning of all-out revolutionary warfare to determine who would next have the power to shape the political order.

NOTES

Abbreviations

AARD Archivo General de la Nación, Archivo de Alfredo Robles Domínguez, Mexico City. Cited, tomo:expediente:folio.

AGM Universidad Nacional Autónoma de México, Archivo de Gildardo Magaña, Mexico City. Cited, caja:expediente:documento.

AGN/AFM Archivo General de la Nación, Archivo de Francisco I. Madero, Mexico City. Cited, caja:carpeta:folio.

AJA Centro de Estudios de Historia de México (Condumex), Archivo de Jenaro Amezcua, Mexico City. Cited, carpeta:documento.

APG University of Texas, Archivo de Pablo González, Austin. Cited, roll:document.

ARM Instituto Nacional de Antropología e Historia, Archivo de la Revolución Mexicana, Mexico City. Cited, rollo:volumen:página.

BN/AFM Biblioteca Nacional, Archivo de Francisco I. Madero, Mexico City. Cited, carpeta:folio.

CPD Universidad de las Américas, Colección Porfirio Díaz, Cholula, Puebla. Cited, rollo:documento.

CS-AY/AFM Catalina Sierra and Agustín Yáñez, eds., *Archivo de Don Francisco I. Madero,* 3 vols. (México, D.F.: Secretaría de Hacienda y Crédito Público, 1960). Cited, volumen:página.

DHRM Isidro and Josefina Fabela, eds., *Documentos históricos de la revolución mexicana,* 27 vols. (México, D.F.: Jus and Fondo de Cultura Ecónomica, 1960-73). Cited, volumen:página.

GBFO Great Britain, Foreign Office, General Correspondence—Political—Mexico, Series 371, London. Cited, file:document.

INAH/AFM Instituto Nacional de Antropología e Historia, Archivo de Francisco I. Madero, Mexico City. Cited, rollo:documento.

RDS National Archives, Records of the Department of State Relating to the Internal Affairs of Mexico, 1910-1929, Record Group 59, Washington, D.C. Cited, roll:document.

RG Archivo General de la Nación, Ramo de Gobernación, Mexico City. Cited, legajo.

NB: In some cases carpeta and folio numbers are missing from the original sources; this is indicated by, for instance, 77:—:—.

1. GBFO, T. B. Hohler to Edward Grey Bart, 10 Aug 1911, 1150:41; Carlton Beals, *Porfirio Díaz, Dictator of Mexico* (Philadelphia, 1932), 376–77; Daniel Cosío Villegas, *Historia moderna de México,* 10 vols. (México, 1955–72), 9:493.

2. CPD, Martínez to Díaz, 3 Mar 1911, 281:5323; Cosío Villegas, *Historia moderna,* 9:449; Ignacio Herrerías, *Sucesos sangrientos de Puebla, 18 de noviembre de 1910* (México, 1911), 5; Miguel Angel Peral, *Diccionario histórico, biográfico y geográfico del estado de Puebla* (Puebla, 1979), 527.

3. Enrique Juan Palacios, *Puebla, su territorio y sus habitantes,* 2 vols. (México, 1917), 1:281. These figures are for 1910.

4. AGM, José Rafael Isunza to Francisco León de la Barra, 26 May 1911, 1:2-Y:750; AGM, Martínez to León de la Barra, 2 June 1911, 7:M-1:39; CPD, Isunza to Díaz, 18 Ap 1911, 282:7161; CPD, Juan N. Pacheco and Sebastian Rocha to Díaz, 8 Mar 1911, 281:5064; *Diario del Hogar,* 19 Feb 1912; *Presupuesto general de ingresos y egresos del estado para el año de 1910* (Puebla, 1909), 9; Crispin Ramos, *Documentos relativos a la acusación presentada ante el honorable congreso del estado por el ex-Gobernador Señor General Mucio Martínez* (Puebla, 1912); Porfirio del Castillo, *Puebla y Tlaxcala en los días de la revolución* (México, 1953), 16, 88; Beals, *Porfirio Díaz,* 376–77.

5. RDS, William S. Chambers to Arnold Shanklin, 17 Ap 1911, 12:1101; *El Imparcial,* 17 Dec 1910; *El País,* 4 Dec 1910; Lucio Tapia and Krumm Heller, *Trilogía heróica, historia condensada del último movimiento libertario en México* (México, 1916), 9; Paul Joseph Vanderwood, "The rurales, Mexico's rural police force, 1861–1914," Ph.D. diss. (University of Texas, Austin, 1970), 339–41; Paul J. Vanderwood, *Disorder and Progress; Bandits, Police and Mexican Development* (Lincoln, 1981), 120–24; Rómulo Velasco Ceballos, *Aquiles Serdán, episodios de la revolución de 1910* (México, 1933), 12.

6. *Nueva Era,* 6 Feb 1912; Luis Casarrubias Ibarra, *Mi patria chica, curso elemental de geografía del estado de Puebla* (México, 1910), 26–28; Enrique Cordero y Torres, *Historia compendiada del estado de Puebla, 1531–1963,* 3 vols. (Puebla, 1965–66), 3:86–89; *Puebla a través de los siglos* (Puebla, 1962), 141; Palacios, *Puebla,* 1:246.

7. AGM, Azpiróz to León de la Barra, 1 Sept 1911, 5:A-4:355; *El*

Demócrata, 19 July 1911; Cosío Villegas, *Historia moderna*, 9:545–46, 733; Peral, *Diccionario histórico*, 67.

8. CPD, Martínez to Díaz, 23 Mar 1909, 257:3339; *Diario del Hogar*, 24 Mar 1909; [Luis Cabrera], *Obras políticas del Lic. Blas Urrea* (México, 1921), 356.

9. CPD, Martínez to Díaz, 14 July 1909, 261:11267.

10. CPD, Martínez to Díaz, 4 June 1909, 260:9885, 16 Aug 1909, 262:12823.

11. For detailed accounts of the Maderista movement in the state from its inception in mid-1909 to the outbreak of the revolution in November 1910, see Atenedoro Gámez, *Monografía histórica sobre la génesis de la revolución en el estado de Puebla* (México, 1960), and David G. LaFrance, "Madero, Serdán y los albores del movimiento revolucionario en Puebla," *Historia Mexicana* 29:3 (Jan–Mar 1980): 472–512.

12. CPD, Serdán to Díaz, 18 Sept 1909, 263:15556; CPD, Martínez to Díaz, 23 Sept 1909, 263:15739.

13. CS-AY/AFM, Madero to Emilio Vázquez Gómez, 10 Oct 1909, 2:448, 14 Oct 1909, 2:452–53, 7 Dec 1909, 2:524–25; Stanley R. Ross, "Un manifiesto de Aquiles Serdán," *Historia Mexicana* 5:1 (July–Sept 1955): 86; Alfonso Taracena, "Galería de la revolución; Aquiles Serdán, iniciación," *Hoy*, 2 Oct 1943, 51; Alfonso Taracena, *Madero, vida del hombre y del político* (México, 1937), 209.

14. AJA, E. Vázquez Gómez to Agustín Díaz Durán, 21 Nov 1909, 1:6; José C. Valadés, ed., "El archivo de Don Ramón Corral," *La Prensa* (San Antonio), 6 Feb 1938; José López Portillo and S. Sánchez to Puebla police chief, 20 Mar 1910; Gámez, *Monografía*, 61.

15. *El País*, 24 May 1910; Joaquín Pita, "Memorias," *El Universal*, 25 June 1948; Gámez, *Monografía*, 110.

16. INAH/AFM, Madero to Francisco Vázquez Gómez, 13 Aug 1910, 10:3; *Diario del Hogar*, 9 Aug 1910; *El País*, 8, 30 June 1910; *México Nuevo*, 5, 7 June 1910; Gámez, *Monografía*, 115–16, 139. Gámez claims that out of 130 Poblanos sent to Quintana Roo, only 6 returned. Another source states that Martínez's two sons shot numerous Maderistas encarcerated in the state penitentiary; see CPD, Pacheco and Rocha to Díaz, 8 Mar 1911, 281:5064.

17. CPD, Miguel E. Márquez to Díaz, 24 June 1910, 271:8156; *El País*, 8 June 1910; Castillo, *Puebla*, 34; Pita, "Memorias," 25 June 1948.

18. *Diario del Hogar*, 20 Aug 1910.

19. CPD, Martínez to Díaz, 23 Sept 1910, 274:13123; CPD, Juan A. Hernández to Díaz, 26 Sept 1910, 274:13737; GBFO, Tower to Grey Bart, 27 Sept 1910, 927:64; *El País*, 18, 20 Sept 1910.

20. CPD, Martínez to Díaz, 23 Sept 1910, 274:13123. Martínez's otherwise almost absolute control in the state did not include all the judgeships.

21. Accounts of the battle are legion; for an eyewitness version see ARM, "Relato de Carmen Serdán sobre los sucesos acaecidos el 18 de noviembre de 1910 en Puebla," n.d., 31:54:248.

22. CPD, Díaz to Martínez, 19 Nov 1910, 366:4549; CPD, Martínez to Díaz, 26 Nov 1910, 276:17379; CPD, Demetrio Salazar to Díaz, 25 Nov 1910, 276:16417; CPD, Díaz to Salazar, 29 Nov 1910, 276:16582.

23. CPD, Martínez to Díaz, 23 Nov 1910, 366:4885, 4893, 24 Nov 1910, 276:17375.

24. CPD, Martínez to Díaz, 16 Feb 1911, 368:3538, 22 Feb 1911, 279:2144; *Mexican Herald,* 8 Feb 1911; *El País,* 8, 18, 19 Feb 1911; Crisanto Cuéllar Abaroa, *La revolución en el estado de Tlaxcala,* 2 vols. (México, 1975), 1:55–60.

25. CPD, Cahuantzi to Díaz, 8 Mar 1911, 281:4683.

26. CPD, Valle to Díaz, 25 Feb 1911, 369:4363, 4406, 27 Feb 1911, 369:4510; CPD, Díaz to Valle, 26 Feb 1911, 369:4409A; CPD, Martínez to Díaz, 3 Mar 1911, 281:5323.

27. *Mexican Herald,* 1 Mar 1911.

28. CPD, Valle to Díaz, 25 Feb 1911, 369:4363; CPD, Díaz to Valle, 26 Feb 1911, 369:4409A; CPD, Isunza to Díaz, 27 Feb 1911, 281:4872; Miguel Angel Peral, *Gobernantes de Puebla* (México, 1975), 164–65.

29. CPD, Valle to Díaz, 27 Feb 1911, 369:4510; CPD, Díaz to Valle, 28 Feb 1911, 369:4511A; GBFO, Hohler to Grey Bart, 1 Mar 1911, 1146:2; *Mexican Herald,* 1 Mar 1911; *El País,* 13 Mar 1911; *Boletín Municipal,* 11 Mar 1911; Francisco de Velasco, *Autobiografía* (Puebla, 1946), 45.

30. *El País,* 13, 29 Mar 1911; *El Imparcial,* 16, 17, 30 Mar, 12 Ap 1911.

31. CPD, Citizens to Díaz, 7 Mar 1911, 281:5063; CPD, Díaz to Isunza, 13 Mar 1911, 281:4889, 29 Mar 1911, 370:7281; CPD, Isunza to Díaz, 23 Mar 1911, 281:4923, 24 Mar 1911, 281:4920.

32. CPD, Isunza to Díaz, 11 Mar 1911, 281:4895; CPD, Díaz to Isunza, 14 Mar 1911, 281:4896; *Mexican Herald,* 10 Ap 1911.

33. CPD, Martínez to Díaz, 3 Mar 1911, 369:5021; CPD, Díaz to Martínez, 3 Mar 1911, 369:5024A; *El Imparcial,* 11 Mar, 15, 16 Ap 1911; Jesús Ferrer Gamboa, *Los tres juanes de la sierra de Puebla* (México, 1967), 22–24.

34. CPD, Isunza to Díaz, 28 Ap 1911, 282:7421, 2 May 1911, 283:

9015; CPD, Luis García Armora to Cahuantzi, 30 Ap 1911, 283:8035; GBFO, Hohler to Grey Bart, 17 May 1911, 1147:413; RDS, Chambers to Shanklin, 21 Ap 1911, 12:1252, 28 Ap 1911, 13:311.

35. CPD, Vicente Popoca to Díaz, 28 Ap 1911, 283:7972; CPD, Filomeno Heinz Argumedo to Díaz, 1 May 1911, 283:8874; CPD, Cahuantzi to Díaz, 5 May 1911, 283:8046.

36. CPD, Isunza to Sec. de Guerra, 29 Ap 1911, 371:10245; BN/AFM, Hilario Márquez to Madero, 19 May 1911, 12:114; *El País,* 16 May 1911; J. Paredes Colín, *El distrito de Tehuacán* (Tehuacán, 1921), 110. At one point Isunza threatened to hand over Puebla to the rebels when Díaz wanted to remove the 29th Battalion; see CPD, Isunza to Díaz, 16 May 1911, 283:8497.

37. RDS, Chambers to Shanklin, 5 May 1911, 13:337; GBFO, Hohler to Grey Bart, 24 May 1911, 1148:22; *Mexican Herald,* 21 May 1911.

38. Jesús Luna, *La carrera pública de Don Ramón Corral* (México, 1975), 160; Francisco Vázquez Gómez, *Memorias políticas, 1909–1913* (México, 1933), 363. The rebels, numbering many thousands, faced a force, according to José I. Limantour, of 2700 in the Federal District.

39. BN/AFM, Eduardo Mestre to Juan Sánchez Azcona, 30 May 1911, 20:—.

40. BN/AFM, Enrique Contreras and Agustín Ramos for Club Central to Madero, 24 May 1911, 7:752; BN/AFM, Madero to León de la Barra, 31 May 1911, 20:—; AGM, Gabriel Soto to León de la Barra, 2 June 1911, 9:S-1:491; Gámez, *Monografía,* 133.

41. AARD, Clemente Escalona to Alfredo Robles Domínguez, 30 May 1911, 4:19:62; AARD, Robles Domínguez to Mendoza, 29 May 1911, 4:19:57; INAH/AFM, L. Francisco García to Madero, 31 May 1911, 20: 2914; *El Imparcial,* 4 Ap, 6 June 1911; Vázquez Gómez, *Memorias,* 321; Donato Bravo Izquierdo, *Un soldado del pueblo* (Puebla, 1964), 19–20; Enrique Cordero y Torres, *Diccionario biográfico de Puebla,* 2 vols. (Puebla, 1973), 1:145–46.

42. AGM, Francisco García to León de la Barra, 23 Sept 1911, 4:G-5:709; AJA, Convocatoria by Benito Rousset et al. to Puebla Citizens, 8 July 1911, 1:27; INAH/AFM, Anonymous circular, 1 July 1911, 20:2051; INAH/AFM, Résumé of conversation between Pedro Orozco and Madero, n.d., 20:2049; ARM, M. A. Salas et al. to E. Vázquez Gómez, 30 June 1911, 34:58:286; *El País,* 4 June 1911; *El Imparcial,* 3 July 1911; *Diario del Hogar,* 9, 11 July 1911; *Boletín Municipal,* 8 July 1911; Vázquez Gómez, *Memorias,* 322.

43. AARD, Robles Domínguez to Francisco R. Bertani, 26 May 1911,

4:19:11; AARD, Felipe T. Contreras to Sánchez Azcona, 28 June 1911, 4:19:130; GBFO, Circular issued by E. Vázquez Gómez to state officials, 16 June 1911, 1150:3; *El Imparcial,* 25 June 1911.

44. *El Imparcial,* 12 July 1911; *Mexican Herald,* 4 Aug 1911; *Periódico Oficial del Estado,* 21 July 1911.

45. The archives and newspapers consulted for this study contain numerous references to the conflict over government posts at the local level; for example, see INAH/AFM, Pedro Leyva et al. to Madero, 22 Nov 1911, 21:3357; AGM, Carmen Castillo to León de la Barra, 17 July 1911, 16:3:241; AGN/AFM, E. Vázquez Gómez to Cañete, 10 July 1911, 77:—:—; *Diario del Hogar,* 15 June 1911; *El Imparcial,* 17 June 1911; *Mexican Herald,* 13 Sept 1911; *Nueva Era,* 26 Aug 1911.

46. AGN/AFM, del Pozo to Madero, 28 July 1912, 7:179:5143; INAH/AFM, Résumé of conversation between Orozco and Madero, n.d., 20:2049; Gámez, *Monografía,* 98; Peral, *Diccionario histórico,* 435; Vázquez Gómez, *Memorias,* 317.

47. AGN/AFM, del Pozo to E. Vázquez Gómez, 3 July 1911, 77:—:—, 16 June 1911, 77:—:—; AGN/AFM, J. Z. Moreno to E. Vázquez Gómez, 29 June 1911, 77:—:—; AGM, Ramón R. de Aguilar to Tesorero de la Federación, June 1911, 19:3:68; ARM, Cañete to Sec. de Gobernación, 8 July 1911, 34:59:149; AARD, Bertani to Robles Domínguez, 27 May 1911, 4:19:16; AARD, Fausto Rodríguez to E. Ortega, 29 May 1911, 4:19:40–41; *El Imparcial,* 9 June 1911.

48. AARD, Madero to Robles Domínguez, 26 June 1911, 1:5:84; AARD, León de la Barra to Madero, 14 July 1911, 17:5:240; AGM, anonymous informe, 31 Aug 1911, 7:M-4:501; ARM, Cañete to Sec. de Gobernación, 8 July 1911, 34:59:149; AGN/AFM, L. A. Guajardo to E. Vázquez Gómez, 29 July 1911, 77:—:—.

49. AGM, José M. Flores and Daniel Bonilla to León de la Barra, 31 May 1911, 28:15:30; AGM, Cañete to León de la Barra, 6 Sept 1911, 14:6:318; RG, Alfredo Ortíz Izquierdo to José M. de la Vega, 18 Dec 1911, 695; RG, del Pozo to de la Vega, 24 Nov 1911, 695; RG, del Pozo to Clemente Villaseñor, 8 Nov 1911, 695; AGN/AFM, Madero to Cañete, 5 Dec 1911, 57:1:35. For the best account of the Zapatistas during the interim see John Womack, Jr., *Zapata and the Mexican Revolution* (New York, 1968), 97–128.

50. For a more detailed account of Madero's policies in Puebla during the interim see David G. LaFrance, "Francisco I. Madero and the 1911 Interim Governorship in Puebla," *The Americas* (forthcoming).

51. AGM, Madero to León de la Barra, 13 July 1911, 17:10:488;

AGM, Eduardo Reyes to del Pozo, 15 July 1911, 28:15:317; AGM, Cañete to León de la Barra, 6 Aug 1911, 2:C-3:459, 7 Sept 1911, 2:C-2:315, 11 Sept 1911, 13:3:123; AGN/AFM, Manuel Mitre to Madero, 31 Oct 1911, 76:—:—; AGN/AFM, Márquez to Madero, 9 Dec 1911, 61:—:568; BN/AFM, various Poblanos to Madero, 29 June 1911, 9:—; INAH/AFM, Epigmenio A. Martínez to Madero, 28 June 1911, 19:726; Vázquez Gómez, *Memorias,* 312–13, 317–18.

52. AGN/AFM, P. S. Ramírez to Madero, n.d., 33:890-1:—; AGN/AFM, Manifiesto by Madero, 28 Dec 1911, 57:1:126–27; AGN/AFM, Juan Sánchez Pontón to Madero, 25 Nov 1911, 61:—:902; AGN/AFM, Rafael Rosete et al. to Madero, 5 Dec 1911, 61:—:911; AGN/AFM, C. Serdán to Madero, 23 Dec 1911, 20:509:—; *Nueva Era,* 10, 20 Oct, 23 Nov, 7, 14 Dec 1911; Castillo, *Puebla,* 87–90.

53. Peral, *Diccionario histórico,* 351–52.

54. AGN/AFM, Madero to Emilio Ibáñez, 20 Feb 1912, 57:1:339; AGN/AFM, Madero to Meléndez, 26 Feb 1912, 57:1:381.

55. AGN/AFM, Jesús Flores Magón to Meléndez, 26 June 1912, 82:—:—; AGN/AFM, Meléndez to Sánchez Azcona, 27 June 1912, 3:77:2246; AGN/AFM, Luis T. Navarro to Madero, 20 June 1912, 44:1192:—; AGN/AFM, Ibáñez to Madero, 5 June 1912, 47:1293-2:—; AGN/AFM, Alfredo Alvarez to Madero, 7 Oct 1912, 1:14:398; INAH/AFM, Elías de los Ríos to Miguel Rosales, 5 July 1912, 10:33; *Nueva Era,* 7 Nov 1912.

56. AGN/AFM, Meléndez to Madero, 6 June 1912, 3:77:2263; AGN/AFM, Navarro to Madero, 23 Mar 1912, 44:1192:—; AGN/AFM, Sánchez Azcona to Luis G. Pradillo, 9 Dec 1912, 56:22:129; AGN/AFM, de la Vega to Comandante del 16º Cuerpo Rural, 13 Jan 1912, 79:—:—; AGN/AFM, Narciso López y C. to Márquez, 23 July 1912, 83:—:—; RDS, D. M. Wolcott to Philander C. Knox, 16 Nov 1912, 21:1652; *La Tribuna,* 27 Jan 1913; *Mexican Herald,* 19 Feb, 20 Sept 1912; Vanderwood, "Rurales," 399.

57. AGN/AFM, Meléndez to Madero, 9 Oct 1912, 3:77:2232; AGN/AFM, Federico González Garza to Meléndez, 20 Jan 1912, 79:—:—; *Mexican Herald,* 8 Oct 1912; Charles Curtis Cumberland, *Mexican Revolution, Genesis under Madero* (Austin, 1952), 198–99.

58. AGN/AFM, del Pozo to Madero, 24 May 1912, 7:179:5138; RDS, Henry Lane Wilson to Knox, 19 Mar 1912, 16:1561; *Mexican Herald,* 7 Feb, 18, 19 Mar, 13 May 1912; *Diario del Hogar,* 26 Mar 1912.

59. AGN/AFM, Baraquiel Alatriste to Madero, 14 Feb 1912, 6:140-1:4130; AGN/AFM, Jesús Rojas to Madero, 12 May 1912, 19:465:—;

APG, Carlos Reyes to F. Díaz, 22 Feb 1913, 36:307; Peter V. N. Henderson, *Félix Díaz, the Porfirians, and the Mexican Revolution* (Lincoln, 1981), 57, 185–86.

60. AGN/AFM, Cruz Olivares et al. to Madero, 15 Nov 1911, 62:—: 1286; AGN/AFM, Sánchez Azcona to Manuel Urquidi, 29 Feb 1912, 53:5:115; RDS, Frederick A. Lendrum to Claude E. Guyant, 30 Mar 1912, 17:0682; *Mexican Herald*, 26 Mar, 18 July 1912; *Nueva Era*, 9 Feb 1912.

61. AGN/AFM, Carrasco to Madero, 21 Nov 1912, 15:349-2:11304; AGN/AFM, Enrique Ibáñez to Madero, 12 Oct 1912, 47:1293-2:—; AGN/AFM, Meléndez to Madero, 2 Oct 1912, 3:77:2235, 9 Oct 1912, 3:77:2232; DHRM, Guillermo and Gustavo Gaona Salazar to Madero, 10 Oct 1912, 8:146–55; DHRM, Gustavo Madero to Madero, 1 Nov 1912, 8:191–92; INAH/AFM, Meléndez to Comisión Permanente del Congreso de la Nación, 16 Dec 1912, 20:2488; *Mexican Herald*, 26 Aug 1912, 2 Feb 1913.

62. AGN/AFM, Sánchez Azcona to Luis Casarrubias Ibarra, 6 Feb 1913, 56:12:331; APG, Rafael Luna Bonilla to F. Díaz, 2 June 1913, 42:—, 18 May 1913, 41B:—; INAH/AFM, Madero to Bruno M. Trejo, 1 Feb 1913, 22:3937; RDS, Wilson to Knox, 3 Feb 1913, 22:1684; *Mexican Herald*, 3, 15 Feb 1913; Peral, *Gobernantes*, 170–73.

President Porfirio Díaz (reprinted from W. E. Carson, *Mexico, The Wonderland of the South*, New York, 1909).

The Plaza, Mexico City (reprinted from W. E. Carson, *Mexico, The Wonderland of the South*, New York, 1909).

General Bernardo Reyes (reprinted from Carleton Beals, *Porfirio Díaz: Dictator of Mexico,* Philadelphia, 1932).

Porfirio Díaz and His Cabinet (photograph by Brown Brothers, New York, 1910).

General Mucio P. Martínez (reprinted from Enrique Cordero y Torres, *Historia de las galerías pictóricas de gobernantes del estado libre y soberano de Puebla,* 3rd ed., Puebla, 1982).

Adobe Huts (reprinted from Dillon Wallace, *Beyond the Mexican Sierras*, Chicago, 1910).

Watching the Train (reprinted from W. E. Carson, *Mexico: The Wonderland of the South,* New York, 1909).

Indian Home in the Hot Country (reprinted from Dillon Wallace, *Beyond the Mexican Sierras*, Chicago, 1910).

Pisaflores, 1895 (reprinted from Frans J. Schryer, *The Rancheros of Pisaflores: The History of a Peasant Bourgeoisie in Twentieth-Century Mexico*, 1980).

Yaqui Indian (reprinted from Dillon Wallace, *Beyond the Mexican Sierras,* Chicago, 1910).

Campesino Ploughing (reprinted from Dillon Wallace, *Beyond the Mexican Sierras*, Chicago, 1910).

Peasant Couple (reprinted from N. O. Winter, *Mexico and Her People of Today* . . . , Boston, 1907).

II

The Rural Economy

During the last half of the nineteenth century, the United States and Europe dramatically increased their purchases of raw materials and foodstuffs from the nonindustrial nations and colonies of the world. This trend reflected the increased ability of industrial consumers to purchase exotic products as well as increased demand for products to fuel industrial growth. Mexico during the age of Díaz sought to profit from this opportunity. The Porfirian regime, through concessions and legislation, modernized the transportation infrastructure and removed many obstacles to economic growth.[1] Industrial expansion occurred, but as a secondary result of the growth of the traditional, agricultural export sector.[2]

Mexico's rural economy was transformed. An international demand for henequen, coffee, cotton, sugar, and other primary products created export-directed economies in Yucatán, Veracruz, Coahuila, Morelos, and elsewhere. Higher prices for these products and the advance of a network of railroads to transport them to markets stimulated production and the desire for land throughout Mexico. The growth in the number and size of haciendas and plantations (occupying slightly more than 70 percent of all landholdings by 1910), often capitalized by foreign investment, was the most noticeable change in the countryside. The quickening pace of national economic growth stimulated the commercialization of small-scale agriculture in many regions as well. By 1910 farms and ranchos represented about 25 percent of all landholdings in Mexico and involved a pattern of production, marketing, and social relations that was different in several respects from that of haciendas and plantations.[3]

Daniela Spenser examines the rise of coffee plantations in Soconusco, Chiapas. The shift from cattle production for local and regional markets to coffee production for international markets was largely the result of developments originating outside the region. Díaz's success in solving a disruptive boundary dispute with Guatemala, actions taken by the government of Chiapas to alleviate a labor shortage, the increase in coffee prices on the international market, and the migration of German entrepreneurs and capital into the region led to a rapid increase in coffee production in the 1890s. The regional economy of Soconusco became vigorous, but at the cost of monocrop dependency, subordination to foreign entrepreneurs and capital, and the deterioration of the status of local farmers and workers.

Frans J. Schryer offers a detailed description and analysis of rural life and economic change in northern Hidalgo. Ranchos in this region led the shift from peasant to commercial agriculture. The rise of small farms at first developed slowly, out of rental arrangements of hacienda land, and later more rapidly, as communal land was converted into private property. Production for local markets was expanded, in time, to take advantage of regional, national, and even international markets. Unlike Soconusco, however, the primary impetus for the commercialization of agriculture came from the rancheros themselves, within the region. The agricultural potential and isolation of northern Hidalgo did not attract large capital investment nor entrepreneurs from outside the region, thereby leaving the regional economy in the hands of small farmers.

Economic change in Soconusco and the Sierra de Jacala during the Porfiriato reflects two basic patterns of the same enterprise: the rise of commercial agricultural production. Although interrupted here and there during the revolution and often forced into new arrangements, commercial agriculture continued to dominate the countryside after 1911.[4] Rancheros in northern Hidalgo and German-Mexicans in Soconusco today compete with *ejidatarios,* but the economies they created during the Porfiriato remain largely intact.

Daniela Spenser was born in Prague, Czechoslovakia, and educated at King's College, University of London, where she received a B.A. in 1972. Formerly professor of history at the Universidad Autónoma de Chiapas and a researcher for the Instituto Mexicano del Café, Spenser is currently a research fellow at the Centro de Investigaciones y Estudios en Antropología Social, in Mexico City. She is a member of a research team studying German political and economic interests in southern Mexico from the Porfiriato to the Second World War. Frans J. Schryer is associate professor of anthropology at the University of Guelph, Canada. He was born in the Netherlands and educated at McGill University, where he received his Ph.D. in 1974. Professor Schryer is the author of *The Rancheros of Pisaflores: The History of a Peasant Bourgeoisie in Twentieth-Century Mexico* (1980).

NOTES

1. John H. Coatsworth, "Obstacles to Economic Growth in Nineteenth-Century Mexico," *American Historical Review* 83 (Feb. 1978): 99.

2. Celso Furtado, *Economic Development of Latin America: Historical Background and Contemporary Problems* (Cambridge, Eng., 1970), 47–49.

3. Percentages of haciendas-plantations and farms-ranchos are taken from John Womack, Jr., "The Mexican Economy during the Revolution, 1910–1920: Historiography and Analysis," *Marxist Perspectives* 1 (Winter 1979): 101, 105.

4. Donald B. Keesing, "Structural Change Early in Development: Mexico's Changing Industrial and Occupational Structure from 1895 to 1950," *Journal of Economic History* 29 (Dec. 1969): 716–20.

5
Soconusco:
The Formation of a Coffee Economy in Chiapas

Daniela Spenser

The integration of Mexico into the global economy in the last third of the nineteenth-century coincided with the regime of President Porfirio Díaz. This historical conjunction was not accidental, since it was Díaz who removed many colonial-era obstacles to economic growth and encouraged foreign investment. At the same time the rise of dependent capitalism in Mexico contributed to Díaz's consolidation of power and to the definitive rise of the modern state by (among other things) expanding the financial resources at the disposition of the regime.[1] The establishment of dependent capitalism in Mexico during the Porfiriato was not the product of an all-engulfing national trend, but the result of a more piecemeal process of regional economic specialization. Sugar production in Morelos, cotton in southwestern Coahuila, henequen in northern Yucatán, coffee in Veracruz, cattle and sheep in Chihuahua, and coffee in Soconusco, to name only the most prominent export-led economies in Mexico, became the peripheral engines of national economic growth, geared to the service of foreign consumers.

The formation of a coffee economy in the department of Soconusco in the state of Chiapas took place between 1890 and 1910, in response to economic *and* political impetus at the regional, national, and international levels. In less than twenty years, Soconusco became one of the most important coffee producing and exporting regions in Mexico and in no small way contributed to the political and economic modernization of Chiapas.[2] The history of Porfirian Soconusco illustrates the interconnective nature of regional, national, and international export-led economic growth in Mexico. The center-periphery nexus was the indispensable element in the formation of a coffee economy in Soconusco during the Porfiriato.

Soconusco extends along the Pacific coast for approximately 140 kilometers, between the plains of the Isthmus of Tehuantepec to the northwest and the Guatemalan border to the southeast. It is a narrow strip of no more than 15 to 30 kilometers wide, divided into coastal lowlands and the mountainous Sierra Madre de Chiapas. It is in this mountainous region, at an altitude of between 200 and 1200 meters, where craggy slopes and fertile soil provide almost ideal conditions for the cultivation of coffee trees.[3]

At the time of the Spanish conquest, Soconusco provided fully one-half of all Aztec cocoa tribute. It became the greatest cocoa-producing province of all the Spanish dominions in the 1530s and 1540s. The ravages of disease, however, decimated the indigenous producers of the bean by mid-century; thereafter the region became a devastated and depressed area.[4] As late as 1823, the Mexican general Vicente Filísola reported that "the land is vacant due to the small number of workers."[5] At the time of independence from Spain, Soconusco repudiated the economic dominance of Guatemala and the political dominance of Chiapas to become autonomous and independent from 1824 to 1842. "During this long period," noted a contemporary oberver in 1843, "[Soconusco] has experienced all the difficulties of an abandoned country surrendered to rivalries and hatred; without laws, without a plan, without a system and with a purely municipal regime very imperfect which still exists and is leading to anarchy."[6] Lack of security for persons and property, armed incursions from Guatemala to reannex the region, and forced

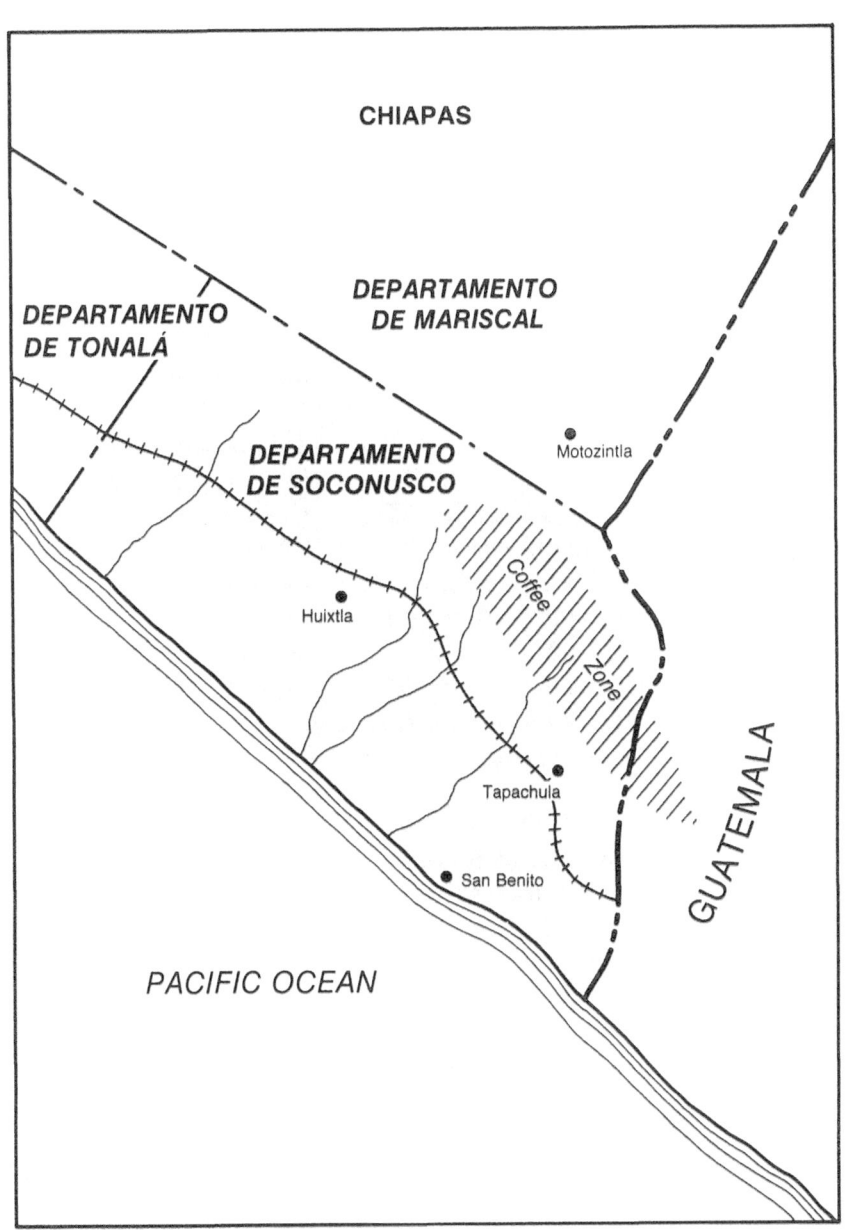

Soconusco, 1910

loans contributed to Soconusco's continuing economic ruin. In 1850 another observer commented that since 1811, "industry, agriculture, and commerce have decayed and are decaying each day more and more."[7] President Antonio López de Santa Anna seized the region by military force in 1842 and made it a department of the state of Chiapas.[8]

Matías Romero, former treasury minister in the Benito Juárez administration and future Mexican ambassador to the United States, first publicized Soconusco's potential for commercial agriculture and pushed for its development. He established a modest plantation of coffee, sugarcane, and cattle in 1872, near the ill-defined Mexican-Guatemalan border. He was attracted to the region because of the appropriate soil and climate for coffee cultivation, abundant land which could be purchased at very low prices, and the proximity to the ocean and easy and inexpensive transport. Romero argued that a coffee plantation could be brought into production in only four years, with little capital. Once the groves began to produce profits were more than satisfactory and yields encouraging: 1.87 kilograms could be harvested from a mature tree in Soconusco, as opposed to no more than half a kilogram in other coffee-producing regions of Mexico.[9]

In the 1870s and 1880s, however, the difficulties outweighed the advantages of initiating commercial agriculture in Soconusco. The most important hindrance was the disputed international status of the area. Guatemala had never recognized Mexico's annexation of Soconusco and still pressed a claim to the region. Soconusco was used by Guatemalan rebels as a base to prepare expeditions to overthrow the government. In the 1870s the Guatemalan president-dictator Justo Rufino Barrios even conceived a plan to cede Soconusco to the United States, which was wisely declined by the *norteamericanos*.[10] Romero's interest in Soconusco apparently threatened Barrios's plans for the region; the Guatemalan dictator had his plantation destroyed and his workers imprisoned.[11] Although this action forced Romero out of business, it also strengthened his resolve to press for a treaty of limits between Mexico and Guatemala. He understood that Soconusco would never attract entrepreneurs and investment as long as the international boundary was uncertain and the region was threatened by Guatemala.

A second drawback to the development of commercial agriculture in Soconusco was the scarcity of workers. In order to attract fieldhands, planters gave cash advances or settled debts with previous employers. Even then a sufficient number could not be secured, since workers would run away to evade paying off their debts. Because of a similar labor scarcity in Guatemala, authorities of that country prohibited Indians from working on the Mexican side of the border.[12] The disputed nature of the region and the undefined border, however, led to confusion over the nationality of the temporary migrant workers. To attract workers the Díaz government offered three hectares of land to any family that would settle in the region.[13]

Yet another problem concerned the pernicious influence of the cacique of Soconusco, Sebastián Escobar. Don Sebastián achieved political power in Soconusco as a result of his military service during the War of Reform (1859–60) the War of French Intervention (1863–64), in Chiapas. He was *jefe político* of the department by 1870, and in 1876 he supported General Porfirio Díaz's successful rebellion against the government of Sebastián Lerdo de Tejada. Escobar, according to some sources, became the undisputed cacique of Soconusco with the assistance of Justo Rufino Barrios. The disputed international status of the region contributed to Escobar's rise to power, and he was not eager to see any definitive settlement of the border, a circumstance which may have contributed to Barrios's procrastination in the boundary negotiations with Mexico.[14] Escobar's autocratic management of local public affairs, furthermore, forced numerous landowners to leave Soconusco and discouraged prospective entrepreneurs from coming.[15] One local *hacendado*, Telesforo Merodio, for example, complained to President Díaz, in 1888, that Escobar impeded "progress and improvement in order to prevent anyone from surpassing his local influence or arousing ideas of equality and true democracy."[16]

The Development of Soconusco

The Mexican government invited the Guatemalan government to reopen negotiations on the border question in 1873. Although Barrios was more interested in uniting Central America under Guatemalan rule than regaining control of Soconusco (or Chiapas, which Guatemala also claimed), he was not prepared to renounce the claim, for domestic political purposes. To aggravate matters even more, from the Mexican point of view, armed parties from Guatemala continued to invade Soconusco, attacking towns and tearing down Mexican boundary markers. Finally in 1881 Mexico sent contingents of the army to the border and Barrios, convinced that his northern neighbor was going to war, appealed to the United States government for assistance and mediation.[17] Through the good offices of the United States, Guatemala renounced all claims to Chiapas and Soconusco in 1882, and a trilateral commission was established to survey the border and draw a boundary line.[18] Although the final border settlement was not reached until 1895, the 1882 agreement significantly contributed to lessening the international tension surrounding Soconusco and in no small way opened the door to the development of the region.

Following the 1882 boundary convention, the Díaz administration took steps to develop and colonize Soconusco. In 1884 the government signed a contract with the Chiapas Mexican Colonization Company of San Francisco, to survey and sell 200,000 hectares in Chiapas, construct a pier at San Benito, and build a railroad from that port to Tapachula, which was the commercial center of Soconusco. Although the company did establish a small North American colony in the region, it did not come close to fulfilling the terms of the agreement.[19] In 1886 the concession was transferred to Luis Huller, director of the Chiapas Mexican Colonization Company. One Chiapanecan newspaper described the work of Huller as follows: "the hour for reforms approaches, capitalists are fixing their sights upon Chiapas, businessmen are beginning to arrive. European colonization is realizing this work. Huller is the motor of Chiapanecan progress; he brings us new customs, he brings us laborious people, he brings us money and interchange."[20]

In exchange for making an accurate survey of all national lands in Chiapas, Huller was granted the right to sell one-third of the total concession and colonize the remaining two-thirds.[21] Thus began the Soconusco "coffee fever" of 1888–95.[22]

The difficult, preliminary foundation of commercial coffee production was initiated by the North American colony—Californians who arrived in Soconusco in the mid-1880s with little capital but imbued with the necessary pioneering spirit. They settled in the mountains north of Tapachula, where they cleared the land, built homes, grew sugarcane and their own food, bred cattle, and planted coffee. These *fincas* were small family operations that also tried to secure permanent Indian workers through allotments of small pieces of land.[23] Toward the end of the 1880s the North Americans were joined by Germans, Englishmen, and Spaniards.

One of the members of the North American colony, Helen Seargeant, recalled that in 1890, "big business coming into the district made it seem that times were looking up."[24] In that year an Englishman named McGee arrived in Tapachula with $45,000, bought and planted 400 hectares in coffee, and built a coffee processing plant (for drying and shelling).[25] German entrepreneurs, who some twenty years earlier had emmigrated to Guatemala from Europe, began to cross the border into Soconusco, buying land and establishing plantations. In Guatemala coffee had been cultivated on a commercial basis since the 1850s on the Costa Chica (the Pacific coast) and in Alta Verapaz and San Marcos, in the northern and western parts of the country. The German colonists in Guatemala, and later in Soconusco, did not pioneer in coffee cultivation, but usually purchased established fincas and enlarged them, improved cultivation methods, and utilized modern processing machinery imported from England and the United States.[26]

These entrepreneurs moved into Soconusco in the late 1880s and early 1890s for two related reasons. The average market price of coffee more than doubled during the decade 1880–90 (see table 1). This favorable trend led planters to expand the size of their operations; since this was more and more difficult to do in Guatemala, given the already developed state of the industry in that country, they were prompted to move to Soconusco, where land was extensive, fertile, and inexpensive.[27] In the late 1880s coffee lands sold for less than one peso per hectare. In 1892 it was estimated that coffee produced for seven centavos a pound in Soconusco could be sold for over twenty centavos. Plantations of 250 hectares could gross from $75,000 to $150,000 dollars per year. There were twenty-

Table 1. Coffee Prices in Mexico, 1880–1910

Year	Price per Kg. (centavos)
1880	.25
1881	.20
1882	.22
1883	.20
1884	.20
1885	.31
1886	.37
1887	.42
1888	.48
1889	.45
1890	.41
1891	.49
1892	.60
1893	.62
1894	.76
1895	.70
1896	.66
1897	.52
1898	.44
1899	.47
1900	.44
1901	.46
1902	.47
1903	.46
1904	.48
1905	.48
1906	.51
1907	.49
1908	.46
1909	.42
1910	.45

Source: *Estadísticas económicas del Porfiriato: Comercio exterior de México, 1877–1911* (México, 1960), 340.

six large commercial coffee plantations in Soconusco by 1892.[28] By 1895 the best coffee lands in Soconusco had been purchased, by Germans for the most part.

International agreement on the status of Soconusco, the placement of national lands in the hands of survey and colonization companies, and the boom in coffee prices all combined to initiate commercial coffee cultivation in Soconusco in the late 1880s. Despite this impressive beginning, obstacles remained to the full and free economic expansion of the region.

First in importance was the continuing shortage of laborers. Indicative of the seriousness of the problem was one attempt to secure fieldhands for Soconusco in 1890–91. Governor Manuel Carrascosa of Chiapas gave permission to one coffee planter to import three hundred natives from the Polynesian Gilbert Islands.[29] The owner of the brig *Tahiti,* which transported the natives, explained that he had obtained a contract from the Mexican government to supply Soconusco with workers. He added that "each man who went on board that brig went on his own free will and with the understanding that if he did not like the work in Mexico he would be sent back to where he came from by that government."[30] Unfortunately, soon after the Polynesians reached Soconusco, all but one died of smallpox.[31] Planters more generally recruited Indian laborers in the highland villages in Soconusco, Mariscal, and on the other side of the border. Workers were attracted to the coffee fields with cash advances and alcohol. Once settled on the fincas, they found that they were unable to pay their debts from the salaries they earned, and were therefore prohibited from leaving. The number of indebted laborers in Soconusco by 1897 was over four thousand, with a collective debt of over five hundred thousand pesos.[32] The permanent laborers (as opposed to the seasonal harvest workers) were considered the property of the plantation; they and their debts were included in the inventory and added to the price when the enterprises were sold.[33]

The state government of Chiapas took two measures that alleviated to some degree the problem of labor scarcity in Soconusco. In 1892 Governor Emilio Rabasa decreed the statewide division of all communal village lands known as *ejidos.* The governor instructed all jefes políticos to set up municipal committees to oversee the survey, division, and sale of plots to individuals. The committees were required by law to apportion five-hectare plots to poor families at no cost. Only the most destitute received the minimum allotment, and even then many obtained no land at all due to corrupt surveys and residency requirements.[34] Between 1893 and 1909 the ejidos of at least eleven villages in Soconusco were divided,[35] leaving many villagers landless and forced into the labor market and debt servitude.[36]

Governor Rafael Pimental of Chiapas gave his permission in 1900 for the recruitment and employment of Indians from the interior central highlands region (the area surrounding San Cristóbal Las Casas) for work in the Soconusco coffee plantations. After enjoying high prices from 1891 to 1897, planters found themselves in a recession from 1898 to 1900 (see table 1). In March 1899 several influential planters hired the attorney Agustín Farrera to lobby before the state government for tax relief.[37] After studying the coffee situation, Farrera reported to Pimentel that coffee planters were selling their product for less than half the price they had received before 1898, yet "the cost of production is the same since wages and transport find themselves at the earlier price."[38] Instead of tax relief, Pimentel gave the planters permission to recruit Indians from the interior of the state.[39]

Regarding the problem of Sebastián Escobar and his *cacicazgo* (domain) in Soconusco, governor Emilio Rabasa appointed Manuel Figuerro of Oaxaca to be jefe político for Soconusco in 1892, in order to clip his wings. In response to Escobar's demands for Figuerro's removal, Rabasa refused to be moved, commenting that "I have confidence in him since he is new to Tapachula and entirely independent of the parties or bands that exist in that city."[40] General Escobar was assassinated in the fall of 1893 by a local political enemy. Rabasa thereafter informed President Díaz that "I have indicated to the jefe político that now with the assassination, he will take this advantage to make sure the Soconusco will never again have caciques."[41] Figuerro made personnel changes in municipal governments and confiscated 211 rifles and over 20 boxes of ammunition, Escobar's personal armory.[42] A way was thus cleared for the oligarchy of coffee barons, cattlemen, and merchant bankers to dominate local government in Soconusco.

Improvement in the international status of Soconusco (and determination of the international boundary in 1895), greater availability of workers, and the disappearance of the Escobar cacicazgo provided the necessary preconditions for the development of the region. The increase in coffee prices and the migration of efficient and experienced German entrepreneurs from Guatemala transformed Soconusco into one of the most productive and wealthy regions in Mexico. The Germans' key to success, however, was their European financial backing. Most of the immigrants originally came from the Hanseatic towns of Hamburg, Bremen, and Lübeck. As the employees of export-import companies, they traveled and lived abroad, pursuing business interests for the firm and themselves. The trading firms often helped their employees become independent landowners, in exchange for regular consignments of the best coffee. Könisberg, Nottebohm, and Schröder were well-known merchants and bankers in Hamburg and planters in Guatemala, by the time the expansion of coffee cultivation began in Chiapas. In Guatemala they were able to amass capital from grain processing and green coffee export, beginning in the 1870s. Nottebohm, for example, produced forty to fifty thousand bags on his plantations, but exported ten times that much. He and Schröder financed other planters who, in time, came to own the largest and best equipped enterprises in Soconusco.[43]

The bankers rarely went to Chiapas themselves, but delegated responsibility to Guillermo Henkel, a fellow countryman who took up residence in Tapachula in 1894. He also represented, as an export-import agent, the Siegmund Robinow and Son Company in Hamburg and, later, merchant houses in New York and San Francisco.[44]

The other source of capital for planters in Soconusco was German trade companies (established in the 1850s) in the Mexican ports of Mazatlán and Manzanillo. One of the most prominent, that of the Melcher family from Bremen, began business in Mazatlán in 1846. Initially the company imported clothes, linen, silk, agricultural and mining implements, arms, and furniture, but it later expanded into insurance and banking. By the 1870s there were forty such German merchant houses in Mexico, with diverse business activities and investments. In 1899 the Melchers began to lend money to Henkel, who in turn lent it to Soconusco coffee planters. Henkel collected the harvests of his debtors and transported the coffee to Mazatlán, where it was sold to European and North American buyers.[45]

German merchants on the Pacific coast were more interested in marketing coffee than producing it, yet occasionally they also became plantation owners. When their Mexican clients were unable to repay loans within the stipulated period, the merchants foreclosed on their properties. By 1910 the Wohler Bartning Company (based in Bremen) in Mazatlán and the Cetling Brothers (based in Hamburg) in Manzanillo owned valuable plantations in Soconusco.[46]

German entrepreneurs either established their own plantations or became so-called industrial partners of a firm in Germany, depending on their credit standing with the commercial companies. Some ambitious Germans, short of capital or financial backing, became plantation managers until they, too, could buy one of their own. One well-connected planter, the nephew of a prosperous Hamburg merchant, established, over the period of three years, three two-partner plantations. The properties were of considerable size—700, 900, and 1,150 hectares—and valued at between 100,000 and 150,000 pesos each. While the nephew traveled between his properties in Guatemala, Soconusco, and Germany looking after larger business concerns, his industrial partners managed the plantations. The partners were responsible for overseeing the laborers, improving the quality of the coffee, preparing it for export, and transporting it to the port of embarkation. They were debarred from pursuing any business initiative of their own while the partnership lasted. On the whole the partners were well paid, receiving about 2,500 pesos a year, which in less than ten years allowed them to become independent landowners and planters. As part of the credit agreement, German planters consigned their coffee crop to the commercial firm through their agents in Tapachula, and the coffee was usually shipped on a German line.[47] After 1890, for example, the Kosmos line of Hamburg carried Soconusco's coffee to Germany, returning with European manufactures to Chiapas.[48]

The German entrepreneurs preferred buying plantations with coffee groves already in full production, equipped with houses, processing machinery, cattle, and servants. The prices paid per hectare could vary from three pesos for virgin land to one hundred pesos for cultivated property. An initial capital investment of 100,000 pesos for a coffee plantation in Soconusco was not unusual in the

1890s, with 8 percent interest a year guaranteed by regular shipments of coffee to the creditor.[49]

Commercial agriculture naturally stimulated the expansion of trade. German commercial companies established branches in Tapachula, where they engaged in moneylending, coffee export, rural and urban property speculation, and the import of housewares, tools, agricultural machinery, and food. German capital and commercial domination of Soconusco is suggested by the following list of enterprises in Tapachula in the 1890s: Luis Thomalen and Cía, shipping agency; Adolfo Buhrmann, processing machinery; Guillermo Henkel, import-export, banking; Othon Marth, import-export; Juan Huthoff, export and shipping agent; Adolfo Giesemann, export agent and planter.[50]

Capital and land in the hands of Germans inevitably led to complaints by Mexicans in the region. One native landowning group became unhappy about the 24 percent yearly interest charged by German moneylenders and the obligation of delivering harvests to creditors at fixed prices.[51]

The growth of a vigorous coffee economy in Soconusco in the 1890s also placed a great strain on the primitive transportation system of the region. Coffee was transported from the plantations to the port of San Benito by mule, which took between two and six days. Although the port was relatively close to Tapachula, it was never adapted to large, ocean-going vessels, nor were there enough warehouses to store the coffee until it was shipped. Once a ship had arrived at San Benito, the loading and unloading of merchandise and coffee was extremely slow, since smaller boats had to transfer the loads between pier and ship.[52] The lack of good port facilities and high Mexican export taxes made it easy for the Guatemalan government to attract Soconusco's agricultural production to its ports. In 1896 President Díaz wrote the governor of Chiapas, concerned that

> for some time now Guatemala has cajoled the residents of Soconusco and has established ports of deposit on the frontier, in which they charge such low taxes on coffee and the other products of Soconusco that it amounts to a free service.
>
> They are, furthermore, bringing a railroad to the frontier and

will ask permission to extend it into Mexican territory. Added to this we have no railroad, nor docks on the coast of Soconusco and the government of the state imposes taxes that appear to be high to the residents of Soconusco. I propose for your consideration that the government of Guatemala is skillfully and slyly breeding a spirit of separatism in the heart of Soconusco.[53]

Díaz proposed that the national government construct a railroad from Tehuantepec to Tapachula, build a modern pier on the coast, and encourage a bank to open in Tapachula, and he suggested that the state of Chiapas "treat Soconusco with a gentle hand and relax a little their taxation."[54] Five years later, the Pan-American Railroad Company was incorporated in New Jersey and obtained a Mexican joint federal-state subsidy totaling $10,000 (U.S., gold) for each mile constructed between Tehuantepec and Tapachula.[55] Construction began in 1901 and was finished in 1908. The railroad permitted shipment of Soconusco coffee to ports on the Gulf of Mexico, thereby reducing shipping costs by more than half, which in turn led to greater production, profits, and commerce (see table 2).

Table 2. Coffee Production in Chiapas, 1904–10

Year	Production (lbs.)	Total Value (U.S. $)
1904–1905	14,042,550	1,053,195
1905–1906	11,852,737	888,955
1906–1907	14,388,870	1,079,165
1907–1908	10,652,274	789,920
1908–1909	18,077,860	1,627,007
1909–1910	21,555,217	2,371,073

Source: "Coffee Crop Conditions in Foreign Countries," 1 Feb. 1912, NARG 84, Tapachula: Miscellaneous Reports

By the end of the Porfiriato, coffee cultivation and German capital dominated Soconusco. According to a North American planter in the region, "seventy-five percent of the coffee growers in this district are Germans."[56] There were around fifty substantial coffee plantations in Soconusco, with an average size of 1,200 hectares, although three or four were over 4,500 hectares.⁵⁷ German capital invested in rural property in Soconusco reached 1,373,414 pesos as compared to United States investment (in rubber plantations and the Pan-American Railroad) of 1,227,120 pesos. Spanish (930,130 pesos) and British (464,814 pesos) capital, generally invested in coffee, held third and fourth places.⁵⁸ In 1906 the coffee planters (predominantly German) had established a private association, the Unión Cafetera de Soconusco, designed to establish a uniform labor policy and to present a united interest-group front to pressure the state and federal governments.⁵⁹ The population of Tapachula rose from 4,750 in 1877 to 16,848 in 1910. In Mexico only the Federal District had more foreign residents than the state of Chiapas in 1910; most of these undoubtedly resided in Soconusco.⁶⁰ A coffee planter, Ricardo Bado, became municipal president of Tapachula in 1909, and another planter, Fernando Braun, was jefe político of the district in 1914.⁶¹

German ownership of the coffee processing plants allowed them to monopolize the export business even when they did not monopolize production or land ownership. A similar near monopoly in credit and strong ties with European buyers facilitated German economic dominance in Soconusco. By 1910 the initial German monopoly over capital was offset somewhat by the establishment of two Mexican banks that financed land purchases and provided short-term credit to coffee growers, yet these banks never became real competitors in the German-controlled export business.⁶²

The Social Impact of Development

The formation of a coffee economy in Soconusco between 1890 and 1910 led to a deterioration in living standards for most workers and villagers in Soconusco. Villagers in Huixtla complained in 1908 that land on which they grew their food had been taken from them when the Pan-American railroad passed through their village. They were unable to buy it back, because the land company had imposed considerably higher prices per hectare of land than had prevailed before the arrival of the railroad.⁶³ A food shortage similarly accompanied the expansion of the coffee economy. In 1895 Soconusco, with a population of 30,333, produced 185,000 hectoliters of maize; by 1909, when the population had grown to 36,631, maize production had fallen to only 48,223 hectoliters.[64] As a result more expensive maize had to be imported during the harvest to feed the temporary workers, while for permanent residents the cost of living soared as wages remained static.[65]

With regard to wages, the United States consul in Tapachula reported in 1910 that in Soconusco, "planters justify the low pay scale by the plea that the more money a Chamula [Indian] is paid the more bad liquor he will drink."[66] In 1911 the consul noted that

> the coffee planters in the majority are Germans and secure their laborers under the peonage system. Their agents or labor contractors, called *"habilitadores,"* go to the tableland and offer the Indians loads of money, principally during the progress of a feast; this money is seldom paid, and cases exist where the debt and peonage conditions have been passed on from father to son. While this system is not legal under Mexican laws, it having been copied from Guatemala, the Indians consider it binding, much more so since the authorities have connived to imprison peons for debt. It is feared that should the masses awaken to the actual conditions of things danger might result to the coffee crop and even to the security of the plantations and planters.[67]

The daily wage for coffee workers averaged about sixty centavos, less if food was provided. During the harvest all pickers were paid on a piecework basis. Each man, woman, and child was assigned a quota and was then paid so many centavos per liter of coffee beans. As a result the working day extended from dawn to nightfall. The work was difficult, the climate of Soconusco is hot and humid, and living conditions for workers were squalid.[68] Only a few benefited from the coffee boom, and most of them were not even Mexican. After all, from the point of view of the German planters, their Indian workers belonged to an inferior race that could be adapted to the service of promoting civilization in Mexico.[69]

Conclusions

The formation of a coffee economy in Soconusco occurred as a result of actions taken not only in the region but also in Tuxtla Gutiérrez (capital of the state of Chiapas), in Mexico City, and in

Hamburg, Germany. The center-periphery nexus was crucial to Soconusco's development in terms of international diplomacy, material improvements, and political stability. The partnership between German planters and the German commercial companies, however, was the decisive element. Germany, like the rest of Europe, recovered from the business depression of the 1870s and 1880s and embarked upon a vigorous course of trade and investment expansion from the 1890s to the beginning of the First World War.[70] The capacity of the European market to absorb Mexican coffee was nearly unlimited, given the Brazilian hailstorm of 1886 that destroyed entire plantations and the 1889 Republican revolution that brought the Brazilian economy to a temporary standstill.[71] The regional economy of Soconusco, driven by German capital, geared to the export of a primary commodity, and tied to an expansive metropolitan economy, was modernized at the expense of local entrepreneurs and a growing working class. It should come as no surprise that the first socialist party in Chiapas appeared in 1920 in this region.

The Porfirian period of Soconusco's history (characterized by the commercial relationship with Germany) did not come to an end until 1914. In that year northern revolutionary soldiers occupied Tapachula, and a number of wealthy families took refuge in Guatemala or Europe. At the same time, young German men, overwhelmed by patriotic feeling, traveled to the gulf port of Veracruz in order to sail to Germany to fight for the Kaiser. They never arrived, however, but were taken prisoners of war by the British navy and locked up in Canada.[72] More importantly, the war cut the marketing-capital tie with Germany; during its course the United States replaced Europe as the primary market for coffee grown in Soconusco.[73]

NOTES

This essay constitutes part of an ongoing research project on German economic and political interests in Soconusco from 1890 to 1950. The author is grateful to Thomas Benjamin for sharing data and for assistance in preparation.

1. *Dependent capitalism* is a system of production and a social order subordinated to the centers of world capitalism. The term generally refers

to a national economy incorporated into the international capitalist market and characterized by strong dependence on external financing and the channeling of resources toward the export of primary products.

Stephen R. Niblo and Laurens B. Perry, "Recent Additions to Nineteenth-Century Mexican Historiography," *Latin American Research Review* 13 (1978): 44–45; John H. Coatsworth, "Obstacles to Economic Growth in Nineteenth-Century Mexico," *American Historical Review* 83 (Feb. 1978): 98–99.

2. *Political modernization* refers to the formation of an effective, centralized, and active state government, capable of bringing about those political and socioeconomic changes desired by the regional elite. *Economic modernization* refers to the establishment of a communications-transportation infrastructure and the removal of obstacles to the greater production of material goods. For an extended treatment of modernization in Chiapas, see Thomas Benjamin, "Passages to Leviathan: Chiapas and the Mexican State, 1891–1947," Ph.D. diss. (East Lansing: Michigan State University, 1981).

3. Leo Waibel, *La Sierra Madre de Chiapas* (México, 1946), 169.

4. Murdo J. MacLeod, *Spanish Central America: A Socioeconomic History, 1520–1720* (Berkeley, 1973), 68–79.

5. Vicente Filísola, "Descripción de la provincia de Chiapas," 28 Nov. 1823, Latin American Manuscripts, Lilly Library, Indiana University.

6. Manuel Larrainzar, *Noticia histórica de Soconusco y su incorporación a la república mexicana* (México, 1843), 79.

7. Quoted in Mario García S., *Soconusco en la historia* (México, 1963), 171.

8. Manuel Larrainzar, *Chiapas y Soconusco con motivo de la cuestión de límites entre México y Guatemala* (México, 1875), 8–19.

9. Matías Romero, *Cultivo del café en la costa meridional de Chiapas* (México, 1875).

10. Daniel Cosío Villegas, *Historia moderna de Mexico. El porfiriato: La vida política exterior* (México, 1972), 118–21.

11. Ibid., 50–51.

12. Romero, *Cultivo del café*, 19.

13. Emilio Rabasa to Porfirio Díaz, 23 Aug. 1892, Universidad de las Américas, Colección General Porfirio Díaz, Cholula, Puebla, roll 85, legajo 17, document 14543; hereafter cited as CGPD.

14. Anonymous, "Análisis situación general estado de Chiapas," 1878, Archivo Histórico de Matías Romero, Banco de México (Mexico City), expediente 28784; Cosío Villegas, *La vida política exterior*, 41.

15. Carlos Gris, *Sebastían Escobar y el departamento de Soconusco, estado de Chiapas: Apuntes para la historia* (México, 1885), 24.
16. T. Merodio to Porfirio Díaz, 11 July 1888, CGPD, 42, 18, 7025.
17. César Sepúlveda, "Historia y problemas de los límites de México; II: La frontera sur," *Historia Mexicana* 8 (Oct.–Dec. 1958): 151–56.
18. U.S. House of Representatives, *Boundary between Mexico and Guatemala*, 48th Congress, 1st Session, Executive Document no. 154 (Washington, D.C.: U.S. Government Printing Office, 1884), 103–4.
19. Ismael Pizarro to Foreign Secretary (Mexico), 20 May 1912, Archivo de la Secretaría de Relaciones Exteriores, Mexico City, expediente 11-2-141.
20. "La Colonización," *El Caudillo* (San Cristóbal Las Casas), 29 April 1888.
21. Albert Brickwood, "Lands in Chiapas (Mexico)," 10 Aug. 1910, U.S. National Archives (Washington, D.C.), Record Group 84, Tapachula: Miscellaneous Reports, hereafer cited as NARG 84. The Huller concession was transferred to the Chiapas Land Company of London in 1895.
22. Albert Brickwood, "Coffee in Soconusco, Chiapas," 26 Sept. 1910, NARG 84, Miscellaneous Reports. See also Carlos Gris, "¿Querías ser rico?" *El Universal*, 30 Dec. 1891; *Chiapas, su estado actual, su riqueza, sus ventas para los negocios* (México, 1895), 8.
23. Helen Seargeant, *San Antonio Nexapa* (Mexico, 1971). The author of this book was ten years old when she arrived in Soconusco, in 1888. The book ends in 1905, when the family left the region for Panama.
24. Ibid., 77.
25. Ibid.
26. Mauricio Domínguez, "The Development of the Technological and Scientific Coffee Industry in Guatemala, 1830–1930," Ph.D. diss. (New Orleans: Tulane University, 1970), 238–39.
27. Brickwood, "Coffee in Soconusco."
28. "Informe sobre el cultivo del café," *La Agricultura* (Tuxtla Gutiérrez), 12 Nov. 1892.
29. Manuel Carrascosa, *Memoria que presenta el ciudadano Manuel Carrascosa, como gobernador constitucional del estado libre y soberano de Chiapas* (San Cristóbal Las Casas, 1890), 5.
30. Cayetano Romero to the Foreign Secretary (Mexico), 8 Sept. 1891, Archivo de la Secretaría de Relaciones Exteriores, 1-e-1634-4.
31. Seargeant, *San Antonio Nexapa*, 67.
32. *Periódico Ofical del Estado* (Chiapas), 30 July 1898.

33. Archivo del Registro de la Propiedad Pública y Comercio (Tapachula), libro 1902; hereafter cited as ARP.

34. *Ley y reglamento para la división y reparto de egidos en el estado de Chiapas* (Tuxtla Gutiérrez, 1893), 1–18; Vecinos de Chiapa de Corzo to Porfirio Díaz, 6 Jan. 1895, CGPD, 112, 20, 936.

35. "Oficina General de Ejidos: Copia del inventario general formado por la Oficina Gral. de Ejidos," 1908, Archivo Histórico de Chiapas (Tuxtla Gutiérrez), Sección de Fomento, 1908, vol. 3, expediente 12.

36. Emilio Rabasa to Porfirio Díaz, 21 May 1894, CGPD, 104, 19, 7417; Emilio Rabasa, *La evolución histórica de México* (México, 1956 [1920]), 237.

37. Adolfo Giesemann, Tapachula, to Porfirio Díaz, 16 March 1899, CGPD, 170, 25, 2870.

38. A. Farrera, "Memorandum sobre el café en Chiapas," 16 March 1899, CGPD, 165, 24, 15132.

39. Brickwood, "Coffee in Soconusco."

40. Rabasa to Díaz, 17 May 1893, CGPD, 92, 18, 6224.

41. Rabasa to Díaz, 14 Oct. 1893, CGPD, 98, 18, 15335.

42. Rabasa to Díaz, 18 Feb. 1894, CGPD, 101, 19, 2678.

43. ARP, libros 1899–1909.

44. Ibid.

45. ARP, libros 1900.

46. ARP, libros 1910. See also Brígida von Mentz, Verena Radkau, Beatriz Scharrer, and Guillermo Turner, *Participación extranjera en el desarrollo de la burguesía en México: El caso de los alemanes en el siglo XIX (1821–1875)* (México, 1981), 147–52.

47. ARP, libros 1899–1909.

48. Ibid., 91.

49. Ibid., libros 1902.

50. *Directorio general de la república mexicana* (México, 1893 and 1900).

51. Manuel Bejarano to Porfirio Díaz, 10 Dec. 1898, CGPD, 156, 23, 17857.

52. Interview with an elderly planter in Tapachula, December 1980.

53. Porfirio Díaz to Francisco León, 5 March 1896, CGPD, 300, 41, 402.

54. Ibid.

55. Fred Wilber Powell, *The Railroads of Mexico* (Boston, 1921), 154; *Moody's Manual of Railroad and Corporation Securities, 1909* (New York, 1909), 755.

56. E. N. Hedin, Tapachula, to U.S. Consul, Salina Cruz, 20 Dec. 1918, NARG 84, Correspondence, Salina Cruz, vol. 61.

57. C. Lesher, "Coffee Crop Conditions in Foreign Countries," 1 Feb. 1912, NARG 84, Tapachula: Miscellaneous Reports.

58. *Anuario estadístico del estado de Chiapas: Año de 1909* (Tuxtla Gutiérrez: Tipografía del Gobierno, 1911), 95–102. In 1910 a total of 52,000 hectares were cultivated in Soconusco, bringing in a total of $2,250,000 U.S., or about $43 per hectare.

59. ARP, libros 1906; "Soconusco Coffee-Growers' Meeting," 1 Oct. 1910, NARG 84, Tapachula: Miscellaneous Reports.

60. *Estadísticas sociales del Porfiriato, 1877–1910* (México, 1956), 34.

61. *Anuario estadístico de Chiapas, 1909,* 307; Antonio García de León, "Lucha de clases y poder político en Chiapas," *Historia y Sociedad* 22 (1979): 68.

62. ARP, libros 1910–1913.

63. Benigno Cárdenas to Porfirio Díaz, 26 Aug. 1908, CGPD, 252, 33, 12841.

64. *Boletín estadístico del estado de Chiapas* (Tuxtla Gutiérrez, 1897); Anuario estadístico de Chiapas, 1909.

65. Paul Furbach, *Die Arbeiterverhältnisse in den Kaffee-Plantagen Süd-Mexikos,* Inaugural-Dissertation zur Erlangung der Doktorwürde der Hohen Philosophischen Fakultät der Ruprecht-Karls-Universität zu Heidelberg (Berlin, 1912).

66. Brickwood, "Coffee in Soconusco."

67. Brickwood, "Memorandum, August 1911," NARG 84, Tapachula Dispatches.

68. Karl Kaerger, *Landwirtschaft und Kolonisation im Spanischen Amerika* (Leipzig, 1901), 543; Friedrich Katz, *La servidumbre agraria en México en la época porfiriana* (México, 1980), 79.

69. Furbach, *Arbeiterverhältnisse.* The author of this book was a planter in Soconusco who received his Ph.D. degree at the University of Heidelberg for this thesis.

70. David Calleo, *The German Problem Reconsidered: Germany and the World Order, 1870 to the Present* (Cambridge, Eng., 1978), 20–21.

71. Fernando Resenzweig, "Las exportaciones mexicanas," *Historia Mexicana* 9 (Jan.–March 1960): 401.

72. Interview with a planter in Tapachula, December 1980.

73. Hedin to U.S. Consul, Salina Cruz, 20 Dec. 1918.

6
La Sierra de Jacala: Ranchos and Rancheros in Northern Hidalgo

Frans J. Schryer

The *rancheros*, a class of small landowners generally ignored in the literature on prerevolutionary Mexico, became an influential rural elite in many remote regions of Mexico during the Porfiriato. While their actual emergence dates back to the middle of the nineteenth century, their social and economic position was consolidated during the Porfiriato, especially in areas where such rancheros did not enter into direct competition with larger, absentee *hacendados*. One such area is the mountainous region of northern Hidalgo. Here, the expansion of such cash crops as coffee and sugarcane, as well as the growing importance of cattle production, gave rise to a new class of commercial farmers. Despite a great variety of legal land-tenure arrangements, the form of agricultural enterprise which became predominant in this region was the small and medium-size estate known as a *rancho*. The owners of such ranchos, usually classified as *agricultores*, or *labradores*, in the censuses, employed day laborers and rented out part of their land to sharecroppers or part-time tenant cultivators. These rancheros, who constituted a local upper class vis à vis the poor peasants dependent on them, exercised paternalistic control over their economic subordinates, many of whom were tied to their employers through bonds of real or fictive kinship. They also occupied all the public posts on the municipal level.

Unlike the hacendados so often portrayed in the literature, the rancheros managed their own estates and were actively engaged in local commerce or the small-scale processing of agricultural products grown on such small estates. They were also characterized by a rustic outlook and culture that contrasted sharply with that of middle- and upper-class urbanites. For example, many rancheros lived in common-law unions like the majority of their peons, and it was not considered improper or unusual for a man who could afford it to have more than one wife, each living in her own separate dwelling or in a different village. Even the wealthiest ranchero of northern Hidalgo frequently wore the same broad-brimmed hat and the silver-buttoned trousers as Emiliano Zapata, who epitomizes the small Mexican farmer or the rural villager—the opposite of the sophisticated *hacienda* owner, born and bred in Mexico City or abroad.[1] Like Zapata, this rich ranchero, the most prominent representative of the landowning farmers of northern Hidalgo and a regional *cacique*, was still considered a peasant, or a backward rustic, during his occasional visits to Mexico City.

While the majority of these rancheros joined the Mexican Revolution, their initial support for Porfirio Díaz was an important factor in helping his regime consolidate its power and extend its control over the countryside during the first two decades after the Tuxtepec revolt. In northern Hidalgo, for example, rancheros supported Porfirio Díaz's rebellion in 1876 and later developed close links with the Díaz regime. These rancheros, whose access to land was ensured by the implementation of the liberal land reforms first introduced by Benito Juárez, also helped to crush the revolt of Indian peasants in the neighboring Sierra Gorda region in the 1870s and 1880s. Despite a lack of modern means of communication, northern Hidalgo experienced a local boom, especially in the decade of the 1890s. Only after 1900 did increasing dissatisfaction among local rancheros pave the way for a new alliance with the middle

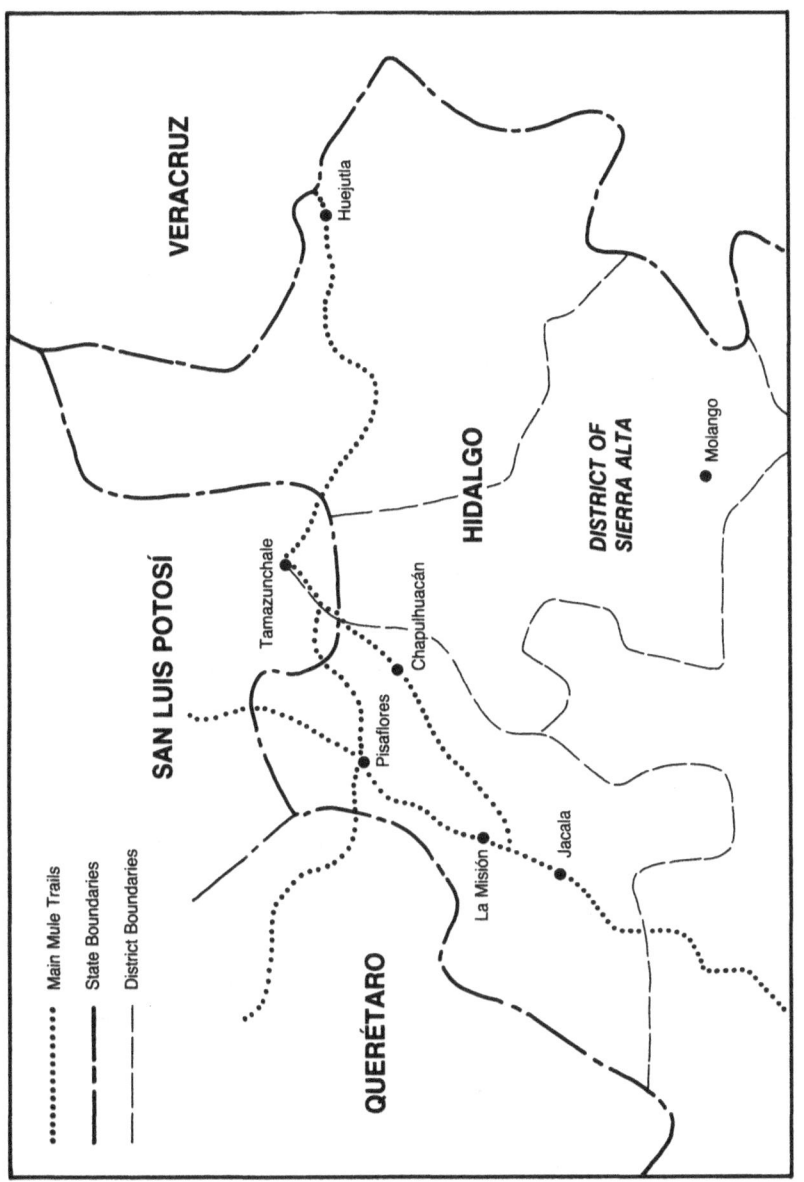

La Sierra de Jacala, 1900

class from northern Mexico, who fought for and gained access to national power in 1917.

The specific area within northern Hidalgo chosen for more detailed examination in this essay is the Sierra de Jacala, which roughly corresponds to the district by the same name, today comprising five *municipios*.[2] Most of this subregion, which belongs to the foothills of the Sierra Madre Oriental, is also considered to be part of the Huasteca, a semitropical region of abundant vegetation that includes parts of the states of Hidalgo, San Luis Potosí, and Veracruz. Special attention will be drawn to the municipio of Pisaflores, which was the object of more intensive investigation by the author.[3] This municipio became the most prosperous part of the Sierra de Jacala and its most thriving commercial center during the Porfiriato. Although a neglected and empoverished region today, this municipio is not only representative of northern Hidalgo during the Porfiriato, but was the birthplace of Nicolás Flores, a guerrilla leader and the first Constitutionalist governor of the state of Hidalgo.

Early Historical Background

Northern Hidalgo constitutes an agricultural frontier that was settled only recently compared to other parts of central Mexico, which had sedentary populations going back to pre-Hispanic days. For example, at the time of the conquest the Sierra de Jacala was inhabited by nomadic Indians who remained outside of the area of effective political control, while the neighboring region of Huejutla, just to the east, had only recently been incorporated into the Aztec state.[4] The first Spanish contacts in the Sierra de Jacala were made by Catholic missionaries belonging to the Franciscan and Augustinian orders. These friars tried to proselytize the native inhabitants and set up small settlements of converts that were repeatedly attacked and forced to disband. The first permanent mission center was a fortified convent established in Chapulhuacán around 1650.[5] The area just north of Chapulhuacán, including part of the municipio of Pisaflores, was then settled by Náhuatl-speaking peasants from the neighboring region of Tamazunchale, in the state of San Luis Potosí. Farther to the south, the valley of Jacala was settled by lay Spaniards in the 1700s. Here a group of miners founded the community and hacienda of San Nicolás. This settlement also served as a military outpost in a frontier war against an enclave of nomadic Indians. Among these Spanish frontier settlers, the Rubio family later established the nearby village of Jacala, which gradually outstripped San Nicolás in numbers and economic importance. Apart from very primitive mining of small copper and zinc deposits, these early settlers raised cattle and grew wheat for export to the Mesquital Valley, a dry region just to the south.

The sparsely inhabited territory between the outskirts of Jacala and the area of Indian settlements along the border of San Luis Potosí was ceded by royal decree to a merchant from Mexico City in 1738.[6] Most of the remaining original inhabitants of the region were abducted or driven away before the end of the eighteenth century, while a few remaining Pame-speaking Indians were assimilated by mestizo newcomers.[7] Their territory was then sold to a Captain Joseph Joaquín Rubio, a resident of Jacala and grandson of the founder of that village. This huge territory, called the hacienda of Tampochocho and covering twenty thousand hectares of fertile but rugged semitropical forest, served as a reserve for further settlement by Rubio's numerous descendants. These settlers, who intermarried with the Indian inhabitants of nearby communal villages, raised cattle on the banks of the Moctezuma and Quetzalapa rivers and in several small valleys within the boundaries of this estate. From Jacala they moved into the neighboring municipio of La Misión; by the end of the eighteenth century they had reached a mountain range just south of the Valley of Pisaflores, where several members of the Rubio family established the village of Álamos.[8] Wage labor was almost nonexistent in this earlier period of expansion, and the tenants, or sharecroppers, of Tampochocho, who cultivated the subsistence crops of maize and beans, were frequently poorer relatives of the founding family, whose direct descendants continued to own the land jointly.[9] One of these co-owners, a grandson of Captain Joaquín Rubio of Jacala, finally settled in the Valley of Pisaflors with a few relatives and friends, during the turmoil associated with the war of independence from Spain. The small residential center they founded in 1817 later became the *cabecera* of Pisaflores. Upon their arrival, the only other nearby population center of even minor administrative importance was the hamlet of Xochicoaco, located on a mountain peak overlooking the valley. This hamlet was surrounded by sparsely populated terrain then communally owned by Náhuatl-speaking peasants who had earlier migrated to the mountainous zone just north of the Valley of Pisaflores, which formed the northern border of Tampochocho (see map). At the time these early settlers built their primitive homes in the valley, most of what is now the municipio of Pisaflores was still covered by thick forests, traversed by numerous mountain brooks.[10]

Emergence and Development of a Ranchero Economy

Between 1820 and 1870, especially during the political turmoil of the War of the Reform and the French Intervention, the Sierra de Jacala was settled by successive waves of immigrants from other parts of Mexico, fleeing from the effects of political persecution or physical destruction in those regions. These newcomers included small merchants and entrepreneurs who started handicraft industries (soapmaking, lumbering, and liquor distilling) while engaging in various agricultural activities, especially the cultivation of sugarcane, an increasingly important regional cash crop that was processed into *pilón*.[11] This sugarloaf, an item of popular consumption, was sold in the highlands of Querétaro and Guanajuato and also provided the raw material for the production of *aguardiente*. Several coppersmiths from Italy, who made equipment used in the processing of sugarloaf or in the distilling of aguardiente, came to live in the recently founded village already known as Pisaflores.[12] The introduction of other cash crops, including tobacco and coffee, further stimulated trade with surrounding regions, and part-time wage employment became an important source of income for local inhabitants who did not own land.[13] The favorable geographic position of the Valley of Pisaflores soon made this part of Tampochocho a flourishing intermediary center between the highlands of Querétaro and Guanajuato and the lowlying areas of the Huasteca region. Earlier paths leading to the neighboring state of Querétaro were improved, and between 1860 and 1870 a mule trail was built, under the auspices of leading citizens, to improve communication between Pisaflores and the town of Tamazunchale. A bustling marketplace developed, and in 1873 the rustic hamlet of Pisaflores became a town (*pueblo de categoría*), as well as the cabecera of a municipio with the same name. This same municipio, which at first included only the Valley of Pisaflores, was expanded in 1878, when it merged with the mountainous zone previously under the jurisdiction of Xochicoaco, just one year after General Porfirio Díaz defeated the government of Lerdo de Tejada.[14] Many prominent rancheros from the mountainous zone moved to the new cabecera or assumed public posts under the new local government.

Although the hacienda of Tampochocho, which now included part of this enlarged municipio, was still officially owned as a single estate by the decendants of the original owner from Jacala, it had evolved into a number of separate farms (ranchos), scattered over three municipios. The typical rancho included a field of sugarcane, a fenced-off pasture for horses and mules, a roofed structure used to house a *molienda* (small sugar mill) during the cane harvest, and an adobe-brick house, where the owner of the rancho lived with his family. This house would be surrounded by thatched-roofed huts used for cooking and sleeping quarters, as well as the humble homes of the landless peasants who were given permission to live in the rancho. Such a cluster of huts frequently formed the nucleus of a hamlet, or ranchería, consisting of several farmers and their day laborers or tenants. Each ranchería, conveniently located near a stream or fresh-water spring, was surrounded by natural pastures for cattle and by forests that provided firewood, timber, and terrain for the perpetually shifting corn plots, or *milpas*. Coffee trees were also planted in the forest, under the protective shade cover of larger trees. There were no fixed boundaries between one rancho and the next when the Valley of Pisaflores was first being settled, in the early part of the nineteenth century. But as the local population expanded, the co-owners or tenants who operated such ranchos set up stone markers to demarcate the limits of their properties.[15] Newcomers who came to Pisaflores after 1850 set up their own ranchos on land belonging to the hacienda and paid rents to an administrative committee representing all the co-owners, established to look after the financial and legal affairs of the old landed estate. Some of these newcomers also became co-owners by marrying members of the founding family, while others bought shares which likewise entitled them to rights of joint ownership.[16]

In the area bordering the old hacienda, including the mountainous zone of the municipio of Pisaflores, the pattern of land tenure changed more dramatically. With the restoration of the liberal government of Juárez, in 1867, and then Lerdo de Tejada (1872–76), the law of *desamortización,* designed to encourage private ownership of land, was implemented in this region. This process of land reform was accelerated during the first two decades of the Porfiriato, with constant edicts to local authorities ordering them to make sure that remaining plots of communal land be transformed into private property. The subsequent granting of titles to specific pieces of communal land reinforced existing wealth differences because wealthy peasants were able to file claims for larger amounts of land they supposedly already possessed, while others sold their land titles to more powerful neighbors. Land records relating to the municipio of Pisaflores and the former municipio of Xochicoaco indicate quite a discrepancy, for example, in the amount of land granted to local inhabitants through such titles.[17] They ranged from three *cuartillos* (the equivalent of approximately two hectares) to ten fanegas (two hundred hectares). Moreover, the number of new landowners (*adjudicatorios*), already smaller than the total number of households in the mountainous zone of Pisaflores, dwindled from 107 in 1872 to 67 in 1887, due to the transfer of such titles from poorer peasants to wealthier villagers or outsiders.

One incident is especially revealing. In the hamlet of Las Moras, an army officer who had come to the region in the 1860s, during the war against the French, filed a claim of ownership in his own name on behalf of the entire hamlet, after persuading the local peasants that they could continue to work rent-free on a portion of this land.[18] The *jefe político* of the district of Jacala also granted land titles to farmers who were already co-owners of the hacienda and who had previously obtained so-called permission to use communal lands of the mountainous zone for pasture and growing maize. In this manner most of the communally owned lands of Xochicoaco were transformed into small, privately owned estates, or ranchos, similar to those located within the boundaries of the hacienda of Tampochocho.

This pattern of increasing concentration of landownership is similar to what occurred just across the border, in the neighboring municipio of Tamazunchale and in other parts of northern Hidalgo, where agrarian communes had seen the influx of outsiders and a process of class differentiation between rich and poor peasants. However, while most communal land in northern Hidalgo was transformed into privately owned ranchos, the majority of rancheros continued to recognize poor peasants' traditional rights of access to tracts of land customarily used for slash-and-burn cultivation. Such de facto communal land, usually located in the hillsides surrounding existing hamlets, could be considered as special reserves for the poor, set aside by commercial farmers in an area of labor scarcity and an abundance of uncleared land.[19] In this way the rancheros were able to maintain the loyalty of the poor peasants who had already become dependent on them for protection and part-time employment. Consequently, no agrarian uprisings occurred in the Sierra de Jacala or the rest of northern Hidalgo, far removed from the sphere of influence of expanding haciendas which were the main objects of attack by militant peasants. In contrast, violent conflicts and at least one peasant movement that started in Tamazunchale spread like wildfire throughout the neighboring region of southern San Luis Potosí and the mountainous region of Guanajuato and Querétaro known as the Sierra Gorda.[20]

After 1870 many landless peasants also came to the Sierra de Jacala from the arid and poorer zones of southern Hidalgo (Valle de Mesquital), attracted by higher wages and the possibility of combining wage labor with subsistence cultivation on virgin slopes. Many of these migrant workers, some of whom spoke Otomí, a language indigenous to many regions of Hidalgo, settled permanently in local ranchos and added to the population of already existing hamlets. In Pisaflores several new population centers sprang up; by 1874 the municipio had over four thousand inhabitants.[21] The fact that these new arrivals came from different regions, with different languages, also reinforced the tendency for Spanish to become the common language of the lower classes in most of the Sierra de Jacala.

The constant influx of newcomers and the rapid expansion of local commerce in the Sierra de Jacala region throughout the second half of the nineteenth century transformed a primarily subsistence-oriented agricultural system—based on a patriarchal relationship between a few so-called Spanish landowning families and tenants or part-time laborers who were poor relatives or so-called Indian peasants—into a commercial type of rural production system characterized by private land tenure and wage labor. This gave birth to a class of rancheros who produced for a national or international market. These commercial landowning farmers, whether they were nouveau riche peasants or the descendants of Tampochocho's original owner, dedicated themselves to overseeing the production of cattle, riding on horseback between hamlets to conduct business, while small stills and stores owned by such rancheros were usually managed by their immediate relatives (for example, by a son, wife, or widowed mother). However, although they did participate in certain kinds of physical labor on occasion, the rancheros all employed wage laborers for clearing the land, harvesting crops, and running their sugar mills. Even the poorer rancheros with very small farms rarely worked in their own cornfields or harvested their own coffee or sugarcane, but rather supervised the peons who carried out these tasks. Local landowning farmers periodically rented out part of their small estates to these same landless peons for the slash-and-burn cultivation of maize. This provided the rancheros with corn (either a fifth or a third of the crop) to use for their own consumption, for animal fodder, or as a means of payment to part-time day laborers. More importantly, such slash-and-burn activities created natural pastures for the rancheros, who drove their cattle into the fields of stubble after the corn harvest had been completed. Some of the landless peasants were also allowed to plant coffee trees for their own use. Because they were given access to land for the cultivation of noncommercial crops, these landless peons were more likely to settle on their employers' estates, thus constituting a local labor force willing to work for low wages during periods of peak demand.

Starting in the 1880s, the production of local coffee and the volume of trade with the surrounding regions greatly increased. Local rancheros who were also merchants ran mule trains to the town of Tamazunchale and then employed barges that navigated by river to the city of Tampico, the port for exporting local coffee. They also carried other commodities, such as pilón, tobacco, chiles, and locally distilled aguardiento to Río Verde, San Ciro, and Ciudad Valles, the terminus of a new railroad in San Luis Potosí. From a biographical account handwritten by a merchant from Pisaflores, it appears that they were provided with credit by Spanish businessmen who owned warehouses in Tampico.[22] On their return trips to the

Sierra de Jacala, these local merchants brought back luxury goods, including imported European liquors and fine linens for sale to wealthy local rancheros or for wholesale to stores in the neighboring state of Querétaro, following mule trails that led from the village of Tilaco to Jalpán and from there to Xichu, in the state of Guanajuato. At the same time, merchants from other states, using mule trains, also converged on the plaza of Pisaflores to buy up local tropical products, in exchange for such highland commodities as palm hats, flour, and textiles. The decade between 1890 and 1900 was the peak in this period of growth and prosperity, coinciding with the high point of the Porfiriato. In the municipio of Pisaflores, major public projects were undertaken, including a telegraph line, and the total population rose from 4,516 in 1880 to 7,804 in 1900, exceeding that of the municipio of Jacala.[23] The Sierra de Jacala was even included in plans for a proposed railroad that was to run from Pachuca, the state capital, through Jacala and Pisaflores to the port of Tampico.[24]

In 1900 the population of the region declined somewhat, as many wage-earning peasants left to seek work for higher wages on a new, modern sugar plantation in El Higo, Veracruz. This first out-migration lasted only a short time, however, because many workers contracted malaria and returned home.[25] Despite these and other setbacks, the local economy continued to expand. Indeed, peasants from the highlands of Querétaro and the Valle de Mesquital region continued to flock to the Sierra de Jacala, and especially to the municipio of Pisaflores, up to and during the revolutionary period. However, the relative prosperity of the Sierra de Jacala, compared to other rural regions, did not provide equal benefits to all of its inhabitants.

The Class Structure in Pisaflores during the Porfiriato

A more accurate picture of the pattern of land tenure and its corresponding system of social stratification during the Porfiriato is provided by data collected for the municipio of Pisaflores.[26] In 1880, when the region can be considered to have constituted a full-fledged ranchero economy, the rancheros made up about one-quarter of the local population. The minimum viable rancho seems to have been one with a fiscal value of approximately fifty pesos. This would represent five hectares of flat land in the valley or fifty hectares of mixed arable land, scrubland, and steep forest slopes in the mountainous zone.[27] Local records indicate that heads of households who owned at least this amount of land also paid taxes on the commercial production of sugarcane or coffee and usually owned cattle. Another five percent of the heads of households were tenant farmers who also paid taxes for producing cash crops but did not yet own their own land. There were, in addition, some small artisans and petty merchants, all of whom lived in the cabecera, who were self-employed but only hired wage laborers to help them cultivate their milpas, an economic activity practiced by practically every family in the area, regardless of socioeconomic status. These small-scale artisans represented 3 percent of all heads of households. Apart from another very small number of men with other occupations (full-time municipal employees, such as scribes and schoolteachers), the rest of the population (60 percent) consisted of day laborers, known as *jornaleros*, who combined wage labor with subsistence farming. This last category, which included some households with small plots of land (less than fifty pesos' worth), did not produce cash crops.

A marked tendency toward greater concentration of landownership, and the virtual disappearance of full-time tenant farmers and part-time subsistence cultivators owning their own plots of land, can be discerned between 1880 and 1910. Both the absolute number and the percentage of peasants with some land, but less than fifty pesos' worth, declined in this period, while full-time tenant farmers, who grew cash crops, dwindled from 5 percent of all heads of households to less than 2 percent.[28] At the same time, the day laborers, most of whom did not own any land whatsoever, represented an increasing proportion of the population, constituting 82 percent of all household heads in 1910. In contrast, the rancheros comprised less than 12 percent of the total number of households in the municipio of Pisaflores at the time of the outbreak of the Revolution. This changing proportion of landowner-employers to day laborers without property reflects the transfer of rural properties from both subsistence cultivators and poorer rancheros to the owners of larger ranchos, as well as the influx of landless peasants from other parts of Mexico.

Up to this point, we have treated the rancheros of the Sierra de Jacala analytically as a single socioeconomic class. The vast majority of these rancheros owned land, and they all raised cattle and produced cash crops using seasonal wage laborers. However, the distribution of rural properties within this class of commercial farmers was highly skewed, as is to be expected in a system of private land tenure, and the rancheros could be subdivided into three substrata. The wealthier rancheros, who were usually classified as *agricultores* in official censuses, owned rural properties with a fiscal value of over 999 pesos.[29] Apart from owning more cattle and growing more sugarcane, they also owned retail stores, urban lots, and local slaughterhouses. Many of these larger landowners were descendants, through the male line, of the founding Rubio family. Some of them owned several ranchos and appointed administrators to supervise some of their agricultural operations. The second category of rancheros, almost as well off as the agricultores, consisted of wealthy merchants and artisans who also owned land (at least 250 pesos' worth). Although they produced cash crops and owned cattle, they tended to dedicate most of their time to commercial and speculative activities, or administered small manufacturing workshops run by apprentices or day laborers. These men left their ranchos almost entirely in the hands of overseers or tenants. For all practical purposes, these wealthy merchants and artisans belonged to the same social stratum as the larger landowners; they all began as farmers and belonged to the same landowning families. Like the wealthiest rancheros, they also had their principal residence in the cabecera. The last category, landowning farmers with 50 to 999 pesos' worth of land, generally resided in their ranchos and did not use overseers. In fact, apart from managing their own ranchos, some of these landowning farmers also administered ranchos for wealthy merchants or larger landowners, who lived in the cabecera.

Wealth differences between rancheros with more land, who generally lived in the small towns of the Sierra de Jacala, and their counterparts in more isolated hamlets, corresponded to certain cultural differences. For example, in the municipio of Pisaflores a little over half of the rancheros who resided in the rancherías of the mountainous zone were illiterate. Although they owned and rode horses and ate better, most of them had not yet built the two-story houses that later became fashionable. In contrast, the supposedly more cultured landowning farmers and merchants of the cabecera lived in adobe and brick houses with tile or copper roofs, surrounding a central patio, and knew how to read and write.[30] Not only did their children attend one of several primary schools in the valley, including one for girls in the cabecera, but the children of wealthier families were sometimes sent to urban centers to continue their education. Despite such differences in life-styles, however, landowning families from both town and hamlet, and even artisans and merchants without land, mingled with one another on social occasions, intermarried, and shared the same aspirations and values. They also tended to distinguish themselves from their economic subordinates, the landless peasants, in terms of language and ethnicity. For example, even rancheros whose parents had been monolingual Indian speakers identified themselves as *gente de razón* and tried to emulate the customs and speech of local representatives of the national culture.[31]

A tendency toward greater inequality of landownership among these various strata of rancheros emerged during the Porfiriato, thus reflecting a more general trend on the national level. After 1880 several already prominent landowning farmers in the Valley of Pisaflores expanded their estates through the purchase of additional ranchos or by foreclosing on mortgages obtained by lending money to other farmers. By 1890, for example, one member of the founding family who lived in the cabecera expanded his landholdings from two hundred to over six hundred hectares. The man who became the wealthiest ranchero, Evaristo Alvarado, was a distant relative of the original owner of Tampochocho on his mother's side; he came to Pisaflores as a young man. He became a co-owner of the hacienda in the 1880s, by purchasing several shares, and later bought tracts of land in other parts of the municipio. This man, who also set up several moliendas and liquor distilleries, then bought up a whole block of houses in the cabecera. By 1900 he had become the largest landholder in the Sierra de Jacala.

Local Politics in a Ranchero Region

The emerging rancheros of the Sierra de Jacala region were consistently Liberals (followers of Benito Juárez's philosophy) and anticlerical in their political orientation around the middle of the nineteenth century.³² This political reputation played no small part in attracting Liberal sympathizers from other parts of central Mexico, who migrated to northern Hidalgo during periods of Conservative reaction and foreign occupation. Such newcomers, as well as leading members of the founding Rubio family and other rancheros, fought on the side of Benito Juárez during the French occupation of Mexico and took part in the siege of Querétaro that led to the final overthrow of the government of Maximilian of Austria. The best known military commander from the Sierra de Jacala region during this struggle was General Joaquín Martínez, a member of a wealthy ranchero family in Jacala.³³ Jacala, at that time the largest town and administrative center of the region, was honored by Juárez himself, who presented its citizens with a wooden plaque bearing the inscription *hijos predilectos de la patria*. With the restoration of the Republican government, in 1867, many former Conservatives and even pro-French politicians throughout Mexico were reconciled to the Liberal faction led by Juárez. This was also true for the new supporters of the Conservative cause in the Sierra de Jacala, including Margarito and Clemente Mata, two brothers who had been minor officers in the so-called imperialist army. During the French occupation, Margarito Mara had taken up residence and started farming in the small hamlet of Las Moras, in a remote corner of what later became the municipio of Pisaflores. Like his immediate superior officer, General Rafael Olvera of Jalpán (Querétaro), Margarito Mata was later reconciled to the Liberal faction and subsequently benefited from the partitioning of communal lands carried out in the region.³⁴ He thus became a leading ranchero and the member of a local elite in the remote municipio of Xochicoaco, as this part of the municipio of Pisaflores was then called.

Starting in 1869, when the second military district of the state of Mexico was transformed into the new state of Hidalgo, politically active landowners and merchants of the Sierra de Jacala had the opportunity to occupy administrative posts on the municipal level, through a procedure of open nominations and free elections among competing candidates.³⁵ Many of these local ranchero politicians, including Margarito Mata (now officially a colonel of the new Liberal government), also supported Porfirio Díaz's rebellion against Lerdo de Tejada in 1876, ostensibly fought to carry out further Liberal reforms. They voted for Díaz a year later. In that same electoral year, several prominent rancheros who lived in the cabecera of Pisaflores set up a small newspaper which criticized interstate tariffs, taxes on locally processed agricultural products, government corruption, and the professional standing army.[36] They also praised the Plan de Tuxtepec, proclaimed earlier by Porfirio Díaz. These same leading rancheros, in cooperation with Colonel Mata, then aided the cause by helping to put down a rebellion of Indian peasants in the neighboring region of the Sierra Gorda and in the municipio of Tamazunchale, just across the San Luis Potosí border.[37] The authoritarian and repressive nature of the Díaz regime did not become apparent to these rancheros until several years later.[38] By that time internal factional disputes arising from personal ambitions and competition among rival landowning families in the Sierra de Jacala overshadowed any preoccupation with larger political issues of national concern. The main rivals in these disputes were the Rubios, direct descendants of the founding family of Pisaflores, and the Alvarados, more recent arrivals who were gradually becoming the wealthiest rancheros of the Sierra de Jacala.

Until 1885 members of the founding Rubio family or people closely associated with them usually won the most important posts in the municipio of Pisaflores. The rising economic power of Evaristo Alvarado and his brother, Ambroisio, however, was gradually eroding the traditional prestige and influence of the founding family. The Alvarados also became increasingly more involved in local politics and ran as candidates for several municipal posts; Evaristo was elected *presidente municipal* in 1893. The first issue in this struggle for local power was control over the committee representing all the rancheros who were co-owners of the hacienda of Tampochocho.

With the gradual transformation of the local economy from an isolated region of primarily subsistence farming and occasional cattle raising to a center of commercial agriculture in the latter half of the nineteenth century, the legal status of the hacienda of Tampochocho, comprising over half the surface area of the Sierra de Jacala region, became increasingly incongruent with its de facto possession by numerous individual farmers. Tampochocho had never been controlled as a single administrative unit by one family, as had many other haciendas in less mountainous regions of Mexico, and consequently had never developed a *casco,* or landowner's mansion.³⁹ On the contrary, the ambiguous legal status of the estate and the lack of clearly demarcated boundaries for the rural properties within its limits led to litigation among the co-owners and shareholders. Because sugarcane plots, coffee orchards, and pastures were sometimes abandoned, and since most cornfields were constantly reverting back to secondary forest, it was not unusual for one ranchero who was legally a co-owner of the hacienda to claim rights of possession over land that had been cleared at an earlier date by another co-owner, thus giving rise to legal disputes.⁴⁰ Increasing competition among local farmers and the gradual expansion of several estates belonging to prominent shareholders aggravated such boundary disputes; one co-owner from Jacala, a widow by the name of Dolores Ledezma, initiated a legal process in 1888 to have the hacienda surveyed and formally divided into separate farms. A new committee of five members was set up to investigate the validity of titles held by some sixty-odd shareholders or co-owners and to hire a professional engineer to carry out the partition of Tampochocho. This administrative committee (*junta directiva*), with two representatives from Pisaflores, two from Jacala, and one from the village of Álamos (in the municipio of Chapulhuacán), was charged with the day-to-day administration of this corporation.⁴¹ The first treasurer of this committee was Mucio Rubio, a wealthy ranchero and leading member of the founding family of Pisaflores. However, the proposed division of the old hacienda only reinforced earlier conflicts over boundaries and aggravated the rivalry between the Rubios and the Alvarados.

At a meeting of co-owners held in Pisaflores in 1895, a group of shareholders closely associated with the Alvarados forced Rubio to resign for alleged incompetence and called for the election of another committee and a new treasurer. Evaristo Alvarado now became the new president of the junta directiva, while Rubio was replaced by Alvarado's brother, Ambroisio, a wealthy merchant and new shareholder as well.⁴² Evaristo also formed personal ties with the powerful Cravioto family, who ruled the state of Hidalgo during the first half of the Porfiriato. Such contacts gave Alvarado a strategic advantage in the ensuing conflicts over the partition of the hacienda and local politics. Indeed, his informal political influence became increasingly obvious, at a time when the process of democratic elections was becoming more and more subject to manipulation by a centralized system of political control. Evaristo Alvarado managed to become municipal president of Pisaflores on two more occasions, as well as to dominate the administrative committee of the hacienda. Political control reinforced his economic power and he soon became a cacique on the regional level.

Disputes over temporary boundaries and the trespassing of cattle increased local tensions until one co-owner, Severo Rubio, was ambushed and killed in 1898. The death of Severo Rubio (son of Mucio, the former treasurer) brought vehement protests by local opponents of Evaristo Alvarado, who according to one witness had ordered this assassination.[43] According to oral tradition, Severo's brother and several other rancheros from the Valley of Pisaflores even traveled to Mexico City to complain directly to Porfirio Díaz himself. However, in the subsequent police investigation, Alvarado was not even summoned to appear as a witness, despite evidence that he might have been responsible for this crime. This immunity even from the due process of law was guaranteed by his friendship with another influential, wealthy ranchero, Margarito Mata, who has already been mentioned in connection with the implementation of the Liberal land reform in the 1870s.

Margarito Mata, the former officer in Maximilian's army who had come to live in the Pisaflores area in the 1860s, had been appointed regional military commander (*jefe de armas*) shortly after Mata's had declared his support for Porfirio Díaz in 1876. He later became an active participant in the politics of Pisaflores, where he attained the post of local tax collector (*recaudador de rentas*) and municipal president on several occasions during the high point of the Porfiriato. While residing in the cabecera of Pisaflores during one of his periods of public office, Mata became a personal enemy of a young man named Nicolás Flores, the son of an Italian coppersmith who had bought a rancho and then set up a liquor distillery in the Valley of Pisaflores. The Flores family belonged to the Rubio faction. Young Nicolás left the area to seek his fortune elsewhere, shortly after a disagreement with Margarito Mata concerning the arrest of his younger brother for minor misdemeanors.[44] These events happened during the same year that Mucio Rubio lost his position as treasurer of the administrative committee of the hacienda of Tampochocho.

Nicolás Flores, now definitely a member of the out-faction, took up his father's trade of coppersmith and merchant, and then set up his own rancho and a small distillery in the hamlet of Zipatla, in the neighboring municipio of La Misión. The contacts he made during his many business trips throughout the Sierra de Jacala, and his popularity, later enabled him to play a leading role in the revolt against Porfirio Díaz and the subsequent struggle to depose Victoriano Huerta.

More conflicts over boundaries and the threat of further violence required the personal intervention of the new state governor, Pedro Rodríguez. At a meeting held in Pisaflores one year after the death of Severo Rubio, the governor was designated legal arbiter of the complex disputes associated with the division of the hacienda.[45] Several years later, in 1902, the hacienda of Tampochocho was finally divided among what had now become two hundred co-owners, about half of whom lived in the municipio of Pisaflores. Each co-owner received one or more lots of land of different sizes (most of them adjacent), according to the number of shares owned. Apart from minor adjustments, this division did not change the prevailing pattern of land tenure, for most rancheros simply obtained full legal rights over land they already possessed and that was already registered as private property in the local tax office. Nor did the implementation of this supposed land reform reduce either the economic power or the political influence of the local cacique. Evaristo Alvarado received many lots, totaling twelve hundred hectares, scattered throughout two municipios. These lots, together with other rural properties he already owned outside of Tampochocho, brought the total size of his estate to over fifteen hundred hectares, compared to from twenth-five to one hundred hectares for many smaller rancheros in the valley.[46]

Despite a temporary reduction in political tensions after the partition of Tampochocho, the factional dispute between the Alvarados and the Rubios continued, with minor switches of allegiance. In 1903, just a year after the division of Tampochocho, a mountain ranchero who had recently befriended the Rubio family was arrested and then drafted into the army when his two sons ambushed the municipal president on his way to officiate at a wedding in a remote hamlet. Several other conspirators, including a young member of the Rubio family also implicated in this plot, were sent off to Mérida to fight against rebellious Mayan Indians.[47] The conflict between Evaristo Alvarado and his opponents involved not only the leading landowning families of the Valley of Pisaflores but many other rancheros in the Sierra de Jacala. For example, in the area of former communal land, the vaguely defined boundaries of ranchos created after 1870, measured in metes and bounds, aggravated conflicts among less influential rival rancheros, who allied themselves with the Matas, the Alvarados, the Rubios, and other factional leaders.

The prevalence of factional disputes during the Porfiriato among the rancheros of the Sierra de Jacala can best be understood by recalling the labor-intensive nature of the agrarian system prevalent in most of rural Mexico at that time. This system put a premium on the control of as much land as possible, so that landowners might assure themselves of an adequate labor supply, receive additional income from rents, and expand their operations to the point where the day-to-day operations of the estate could be relegated to an overseer or administrator.[48] Wealthier landowning farmers, like Evaristo Alvarado, also sought to monopolize the lucrative business of liquor distilling in the region. Such economic control was reinforced by control over public office and favorable connections to the conservative, prolandholder government of Porfirio Díaz, as we have seen. It must also be remembered that, in this period of local economic expansion, agricultural and commercial activities still provided a potentially important means of personal advancement for wealthier rancheros who aspired to become real hacendados, even though the extent to which this process of land concentration could proceed was severely limited by the accidental nature of the terrain in such a mountainous region. Factional disputes continued during and after the Mexican Revolution, which simply changed the nature of the formal political system under which competition among rival landowning families could occur, and which tipped the balance of power in favor of the out-faction, led by the Rubio, Flores, and other ranchero families.

The Mexican Revolution in the Sierra de Jacala

Unlike other regions characterized by a high rate of landlord absenteeism or a much higher degree of concentration of landownership, the Sierra de Jacala did not experience violent clashes between landowners and landless peasants during the ten years of civil war following the downfall of Porfirio Díaz. There were no foreign landowners, nor were the economy and the social life of the Sierra de Jacala controlled by a handful of wealthy Mexican families residing in provincial capitals; the numerous descendants of the Rubio family, who originally bought the lands of Tampochocho, had long ago intermarried with the predominantly mestizo and Indian population. Moreover, many landowners in the Sierra de Jacala were nouveau riche peasants who had been able to accumulate some capital. Apart from the purely economic ties of dependency between these local landowning rancheros and the wage-earning peasants, with whom many employers shared a common origin, there were usually personal bonds of kinship or *compadrazgo* between rich and poor. However, while the landless peasants of northern Hidalgo considered themselves relatively well-off, compared to indebted peons in other regions, the rancheros shared many grievances with other segments of Mexico's population against the regime of Porfirio Díaz. Apart from the general economic crisis of the country following the booming 1890s, they resented the widespread corruption associated with the regime. Members of the out-faction, led by the Rubio family, and many rancheros not actively involved in local politics especially resented the favored treatment of such powerful men as Evaristo Alvarado. Apart from allowing local inhabitants to vent general grievances, the Mexican Revolution also provided the rancheros of the Sierra de Jacala with a unique opportunity to destroy the economic power of personal rivals and to initiate their own political careers in the vacuum of power left after the downfall of the Porfiristas.

During the Revolution many rancheros became self-appointed officers associated with one of several revolutionary factions. They recruited their own subordinates, some of whom were relatives as well as employees and tenants, to fight for the so-called revolutionary cause, using guerrilla tactics and returning home periodically to tend to their farms. Such revolutionary rancheros had several advantages vis-à-vis rebels who came from urban areas. They were quite adept at horseback riding and using firearms, and were thoroughly acquainted with the physical terrain of a mountainous region of strategic military importance.[49] Revolutionary leaders from this local upper class of landowning farmers were also able to utilize a wide network of social contacts with other ranchero families, previously established through intermarriage, in order to recruit additional allies and supporters. Rancheros who were involved in regional trade by means of mule trains as a seasonal activity, like Nicolás Flores, were in a particularly favorable position to obtain political benefits from the Revolution. These local revolutionaries also became involved in politics on the regional and state levels, using their military careers as stepping-stones toward more influential posts within the establishment that took the place of the old Díaz regime. Nicolás Flores, who had already been appointed provisional governor of the state of Hidalgo by Venustiano Carranza, was thus elected the first constitutional governor of his home state in 1917; another young ranchero from Pisaflores later became governor in the neighboring state of Querétaro.[50]

Conclusions

The class structure that developed in rural Mexico during the Porfiriato has been grossly misrepresented by an oversimplified model that portrays a small handful of hacendados pitted against an equally downtrodden mass of peons, impoverished smallholders, and a few remaining communal villages. A close examination of the history of northern Hidalgo, as well as a growing number of case studies from other parts of Mexico, indicate that the development of capitalist agriculture in rural Mexico and the accompanying changes in land tenure gave rise to a complex social structure, characterized by a new class of rich peasants, or small, landowning commercial farmers, generally referred to as rancheros, as well as to a new kind of large latifundist.[51] Elsewhere I have argued that such rancheros probably controlled as much as a third of Mexico's arable land and a third of its population at the end of the Porfiriato.[52] However, because the rancheros had such low status in the eyes of the metropolitan elite, and because of the relatively small size of the estates owned by even the wealthier rancheros in comparison to the huge haciendas, this rural class was socially almost invisible to those revolutionaries who came from urban areas and to the intelligentsia who formulated the ideologies of the Mexican Revolution. Although rancheros were also found in other parts of Mexico where the political and economic life was clearly dominated by hacendados, northern Hidalgo is typical of those regions where rancheros had gained both political and economic ascendency on the regional level during the Porfiriato. The economy of this region, far removed from modern means of communication and roads, was just as profoundly transformed during the Porfiriato as was that of Mexico as a whole. Moreover, contrary to the consensus of much of the literature, by the end of the Porfiriato the rancheros of such isolated regions more closely resembled the *kulaks* of Russia than the family farmers of North America.[53] Ironically, this social class was created by the policies of the same government they would later help to overthrow.

NOTES

1. See John Womack, *Zapata and the Mexican Revolution* (New York, 1969). The photographs of Zapata and this wealthy ranchero, Evaristo Alvarado, are strikingly similar.

2. Jacala, Pacula, La Misión, Chapulhuacán, and Pisaflores.

3. See Frans Schryer, *The Rancheros of Pisaflores* (Toronto, 1980). Sections of this chapter dealing with the early history and the emergence of a ranchero region were previously published by Duke University Press, in Frans Schryer, "A Ranchero Economy in Northwestern Hidalgo," *Hispanic American Historical Review* 59, no. 3 (1979): 418–43.

4. The nomadic tribesmen of northwestern Hidalgo were referred to as Jonaces, and included both Náhuatl and Otomí speakers, who inhabited a larger region known as the Cíbola; see *Catálogo de construcciones religiosas del estado de Hidalgo* (Pachuca, 1932), with an introduction by Manuel Toussaint. The northeastern half of Hidalgo, corresponding to the district of Huejutla, was one of several small states originally populated by Huasteco-speaking people; see Lorenzo Ochoa, *Historia prehispánica de la Huaxteca* (México, 1979).

5. *Catálogo de construcciones religiosas;* see section dealing with Chapulhuacán.

6. Archivo General de la Nación, México, ramo tierras, vol. 2255, Meztitlán.

7. Hector Samperio Gutiérrez, "Missiones del Colegio Apostólico de San Francisco de Pachuca en la Sierra de Zimapán," in *Historiografía Hidalguense* 2 (Pachuca, 1978).

8. Theodomiro Manzano, *Geografía del estado de Hidalgo* (México, 1897).

9. These and other statements concerning the early history and founding of Pisaflores are partly based on a handwritten account by a local merchant, Luciano Cruz, "Apuntes históricos de Pisaflores: Su fundación, desarrollo económico, social y político hasta su erección en pueblo," unpub. ms., n.d. (ca. 1910).

10. Cruz, "Apuntes."

11. The price of sugarcane increased dramatically after 1867, as a result of the war for independence in Cuba. Diego Lopez Rosado, *Historia y pensamiento económico de México* (México, 1968).

12. These Italian immigrants, followers of Garibaldi in Italy, had come to Mexico because of political persecution at home. One family of French origin and an Arab who married a local girl also became Pisaflorenses.

13. Arabic coffee trees were introduced on an experimental basis in 1845. The first coffee orchard was planted in the valley in 1859, but coffee beans produced in the Sierra de Jacala were not sold in Tampico until 1871. See Cruz, "Apuntes."

14. In the early nineteenth century, when the area still belonged to the state of Mexico, Xochicoaco and Pisaflores were both under the jurisdiction first of Meztitlán, and later of Zimapán. Pisaflores actually became a municipio in 1863, although its cabecera retained the legal status of ranchería, prior to the formation of the state of Hidalgo in 1869. In 1878 the former municipio of Álamos also became part of Chapulhuacán.

15. Several references are made to such *mojoneras* (some of which still exist) in local archives.

16. The institution of joint ownership (*codueñazgo*) is a land-tenure arrangement whereby a number of persons own shares in a single property that has legally remained undivided after the death of the original owner. Frequently its de facto division by inheritance or sale has been carried out without the prescribed legal formalities. Each shareholder has the right to occupy and cultivate any unused portion of the property and to enjoy the use of pastures, woods, waters, or forests of the place. See George McBride, *The Land Systems of Mexico* (1923; reprint ed., New York, 1971), 103–4.

17. These *títulos de adjudicación* and other documents were found, unbound, unsorted, and frequently unlabeled, in the attic of an old schoolbuilding in Pisaflores and in a storage room in the district jail, in Jacala. Officially the first set of documents belong to the archive of the municipal government of Pisaflores, the second set to the district judicial office; hence, the sources for these documents will be cited as Archivo Municipal de Pisaflores and Archivo del Juzgado de Primera Instancia de Jacala (hereafter cited as AMP and AJJ, respectively).

18. Petition of the hamlet of Las Moras to *jefe político*, 18 Aug. 1874.

19. Some of these lands, which were not claimed by individual farmers, were later registered as properties belonging to the municipal government. Other sections were legally owned by rancheros but were loaned to their employees at nominal rates of rent.

20. See Leticia Reina, *Las rebeliones campesinas en México (1819–1906)* (Mexico, 1980).

21. Data obtained from population censuses, listing place of residence, sex, age, marital status, occupation, and literacy, carried out in 1869, 1872, 1873, and 1874 in the municipio of Pisaflores; AMP.

22. Cruz, "Apuntes."

23. "Memorias administrativas," 1890 and 1901; AMP.

24. *Periódico oficial del gobierno de Hidalgo,* 1 Mar. 1904.

25. This information is based on interviews conducted with Fausto Cruz Ángeles, Severino Orosco Rubio, Irene Flores, Noradino Rubio Ortiz, Elpidio Rubio Nieto, Leobardo Morales, Antonio Reséndiz Estrada, Aurelio Rubio Márquez, and Juan Aquino Chávez at various times between May 1971 and August 1977. All of these people were alive at the time of the Revolution.

26. For a more detailed treatment see Schryer, "A Ranchero Economy."

27. The fiscal values of rural properties listed in a census compiled in 1908 were used as a common basis for comparison—"Causantes, predios rústicos y urbanos, pago de contribuciones," 1908, Oficina de Recaudación de Rentas, Pisaflores; AMP. These fiscal values did not change from 1880 to 1911 (prior to 1880, local documents recorded land values in terms of the number of bushels of corn that could be sown thereon, following local custom). Because of the great variation in quality of land, especially between valley and hillside, this standard fiscal value is a more meaningful figure for comparing the real worth of land than the actual size of the rural properties in number of hectares.

28. *Full-time tenants* includes all heads of households who produced cash crops or cattle but did not own land and who were also not members of landowning families. There were considerable variations in the scale of operation among such tenants, ranging all the way from small family tenants, who must have recently worked mainly for wages, to capitalist farmers. Their decreasing proportion in the population in this period represents both the process of purchase or inheritance of land by wealthier and more successful tenant farmers (who frequently married daughters of landowning farmers) and the financial ruin of many smaller tenant farmers.

29. Such labels as *agricultor, labrador, peón del campo,* and *jornalero* were not used in any consistent fashion in official censuses. For example, while

most rancheros with less than 999 pesos' worth of land were referred to as labradores at least once in various written records, they were often called jornaleros and sometimes even agricultores. In fact, even some of the wealthiest rancheros were sometimes listed as jornaleros! Not only were there variations according to the type of census (electoral, general population, or for taxation purposes, but during the volatile revolutionary period nearly everyone, including wealthy landowning farmers, was listed as peón de campo.

30. Local records indicate that 58 percent of the landowning farmers of the municipio born before 1875 were illiterate, but only one of these illiterate landowners lived in the cabecera.

31. Although the Sierra de Jacala is 99 percent monolingual Spanish-speaking today, relations between Náhuatl-speaking peasants and Spanish-speaking farmers and merchants in the Huejutla district of northeastern Hidalgo is still characterized by the use of such racial and linguistic terms. If, as I believe, interethnic relations in the Huejutla region can be used as a basis for speculating about relations between such groups in northwestern Hidalgo in the past, rancheros probably emphasized their non-Indian status even if they were completely bilingual and had relatives who spoke only Náhuatl.

32. Cruz, "Apuntes."

33. Numerous documents referring to him, including the execution of his last will, were found in the archives of Jacala (AJJ).

34. Petition of the hamlet of Las Moras to jefe político, 18 Aug. 1874. Mata had already been appointed *recaudador de rentas* of the municipio of Xochicoaco earlier that same year; AMP.

35. This is indicated by electoral records showing the number of votes received by competing candidates for municipal posts; AMP.

36. *El Instinto del Pueblo,* published in Pisaflores in 1877 and 1878.

37. Acuerdos de la Asamblea Municipal, 1976; Margarito Mata to Joaquín Rubio, Mucio Rubio, Timoteo Rubio, y Ciriaco Angeles, from Tamazunchale to Pisaflores, 1979 (sin fecha); both in AMP. These men, who were asked to send money and provisions to Mata in order to put down the so-called rebellion, had earlier helped to put down another uprising in the Sierra Gorda. Presidente Municipal de Xochicoaco to Jefe Político, 1868, AMP.

38. An anonymous writer from Pisaflores contributed at least one article to a newspaper critical of the government well into the Porfiriato: *El Estado de Hidalgo—Semanario Político, Literario, Commercial y Agricultor,* 9 Aug. 1885, "Remetido mandado de Pisaflores por M.V."

39. This was largely due to the irregular terrain of the Sierra de Jacala,

as well as to the lack of an effective communications network in such a mountainous region. These conditions were not conducive to centralized control and thus tended to favor smaller units of production. David Brading has shown that haciendas in the neighboring region of the Bajío in the nineteenth century were likewise unable to compete with maize-growing ranchos in areas that were not amenable to irrigation; see David Brading, *Haciendas and Ranchos in the Mexican Bajío* (*León 1700–1860*) (Cambridge, Eng., 1978).

40. The details of several of the more serious disputes over competing land claims are found in the records of the district judicial office; see, for example, Juicio verbal, Vicente Villanueva contra Ambroisio Alvarado, Sept. 1893, AJJ.

41. Testimonio de las diligencias mandadas protocolizar en el juicio promovido sobre la división de la Hacienda de Tampochocho, 3 Oct. 1888, AJJ.

42. Acta de elección de los miembros de la Hacienda de Tampochocho, elevado a instrumento público, Libro de Protocolos no. 15, AJJ.

43. Details concerning the assassination, including a statement by this witness that the gunman responsible for the murder had been paid by Evaristo Alvarado, were recorded in a lengthy investigatory report: En averiguación del homicidio de Severo Rubio, 1899, AJJ. News concerning these events even appeared in several daily newspapers in Mexico City: *El Universal*, 6 Nov. 1898 and *El Popular*, 8 Nov. 1898; but charges of a cover-up were vehemently denied by the official state newspaper. *Periódico Oficial del Estado de Hidalgo*, 8 Nov., 16 Nov. 1898.

44. This incident has become part of oral tradition. According to official records in Jacala, Nicolás's brother had been arrested by a local constable for disorderly behavior and drunkenness at a circus held in the cabecera. Nicolás then intervened in this arrest and tried to persuade the constable to let his brother sleep it off at home before a fight broke out. The constable was shot in an ensuing brawl by a third party, who was never caught. See Criminal por homicidio, 22 Oct. 1895, Libro de Exortos no. 79, AJJ.

45. *Periódico Oficial*, 20 July 1899. A detailed map, indicating the location and sizes of the various lots, is located in the Mapoteca del Servicio Metereológico Nacional, in Mexico City.

46. Registro de una información ad perpetuam sobre hechos y derechos de la Hacienda de Tampochocho, Registro Publico, año de 1902, sección primera, no. 1, AJJ.

47. This information is based on the recollections of older people alive at the time of this incident. The exact date and some details concering

this ambush were confirmed by a written report found in the regional archives: Instruida contra Gregorio Balderas y socios por homicidio de don Miguel Acosta, 22 Aug. 1903, Libro de Exortos, no. 79, AJJ.

48. Eric Wolf and Edward Hansen have made similar observations about the hacienda system in the early nineteenth century. Although their analysis applies to the national level and to the large *criollo* haciendas, some of their comments are applicable to the type of land-tenure system found in the Sierra de Jacala prior to the Revolution. See Eric Wolf and Edward Hansen, "Caudillo Politics: A Structural Analysis," *Comparative Studies in Society and History* 9 (1967): 168–79.

49. In the neighboring district of Molango and in the region of Huejutla, local rancheros were also able to speak the local dialect of Náhuatl. They thus had a monopoly on communication with the majority of peasants who did not speak Spanish in that part of northern Hidalgo.

50. Noradino Rubio Ortiz was governor of Querétaro from 1939 to 1945. See Schryer, *Rancheros,* ch. 6.

51. See Hector Aguilar Camin's study of Sonora, Luis Gonzáles's monograph of San José de Gracia, David Brading's study of the Bajío and Ian Jacob's dissertation dealing with the rancheros of Guerrerro.

52. Schryer, "A Ranchero Economy," 441.

53. For a discussion of the literature depicting rancheros as family farmers, see Schryer, "A Ranchero Economy," 418.

III

And the People

Few contemporary observers of Porfirian Mexico acknowledged that the *gente ordinaria* were the victims of political and economic modernization. As elite opinion would have it, the popular classes, by their laziness, ignorance, and drunkenness, were responsible for their low state and Mexico's underdevelopment. The Indian peon, wrote W. E. Carson in 1909, "is essential to agriculture, yet his tropical surroundings and his mental characteristics unfit him for energetic work or the adoption of modern improvements. . . . His ideal of life is to be idle."[1] A profound tension existed between the preindustrial and precommercial social structure and modernizing processes and institutions both in Mexico and, as Herbert G. Gutman has shown, in the United States. Older work habits and rhythms of life were forced into new and disrupting patterns.[2]

The people of Mexico were not so much the obstacles to development as its expendable fuel. Economic growth and modernization entailed deplorable consequences for Porfirian Mexico's *campesinos,* the country people. Village land was expropriated for commercial agriculture, real wages for hacienda laborers decreased between 1876 and 1910, indebted servitude increased in some regions, as did tenantry and sharecropping, and levels of health, nutrition, and consumption among the rural masses deteriorated. It is not simply that elite Mexico did not invest in its human resources—it sacrificed its people for the ideal called modernity.

One common perception of the peon, as reported by Dillon Wallace in 1910, was that "his needs are small, his opportunities limited, and he is content with what he has."³ Beneath a thin veneer of apparent contentment and passivity, however, existed defiance, resistance, and rebellion on the part of villagers, peons, Indians, and workers. Laziness, drunkenness, violence, and rebellion were all forms of opposition to the destructive nature of elite-directed modernization and growth.

Evelyn Hu-DeHart examines the status of two ethnic minorities in Porfirian Sonora: Yaqui Indians and Chinese immigrants. The treatment these two groups suffered at the hands of Sonora's leadership underscores in unmistakable terms a major trend of Porfirian Mexico: economic development at the expense of social justice. The Yaqui, and to a lesser extent the Chinese, were subject to harsh treatment and persecution that, for the Yaquis, culminated in the deportation of thousands to Yucatán's henequen plantations. Growing resentment of Chinese merchants during the Porfiriato erupted into anti-Chinese riots during the Revolution.

Hu-DeHart's analysis of Yaqui reaction to the changes which transformed Sonora between 1876 and 1911 revels the refusal on the part of the Yaquis to withdraw into isolation. Rather the Indians, taking advantage of the frontier's chronic lack of labor, sought to function within the increasingly modern economic system. Their ultimate turn to guerrilla warfare was a last resort. Hu-DeHart stresses that the anti-Yaqui policy carried out by state leaders and supported by Porfirio Díaz was a glaring example of the regime's lack of consideration for local elite interests. Just as Díaz's personalistic view of politics helped foster Madero's challenge in Coahuila, his Yaqui policy contributed to the rise of an elite opposition in Sonora. Chinese immigrants, similarly, were tolerated as unskilled laborers, but their achievement of a more independent and economically rewarding position as shopkeepers led to resentment, discrimination, and later, persecution.

Allen Wells offers a detailed examination of debt peonage in Yucatán. The changing relationship between hacendado and peon during the Porfiriato was tied to Yucatán's rapid rise to preeminence in henequen production. An expanding regional economy, as Wells argues, only emphasized the tension and resentment that marked the core of the hacendado-peon relationship. The theme of accommodation which other writers suggest characterized hacienda social relations during the Porfiriato was absent on Yucatán's plantations. Rather Wells suggests that violence—directed at local authority figures—was commonplace in Yucatán during the latter stages of the Porfiriato. The Yucatecan system of labor control both engendered persistent unrest and prevented social revolution, until the latter was initiated from outside in 1915. The isolation of Yucatán in Mexico, of henequen plantations from the contagion of so-called dangerous ideas, and of peons from each other permitted the survival of a harsh labor system and prevented unified action on the part of peons in defense of class interests.

A very different set of circumstances emerged in the Laguna region of north-central Mexico. William K. Meyers discusses the phenomenal economic transformation of this region after 1880 and the accompanying increase in rural unrest. Small landholders in the Laguna, in contrast to their counterparts in northern Hidalgo, fought a losing battle against the encroachment of large plantations. More important in terms of numbers were the landless workers, who frequently resorted to violence as a response to economic insecurity, low wages, poor working conditions, and the high price of food. Unlike those in Yucatán, however, agricultural workers in the Laguna possessed greater mobility, were accessible to outside political agitators and ideas, and were more vulnerable to drought, inflation, and unemployment. They also tended more toward unified action and rebellion. As a result this region produced one of the most important and enduring peasant and worker movements in Mexico.

The following essays on Sonora, Yucatán, and the Comarca Lagunera exhibit regional social responses to economic growth and modernization. These discussions of regional variants help explain the disparate nature of the Mexican Revolution. Not surprisingly, Yaqui Indians in Sonora joined and fought for revolutionary leaders, while Chinese immigrants became the target of abuse and persecution. The mobilization of workers in the Laguna, and the absence of such mobilization in Yucatán until much later, is explained by differences in geography, systems of social control, and openness vs. isolation.

Evelyn Hu-DeHart is associate professor of history at Washington University, St. Louis. She received her Ph.D. in 1976 from the University of Texas at Austin and has written several articles on Mexican history. Her book *Missionaries, Miners, and Indians: History of Spanish Contact with the Yaqui Indians of Northwestern New Spain, 1533–1820* was published in 1981. Allen Wells, assistant professor of history at Appalachian State University, received his Ph.D. from the State University of New York at Stony Brook in 1979. Professor Wells is author of *Yucatán's Gilded Age: Haciendas, Henequen, and International Harvester, 1860–1915* (Albuquerque, 1985) and currently is editor of the *South Eastern Latin Americanist*. William K. Meyers is assistant professor of history at the University of Oklahoma, Norman. Professor Meyers received his Ph.D. in 1979 from the University of Chicago and is director of Latin American Studies at the University of Oklahoma.

NOTES

1. W. E. Carson, *Mexico: The Wonderland of the South* (New York, 1909), 187–88.
2. Herbert G. Gutman, *Work, Culture and Society in Industrializing America* (New York, 1977), 3–78.
3. Dillon Wallace, *Beyond the Mexican Sierras* (Chicago, 1910), xxiv.

7
Sonora: Indians and Immigrants on a Developing Frontier

Evelyn Hu-DeHart

The northwestern frontier state of Sonora was unquestionably one of the most interesting and dynamic regions of Mexico during the dictatorship of Porfirio Díaz (1876–1911). Long neglected and subordinated to more pressing priorities by the federal government, and isolated from the rest of the nation while establishing closer ties with the United States just to the north, Sonora finally moved into the forefront of Mexican development during the Porfiriato. Upon assuming power, the dictator and his associates in the state immediately set about realizing the development potential of this resource-rich frontier region, making it attractive for foreign, notably North American, investment, enhancing its links with international markets through infrastructural improvements, and promoting immigration and colonization of its sparsely populated and underexploited land.

The peculiarities and uniqueness of the so-called Sonoran traditions quickly become evident to those who study the state's history. Also noteworthy is the fact that three Sonorans—the so-called Sonoran Triumvirate, or clique, of Álvaro Obregón, Adolfo de la Huerta, and Plutarco Elías Calles—captured national political power after the Revolution of 1910 and retained it until they were overthrown by Lázaro Cárdenas in 1934. How is it that little-known men of modest fortunes from a previously underdeveloped, isolated region could become the most forceful, compelling national leaders of a modern Mexico in the twentieth century? What is it about their personal background and about the history of their state that endowed them with broad perspectives on their nation and the world, and with the comprehension and ability to deal with a range of political, economic, and social issues?[1]

With one important exception, the Sonorans were acquainted with all the major problems confronting Mexico. Pacifying the Apaches on the frontier and subjugating the Indian communities along the fertile Yaqui and Mayo rivers taught the Sonorans about Indians, peasants, land, and agrarian reform, which to them included colonization of the underexploited river valleys. As landowners they were of the progressive, modern entrepreneurial type, committed to the promise of commercial agriculture as the basis of the nation's wealth.

Sonorans became familiar with massive foreign investment, early industrialization, and the rise of a modern working class accompanying the proliferation of mines and the feverish construction of railroads. Among the revolutionary leaders the Sonorans were the first to recognize the necessity of both fostering and controlling organized labor.

Contact with foreigners and foreign interests was another major Sonoran experience, one which actually predated the Porfiriato by many years. Because of its long-time isolation from the rest of Mexico, the northwest frontier had always been more oriented toward North America. Furthermore, geographically and culturally, as far as its native peoples are concerned, Sonora belongs to the same larger environment as does the southwestern United States. During much of the nineteenth century, Sonorans had to deal with French and American filibusters from the north, as well as with the French Interventionists invited by the Mexican Conservatives during

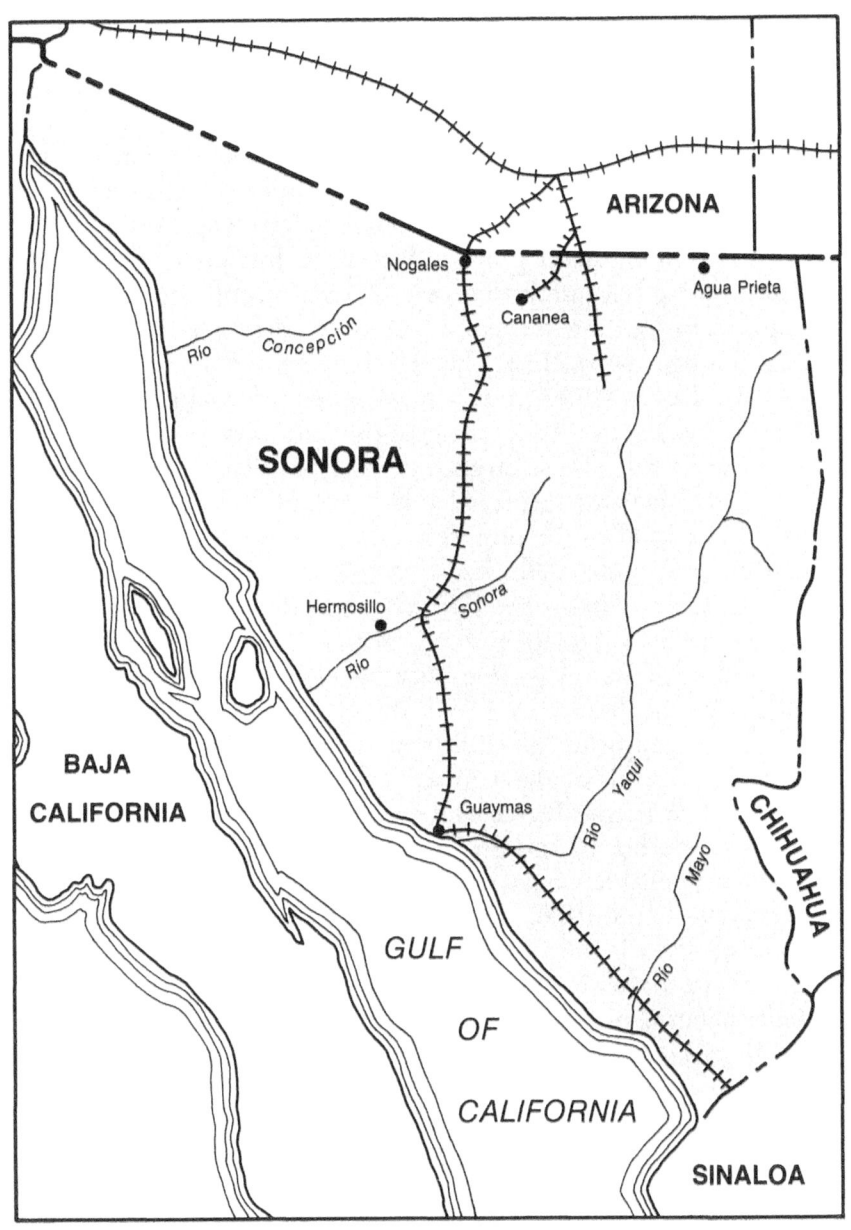

Sonora, 1910

the Reform Wars. Also, as soon as Mexican independence was achieved, British, North American, and other foreign speculators and business agents traveled up and down the Pacific coast, looking for lucrative resources to exploit and market, although political and social conditions did not favor successful foreign investment until the Porfiriato. This long history of contact with foreigners produced a complex and often ambivalent set of relationships and attitudes, ranging from an easy acceptance of alien ideas and cultures to a highly charged nationalism characterized by virulent xenophobia. Spaniards, North Americans, and especially the ubiquitous alien Chinese, who began immigrating to the northwest during the Díaz regime, were the major targets of this peculiar brand of North Mexican nationalism. It played a key role in mobilizing a revolutionary opposition to the proforeign dictatorship, and, later, to the formation of a modern Mexico.

In one crucial area—the Church and Church-related issues—Sonorans did lack understanding, primarily due to their limited experience with an institution that had never recovered from the expulsion of the Jesuits in 1767. Because of the hegemony Jesuit missionaries established on this desolate frontier during the colonial period, a powerful secular Church never developed alongside the missions. Thus Benito Júarez's Liberalism gained an early and strong foothold in the north, and Sonoran revolutionary *caudillos,* notably Calles, were well-known anticlericals. Not surprisingly, when Calles was president in the 1920s, he was least adept and most controversial when dealing with the Church-related Cristero conflict.[2]

The above discussion is intended to give a general appreciation of the Sonoran historical experience. In the remainder of this essay, we shall look closely at two important social groups that figured prominently in the course of Sonoran development during the Porfiriato. One, the Yaqui Indians, constituted the most serious obstacle to large-scale commercial agricultural development in the state. As original inhabitants and vociferous claimants of the land in the Yaqui River Valley, they refused to submit peacefully to plans for the division and colonization of this territory. Instead, they reacted with force and cunning, in effect conducting a protracted armed uprising characterized by guerrilla warfare tactics and culminating with their massive deportation from the state. However, the Yaquis did not present the same kind of pacification problem as did the seminomadic Apache warriors on the U.S. border. Whereas the latter were considered totally unassimilable and of absolutely no redeeming social value, the Yaquis were highly valued as diligent, skilled, and cheap workers in a sparsely populated region. Hence the difficult dilemma confronting state and federal authorities was how to subjugate the rebellious Indians without having to exterminate them.

The second social group we shall consider are the Chinese immigrants, who began arriving in Sonora at the onset of the Porfiriato. Their eventual diffusion throughout the state and the commercial roles they assumed reflected the rapid expansion of population, towns, and the internal market, consequences in turn of the accelerated growth of the mining, railroad and infrastructural, industrial, commercial, and agricultural sectors of the local economy toward the end of the century. At first tolerated as a source of cheap labor, the Chinese turned increasingly toward business, becoming by the end of the Porfiriato the ubiquitous petite bourgeoisie of the region: owners of small retail stores and service operations such as laundries, hotels, and restaurants. Just as Chinese immigration paralleled in time and followed in demographic movement the influx of North American capital, so did the Chinese become the target of growing antiforeignism. In fact, Sonorans from politicians to workers discovered that it was much easier to vent their nationalistic frustrations on the highly visible but virtually defenseless Asian shopkeepers than on the powerful and often absent American investors.

Intensification of the conflict with the Yaqui Indians and the introduction of Chinese immigrants to this frontier region must both be examined within the context of the nature and scope of local economic development. As soon as the Porfiristas came to power in the state, they set the economy on a dynamic course. By 1886, working closely with U.S. military authorities, they had pacified the Apaches on the frontier. In the same decade, they saw the American-owned and built Sonoran Railroad link the Pacific coast port of Guaymas with Nogales on the Arizona border, a stretch of 422 kilometers that greatly facilitated internal communication and transportation to North American markets. Steamships plying the coastline connected Sonora with San Francisco to the north and with Mexican ports as far south as Manzanillo. Furthermore, North Americans invested heavily in mines. By 1902 Sonora had the largest U.S. mining investment of any Mexican state—$27,800,000. It was third in total U.S. investment, after Mexico City and Chihuahua.

Another area of major development concern, and the one that most affected the Yaquis, was land and agriculture. With a total of some 3.7 million dollars, Sonora ranked second among Mexican states receiving U.S. capital in "haciendas, ranches and farms."[3] Within the state, perhaps the most coveted land, and at the same time the most inaccessible, was the Yaqui territory. In 1894 the Díaz government made a generous concession to the Sonora and Sinaloa Irrigation Company: 547,000 acres of land in the Yaqui Valley, 400,000 of which to be irrigated by water from canals the company would build. The company was later bought up by the Richardson Construction Company, which also operated mines in northern Sonora. These large investors were primarily interested in commercial agricultural development of the Yaqui Valley through colonization and irrigation.[4] Another type of interested party was represented by Colonel Ángel García Peña of the Army Corps of Engineers, who headed the scientific commission charged with surveying and dividing up Yaqui land. After he completed his task, he became one of the valley's largest landowners. As will be discussed later, Yaqui Indian resistance to the colonization plans made progress slow and uncertain. In 1902 land in the valley was still being sold at the incredibly cheap price of 6.60 pesos per hectare.

The Yaqui projects fell within Díaz's general agrarian and land policies—to break up communal Indian lands and open up *baldíos,* or public lands, for private exploitation. These policies benefited Mexican hacendados as well as foreigners. Old landowning families increased their holdings, new families acquired land; meanwhile, agricultural production was stimulated both by increased foreign trade and by expansion of the internal local and national markets.

Representative of the local entrepreneurial agricultural families were the Maytorenas of Guaymas. Led by the patriarch José María Maytorena, Sr., by the early Porfiriato the family was well established as one of the state's richest and most respected landowners. Their haciendas in the Guaymas area alone included San Antonio de Abajo, La Misa, La Huerta, and Santa María, all of which relied heavily on Yaqui agricultural labor. Later, some of the younger Maytorenas moved to the newly developing northern districts, in search of more cattle land and wealth.

During the Porfiriato, old landed elite families such as the Maytorenas were for the most part deliberately excluded from the highest echelons of state power, which was in turn tightly controlled by a ruling triumvirate composed of the Díaz loyalists Luis Torres, an outsider imported into the state, Ramón Corral, and Rafael Izábal, the latter two native Sonorans. From the very beginning of the dictatorship until its closing days, Torres alternated between the two highest posts of governor and coommander general of the First Military Zone (Sonora, Sinaloa, and Baja California), headquartered in Sonora. In the case of Corral, a brilliant Sonoran journalist who began his political career at the age of nineteen and rose to become governor, it is important to note that Díaz selected this northerner to be his vice-president during the last decade of his rule. Meanwhile, Izábal, who never left the state, held down the fort back home. While in office, all three men became leading landowners and industrialists in the state, thereby acquiring considerable personal wealth.

This pattern of political exclusion on the state level was not unique to Sonora, of course. Exceptions such as Luis Terrazas of Chihuahua notwithstanding, in most states Díaz bypassed the old local elite to install his own loyalists, often outsiders. The traditional gentry could keep their social positions. If they shared any political power under the dictatorship, it was usually limited to the ayuntamiento, or municipal, level. In Sonora, for example, in 1887 Maytorena, Sr., and Adolfo Almada—scion of an old, prestigious family in the once glorious but now decadent mining town of Alamos—challenged the Díaz ticket of Torres and Corral for governor and vice-governor. Although Maytorena and Almada apparently won the popular vote, the State Congress awarded the election to the Porfiristas.[5] Henceforth, Díaz's men maintained firm political control, his candidates never again seriously challenged. The reasons for exerting such political control were quite obvious. By installing loyalists in power in every state, he not only ensured trust and reliability, but through a shared ideology greatly facilitated the political integration of Mexico into one federal entity, a hallmark of the Porfiriato.

While politically repressive toward the local elites, Díaz at the same time offered them economic benefits, a chance to share in the prosperity ushered in by his development policies. Thus in the beginning of his rule, political disenfranchisement did not necessarily bring discord between the center and the periphery, as long as there was no concurrent economic monopoly in the hands of a few. Toward the end of his reign, however, political and economic power were joined: it became increasingly difficult to maintain or advance any economic interest without political support. The center and the periphery drew apart again, leading to the outbreak of the Mexican Revolution in 1910. The entire Yaqui question in Sonora provides a good illustration of the changing dynamics in this center-periphery relationship.

The Yaqui Problem

Initially there was little disagreement between the ruling clique in Sonora and the local elite over the issues of pacifying the Yaquis and opening up land in the Yaqui Valley south of the river for colonization and commercial agricultural development. All agreed that these were prerequisites for the progress and improved welfare of the state. Understandably, the Yaquis adopted the opposite stance toward the development projects and fought hard to maintain their position throughout the period.

The Indians' reaction to their imminent displacement and social dislocation was a continuation of their ongoing resistance against political domination and cultural assimilation by the larger, more powerful Mexican state and society. What is unique about the Yaqui rebellion is that for most of the nineteenth century it was not a movement of withdrawal and isolation from the rest of the society that they were at the same time rejecting. Rather, while Yaquis consistently repelled incursions into their tribal territory, a significant number of them could always be found in all corners of the state, hiring out their labor in all conceivable types of employment. The only exception to this pattern occurred during the reign of the chief José María Leyva Cajeme, who single-handedly organized a Yaqui state-within-a-state from 1875 to 1886. During this period, Cajeme recalled most of the Yaquis to the Yaqui River and drastically curtailed their interaction with the outside world. When the Yaquis' de facto separate republic was finally crushed by a series of ruthless federal campaigns, they once again dispersed themselves throughout the state.

In a rapidly developing but sparsely populated region (including Arizona), Yaquis fleeing from their *pueblos* readily found employment in burgeoning enterprises in mining, railroad, and agriculture everywhere. For a short while after Cajeme's defeat, the Díaz government thought it had definitively pacified the Yaquis, just as it had the marauding Apaches. In its brief euphoria, as it launched plans to develop the Yaqui Valley, the government actually envisioned transforming the Yaqui people into the "principal colonist on intensely cultivated soil."[6] Private developers such as Walter Logan, president of the Sonora and Sinaloa Irrigation Company, echoed similar sentiments. In a promotional pamphlet published in 1894, he confidently predicted that the Indians would settle on their contested homeland as hardworking colonists.[7]

Reducing the Yaquis to happy colonists was not an automatic consequence of the crushing defeat of Cajeme, however. As noted earlier, most of the Yaquis fled the river region after Cajeme's demise. At the same time, a small group under chief Juan Maldonado, alias Tetabiate, continued to wage war against the government. After a decade of fruitless military action against these tenacious, elusive guerrillas, General Luis Torres negotiated a peace settlement with Chief Tetabiate. The Mexicans believed that in the Ortiz Peace of May 1897, the rebellious Yaquis agreed to lay down arms and return to the river as peaceful colonists, alongside other Mexican and foreign colonists. A gross miscommunication must have occurred during the negotiations, however, for the Yaquis understood the peace terms quite differently. They thought it guaranteed their long-sought independence and autonomy; in effect, that the government would withdraw *yori,* or alien colonists, as well as the federal occupation force. Not surprisingly, the Ortiz Peace did not endure.

In 1898 some three thousand Yaqui Indians were officially listed as colonists in the Yaqui territory. But by 1899–1900 fighting between Yaquis and government troops broke out anew, culminating in the Mazocoba massacre of 18 January 1900, in which four hundred Yaquis were killed and another eight hundred taken prisoners. After this tragedy, both the government and Yaquis concluded, of course for different reasons, that the attempted colonization of Yaqui land by Yaquis themselves was a dismal failure. The Indians resumed guerrilla warfare, starting out with a core estimated at nine hundred, but reduced to three hundred by the end of 1900. Once again the bulk of the Yaqui population dispersed throughout the state, much to the relief of their former employers.[8]

Governor Izábal formulated in 1902 the next set of pacification plans, aimed simultaneously at protecting Yaqui workers while ferreting out the guerrillas. It involved search-and-seizure maneuvers, both in the Sierra de Bacatete, flanking the north bank of the Yaqui River, which served as rebel stronghold, and in the haciendas and other workplaces where Yaqui guerrillas might be hiding. This approach called for employers to keep their Yaqui workers in closely guarded camps, and for local prefects to maintain a meticulous, up to date register of all Yaquis in their respective districts. Moreover, prefects issued passports to Yaqui workers—known as *mansos* or *pacíficos*—to distinguish these ostensibly peaceful elements from the troublesome armed guerrillas—the *broncos*—marked for extinction.

As Izábal soon discovered and reluctantly admitted, the problem was that it was impossible to distinguish between the two categories of Yaquis, for pacíficos and broncos were all collaborators in the same resistance movement that took the form of guerrilla warfare. The widely dispersed pacíficos constituted the indispensable base of support for the core of broncos, supplying them with food, money, arms, intelligence, and refuge. The countryside also provided an unlimited recruiting ground, as rested workers traded places with exhausted fighters. Operating on their home turf, the guerrillas enjoyed certain advantages over government forces, who had difficulty maneuvering in the tortuous mountain routes of the sierra. Furthermore, the Yaquis took every advantage of the convenient border with Arizona as an escape route and as a source of employment, supplies, and arms. Inevitably, then, the Izábal government arrived at the decision to resort to more drastic measures to deal with the Yaqui problems. When this happened, discord grew among the state's various interest groups over the proper policy to follow in dealing with these Indians.

Izábal stepped up his search operations and made increasingly false and arbitrary arrests, much to the distress of employers and Yaquis alike. Wandering bands of Yaqui women and children were apprehended as rebel suspects, as were Pima, Ópata, Pápago, and Mayo Indians, mistaken for Yaquis. Complaints from hacendados and other employers affected by the indiscriminate arrests poured into the governor's office, decrying the "extreme shortage of laborers" caused by the intensified campaign. Hacendados squabbled over good Yaqui workers. Others accepted and protected all Yaquis who sought work with them, no embarrassing questions asked. Obviously exasperated, the state government accused the hacendados of obstructing its pacification efforts. Izábal characterized Sonora's hacendados as "if not content, then indifferent to the anti-Yaqui wars, which worked in their favor. When the Indians are at war, they have cheap peons, for in their haciendas they find refuge. . . . On the other hand, when they are at peace, they migrate back to the Río Yaqui, and consequently [the hacendados] lose this valuable asset for prosperity on their properties."[9]

To the hacendados, however, it was Izábal's increasingly arbitrary search-and-seizure operations, bordering on terrorism, which really destablized the countryside. The problem was that while hacendados still insisted that the government could deal with the few active rebels without seriously affecting the many working Indians, Izábal had already seen the connection between Yaqui broncos and pacíficos. Thus, in 1904, he accelerated his campaign even as he grudgingly acknowledged complaints from Yaqui employers. But by this time he seemed determined to settle the Yaqui question once and for all, and at all costs. In pursuing this course, he received no signs of disapproval from superiors in Mexico City.

Despite mounting criticism against his arbitrary and high-handed methods, he raided more and more haciendas and some ranches and mines, often rounding up the entire *yaquería* on charges of collusion with guerrillas. His orders began to call for the arrest of Yaquis "with all their families, so that not a single Yaqui remains, neither big nor small."[10] Thus what had begun as a system of selected arrests developed into a reign of terror against all Yaquis. What had begun as a response to widespread public pressure to extirpate the handful of Yaqui broncos had become a source of growing conflict between the government and certain local entrepreneurs who were largely dependent on Yaqui labor for their economic well-being. Complaints from hacendados concerning loss of all their workers, often just before harvest time, continued unabated. In addition to losing workers to Izábal's indiscriminate roundups, employers lost valuable Yaquis when they began fleeing across the border to Arizona to evade arrest. One hacendado, the American Carlos Johnson, carried his case all the way to the U.S. State Department, hoping for some influential intervention from that quarter.[11]

Once they were detained, something had to be done with the large number of Yaqui prisoners, far more numerous than the state penitentiary in Hermosillo could hold. Deportation seemed a logical solution. Since the early part of the nineteenth century, the government had occasionally deported rebel leaders out of the state. It was proposed as a neat solution to the Yaqui problem early in the Porfiriato, but none other than President Díaz himself vetoed the idea as impractical and cruel. By the dawn of the twentieth century, as the pacification process stalled, the plan was revived and this time accepted.

During the 1900s several thousand Yaquis were deported, mostly to the flourishing and chronically labor-short henequen plantations of Yucatán. After a brief trial period, the planters unanimously acclaimed the imported Yaquis as superior to their own vanquished Maya Indians in "hard work and vigor."[12] (For an extensive treatment of labor conditions and of the importance of Yaquis to Yucatán, see chapter 8.)

Concurrent with massive arrests and deportation, Governor Izábal began to apply pressures on U.S. authorities in Arizona to curtail the movement of Yaquis across the border and to turn back illegal Yaqui entries and on Arizona businessmen not to sell arms and ammunition to Yaquis. He also pressured Arizona mineowners not to give rebels employment. He made it harder for Yaquis to cross the border by removing all Yaquis in districts north of Hermosillo and adjacent to the border—Sahuaripa, Arizpe, Ures, Magdalena, and Altar. Even those with passports were to be arrested in these districts. Furthermore, Yaquis were forbidden to work on the railroads. In 1907 persecution of the sierra, or bronco, Yaquis further intensified with the formation of the Eleventh Rural Corps, a special counterguerrilla force with a monthly budget of 10,000 pesos.[13]

The accelerated campaign against all Yaquis, guerrillas and peons alike, produced the desired and expected result of drying up the social base in the countryside. At first there was a counterproductive effect as well, for in order to survive the hardpressed rebels resorted to more violent actions. Unable to count on their usual supply network, the broncos had to increase their own raids on company stores and on travelers on the open roads. As they looted for arms and supplies, they also tended to kill more readily.

In May 1908, Luis Torres, once again governor, tried to negotiate a settlement, this time with Chief Luis Bule of the sierra Yaquis. When Bule missed the deadline for turning in arms, the government signaled all-out war against the Yaqui people. One state official put it succinctly to Ramón Corral, then vice-president of the nation, that only the complete deportation of the tribe could solve the Yaqui problem. Corral wired back that both he and President Díaz approved of the decision.[14] The reservation Díaz had expressed at the beginning of the decade regarding deportation as cruel and impractical apparently dissolved in the face of repeated failures to pacify the Yaquis by less draconian measures. Perhaps, also, his Sonoran vice-president, who allegedly received a bounty of several pesos for each Yaqui sold in Yucatán, and his secretary of development, Yucatán's henequen king Olegario Molina, helped change his mind. There is no evidence that Izábal or Díaz even considered the opinions or interests of local hacendados and other Yaqui employers when deciding on deportation.

The year 1908 saw the height of the Yaqui deportation. In one July shipment alone, some eight hundred Yaqui men, women, and children were loaded on board the steamship appropriately named the *Corral*. The exact number of deported Yaquis has never been officially tabulated. Turner, in *Barbarous Mexico,* cited a probably inflated figure of over fifteen thousand, based on the boastful testimony of a deportation officer. The census of 1910 noted 2,757 Sonorans living in Yucatán; it is not clear whether and to what extent this figure included deported Yaquis. And there is no precise accounting of the reputedly large number of Yaquis who died while in transit or in exile.[15]

Also by 1908, more stringent border control measures went into effect, due primarily to the U.S. Department of Commerce and Labor's decision to intervene in Arizona. It ordered the detention and deportation to Mexico of all illegally entering Yaquis. It strictly prohibited merchants in Arizona from selling arms and ammunition to Yaquis. The timing of this long awaited cooperation had much to do with changing economic circumstances in the United States. November 1907 was the beginning of an investment and banking crisis that had serious repercussions on the railroad and mining sectors of Arizona and Mexico. So where once Arizona welcomed the influx of cheap Mexican laborers, including Yaquis, it now eagerly turned them back. Unlike reactions of earlier years, Arizona newspapers no longer rebuked the Mexican government for unfair treatment of Yaquis. The American mining and railroad companies in Sonora also stood mutely by while the pace of deportation accelerated.[16]

The Yucatán economy suffered a similar setback from the 1907 crisis, as henequen prices dropped on the world market.[17] This largely explains the abrupt cessation of large shipments of Yaquis to the Yucatán at the end of July 1908. Only then did the government begin to respond to the many protests Sonoran hacendados had been sending directly to President Díaz, imploring him to revoke the deportation orders to avoid a real economic crisis in the state. Unlike the foreign-dependent mining and railroad sectors, the locally controlled internal agriculture market was relatively free from the effects of the U.S. investment crisis. Local hacendados continued to experience labor shortages; the problem had reached such proportions that in July two Maytorena brothers were caught trying to smuggle several Yaquis to Sinaloa to avoid deportation.[18]

By January 1909, Yaquis in the urban areas of Hermosillo and Guaymas were once again issued passports and permitted to seek employment in haciendas, mines, and other businesses. At the same time, Chief Luis Bule and his faction of sierra Yaquis surrendered to the government, to be promptly incorporated into a special auxiliary federal force charged with persuading their less repentent brothers to abandon the struggle. Furthermore, the government offered bounties of from one hundred to five hundred pesos for every rebel captured dead or alive. After waging a relentless war against the Yaquis for over a quarter of a century, the Díaz regime finally seemed on the verge of breaking them. Then came the Mexican Revolution of 1910, which gave the Yaquis a new chance for survival, as they integrated their historical struggle into the movement to overthrow the Díaz regime.

The pacification of the Yaqui people and the colonization of their homeland illustrate the Díaz government's push for economic development at all costs and with considerable foreign, particularly North American, input. The Yaquis saw their land removed from their control, divided into private lots, and occupied by Mexicans and foreigners. At first, because Yaqui labor was useful and practically indispensable for the burgeoning new enterprises in the state, the government did not wish to exterminate them, but merely to destroy their independent spirit, while incorporating them socially into the general working class. Only when this plan failed, when the dispersed Yaqui population became the social base of support for protracted guerrilla warfare, did the state enact massive, indiscriminate deportation. Carried out without regard to family unity and compounded by forced, virtually slave labor in the extremely harsh and alien conditions of Yucatán's henequen plantations, deportation was the hardest trial Yaquis had to suffer in their entire history.

Were Yaquis the only ones affected by the pacification program, especially the deportation phase, it probably would not have become so controversial. But local Sonoran hacendados and, to a lesser extent, foreign mine and railroad owners, were also victimized by the campaign, which deprived them of valuable workers with no suitable substitutes available. Denied access to the tightly controlled political system, these enterprising local landowners—who had initially been bought off by the regime's willingness to spread economic benefits more evenly—began to fear for their continued prosperity by the opening of the twentieth century. Sharing the sentiments of many of their counterparts in other northern states, they felt they should have political power more commensurate with their economic importance. The Yaqui policy, culminating in the massive deportations, was one glaring example of the regime making political decisions without sufficient consideration for local elite interests. Families such as the Maytorenas of Guaymas, who owned extensive landholdings and depended heavily on Yaqui labor, were among the first Mexicans to join with Francisco Madero to overthrow the Díaz dictatorship.

The Chinese in Sonora

The Chinese and the Yaquis in Sonora had more in common than might superficially meet the eye. Whether natives or immigrants, peons or small entrepreneurs, both remained outside the mainstream of Mexican culture and society, while participating actively in the developing economy of the northwest frontier region. The two peoples had occasional contacts, usually in the form of Yaquis attacking Chinese travelers or looting Chinese stores, even in the Yaqui Valley, as Chinese businessmen kept pace with colonization there. Both groups were the objects of intense persecution by Mexicans. In the case of the Chinese, although actual organized campaigns were more a phenomenon of the revolutionary and postrevolutionary periods, hostility definitely surfaced during the Porfiriato.

There was one important difference in official attitude toward the two groups. Taking a longer view of what was good for colonization and commercial agriculture, the Díaz government decided on total pacification of the Yaquis, even if in the short run it meant hurting certain local interests dependent on Yaqui labor. By contrast, the same federal government promoted Chinese immigration, partly intended to meet the growing labor demand, in spite of mounting popular resistance in Sonora to these excessively industrious immigrants with uncanny business acumen. Difference in attitude notwithstanding, both the Yaquis and the Chinese represented examples of the Díaz dictatorship's insensitivity to certain local sentiments while forging ahead with its own, federally oriented perspective on national development. Federal policy toward both groups provides a good illustration of center-periphery tension.

At its inception, the Díaz dictatorship accelerated reforms already set in motion by the preceding Liberal regime and brought about new changes. In the north, it mounted the last and finally successful drive against the Apaches, assumed federal responsibility for the pacification of the Yaquis, encouraged the opening of mines as well as the construction of railroads and other infrastructural improvements, and facilitated the alienation of communal lands and the transformation of Indians, peasants, and debt peons into wage laborers. These developments in turn stimulated significant demographic changes: the censuses of 1895, 1900, and 1910 showed marked rises in the state's population, from 191,281 to 221,682 to 264,383, an increase of forty percent in fifteen years. Between 1900 and 1910, the number of *localidades*, or places of residence, of all sizes increased from 1,568 to 2,553.[19] Natural reproduction, migration from other parts of Mexico to the northwest, and to a lesser extent foreign immigration, accounted for the upward demographic trend. Among foreigners, North Americans, Englishmen, Frenchmen, Germans, and Spaniards had been present in the state since the early nineteenth century, although their numbers, especially of Americans, increased substantially during the Porfiriato, along with their higher investments. The mining boom and new rail lines accounted for many of the new population centers. The relatively smooth colonization of the Mayo Valley, and even the more turbulent history and fitful progress in the Yaqui Valley, also contributed to these demographic changes.

It is probably no coincidence that Chinese immigrants began arriving in Northern Mexico at the dawn of this new era. Besides Mexico's own attractions, following the passage of the first anti-Chinese Exclusion Act in the United States in 1882, Mexico became an alternative destination for Chinese seeking a new beginning in the New World. In the 1880s a small Chinese colony was already present in Guaymas, the port of entry on the Pacific coast. At first California immigration authorities were convinced that the Chinese were merely using Mexico's west coast as an illegal route into the United States. The American consul in Guaymas, A. Willard, viewed the situation with less alarm. While he noted occasional attempts by Chinese to steal across the border, he concluded in numerous reports to Washington that most of the Chinese arrivals appeared to be prepared to stay and work in Sonora.[20]

Local Sonoran authorities certainly did not appear perturbed by the Chinese immigration. Governor Ramón Corral included in his 1890 annual report a roster of all foreign residents in the state. The

229 Chinese were second only to the 339 North Americans and well ahead of the number of Germans, Englishmen, and Spaniards. Not surprisingly, most of the Americans were listed by occupation as *minero* (mine owner or speculator), followed by rancher, railroad employee, manufacturer, merchant, and skilled tradesman; there was only one cook. By contrast, only one Chinese was listed as *minero*, and, interestingly, over half (161) as shoemaker, tailor, or ironer—all, as it turned out, employees in several Chinese-owned shoe and coarse clothing factories in the state. Other occupations listed for the Chinese were day laborer; truck, or vegetable, farmer; cook; baker; and even *cirujano*, or surgeon (probably a traditional Chinese healer). Only 20, or less than 10 percent, were *comerciantes*, merchants or businessmen. No Chinese was specifically noted as a mine or railroad worker, two types of jobs typically associated with Asian immigrants in the American West and Southwest in the nineteenth century.[21] Significantly, Governor Corral did not accompany this survey with any negative editorial comments that might reflect misgivings about the Chinese. Indeed, Corral—who later as vice-president helped deport Yaquis to Yucatán—was keenly interested in locating alternative sources of cheap labor for the state's many new enterprises.

From the beginning, President Díaz himself actively encouraged foreign immigration, especially to the more sparsely populated regions, as a critical component of the development process. To be sure, he and his advisors would have preferred only European Catholics. But Mexico could not attract such immigrants in significant numbers because of the scarcity of available good land or well-paying jobs. Mexico agreed, therefore, to accept some less attractive settlers, including the Chinese, who had a reputation for docility and industriousness. The Díaz government also had hopes of improving trade with the populous empires of China and Japan. Toward these ends and after years of negotiation, Mexico and China signed, in 1893, a Treaty of Amity and Commerce, which included a "most favored nation" clause.

The treaty definitely helped accelerate Chinese immigration to Mexico and especially to Sonora. From a mere 229 in 1890, the number of Chinese residents in the state rose to 850 by 1900, to 2,414 by 1904, and to 4,486 by 1910. Table 1 compares these numbers with some figures for the total population in the state and with the total number of Chinese in Mexico.

Table 1. Chinese Population Figures

Year	Population of Sonora	Chinese in Sonora	Chinese in Mexico
1890		229	
1894	191,281		
1900	221,682	850	2,719
1904		2,414	
1910	265,383	4,486	13,203

Sources: Mexican censuses of 1895, 1900, 1910; Ramón Corral, *Memoria de la administración públlica del estado de Sonora* (Guaymas, 1891), 1: 586–602; state district reports to "Comisión oficial encargado del estado de la inmigración asiática en México, 18 nov. 1903," submitted in 1904, Archivo Histórico del Gobierno e Estado de Sonora, tomo 1900.

In the thirty years from 1880 to 1910, besides increasing in numbers, the Chinese had also redistributed themselves demographically and occupationally. From an initial concentration in the port city of Guaymas, they had moved to practically all population centers large and small, from older, established towns such as Hermosillo and Magdalena, to new ones such as Cananea and Nogales. At the same time, while many Chinese continued to be employed by their own countrymen in shoe and clothing factories, by the end of the century the majority had decidedly moved into local commerce and into business for themselves. With a few notable exceptions, these businesses were run on an extremely modest scale. At the end of the Porfiriato, the Chinese had distinguished themselves as the basis of a new social class—the petite bourgeoisie—in the flourishing, rapidly urbanizing, export-oriented economy of the northwest, a development stimulated in large part by heavy foreign investment. The Chinese became the foundation of the petite bourgeoisie by following an interesting course, during which they formed working relationships with three important groups in Sonora: the emerging working class, traditional local Mexican hacendados, and North American investors.

From the beginning, there were two distinguishable groups of Chinese immigrants—those very few with some investment capital who opened shoe and clothing factories or well-stocked wholesale-retail commercial houses, and the majority who came with little or no money. The first Chinese factory, Fung, Chung, Lung, was established in Guaymas in 1876, followed shortly by Siu Fo Chong. By 1903 ten of the thirty-seven shoe and clothing manufacturers in the state were Chinese-owned, producing over one hundred thousand dollars in goods each year.[22] These Chinese entrepreneurs capitalized, literally, on the growing demand for cheap, ready-made clothing and shoes, catering quite clearly to the needs of the emerging working class.

If exceptional in terms of their relative wealth, the richer Chinese nevertheless established business patterns closely followed by other Chinese immigrants: they preferred to operate their own businesses, and, if they needed workers, tended to hire their own compatriots. Thus the 229 Chinese noted in Governor Corral's 1890 report were almost all employed by other Chinese. After the 1880s, as Chinese moved out of Guaymas to other towns (especially in mining areas and along railroad lines), those with less capital opened much more modest kinds of businesses, some requiring practically no investment other than labor: laundries, restaurants and canteens, hotels and boarding houses, vegetable, or truck, farms.

Partnerships were also common among Chinese with poor immigrants contributing labor rather than capital to a joint enterprise. Large Chinese firms also set up poor partners in branch stores in new, small interior towns. Or, outside the formal partnership arrangements, they readily extended merchandise on long-term credit to traveling Chinese salesmen and independently owned small stores. These practices, engaged in by surprisingly few European commercial houses, reflected Chinese efforts to penetrate and then corner new internal markets. In some towns such aggressive business activities provoked hostility from local Mexican merchants; in other places the Chinese were the first to set up a commercial business of any kind.

On the other end, the large Chinese merchants bought from Mexican, European, and North American suppliers, in effect helping to distribute their products through the Chinese commercial network and by extensive use of the railroads. The firm of Quan, Gun, Lung y Cía. of Alamos, established in 1894, sold a wide variety of goods, ranging from groceries and canned goods to clothing and notions; it dealt in imported as well as domestic products; and it had its own "well mounted factory" to manufacture shoes. The company served as agent for national and foreign products and traded directly with New York, Chicago, San Francisco, St. Louis, and Hamburg, Germany. Within Mexico its sphere of operation extended beyond Sonora to the adjacent states of Chihuahua and Sinaloa, where it opened a branch store. Guillermo Leytón—an obviously Hispanicized name—was the leading *socio*, or partner, of the company. His assistant manager was Chinese, although his chief clerk was a "conscientious and intelligent" Mexican.

Two partners founded the firm of Juan Lung Tain in Magdalena in 1890. Eventually it opened branches in Santa Ana, Imuris, Estación Llano, Guaymas, Hermosillo, Cananea, Navojoa—in short, in practically every corner of the state affected by mining, railroad, or agricultural development. A general merchandise store, it too had its own shoe factory. It bought and distributed domestic and foreign goods to its own branches as well as to other, smaller Chinese merchants. It bought agricultural staples such as wheat and corn from local Mexican hacendados, and imported hardware and luxury items from Europe and the United States. A typical transaction with local hacendados or *molinos* (mills) involved receiving, for example, sacks of flour or corn *en consignación* (on consignment), for resale *en comisión* in smaller quantities to keepers of smaller Chinese stores.[23]

At no time during the Porfiriato did major European commercial houses, primarily those of Germans and Spaniards located in Guaymas and Hermosillo, express alarm at Chinese competition. In fact, judging from John R. Southworth's commercial survey of Sonora in 1897, which listed all the important enterprises by district, only the shoe manufacturer Siu Fo Chon of Guaymas merited inclusion. Eight years later, in 1905, the official business directory took greater note of the progress the Chinese had made: of 968 listings, 52 were Chinese, operating in 21 of 86 municipalities. In the directory, business was interpreted loosely to include all persons of some means and stature—doctors, lawyers, hacendados, and ranchers as well as merchants—thus explaining the long roster. All 52 Chinese were listed as *comerciantes*.[24]

In fact, by middecade there were many more than 52 Chinese businesses, but the majority were simply too insignificant to be included in such a directory. By 1904 the Chinese population in the state had risen to 2,414, distributed among all eight political districts (see table 2).

Table 2. Chinese Population by District

District	Number of Chinese
Álamos	57
Altar	10
Arizpe	1,106
Guaymas	427
Hermosillo	409
Magdalena	350
Moctezuma	39
Sahuaripa	5
Ures	11

Sources: State district responses to "Comisión oficial encargado del estado de la inmigración asiática en México, 18 nov. 1903," submitted in 1904, AHGES, tomo 1900.

The Chinese maintained a strong presence in towns such as Guaymas, Hermosillo, and Magdalena. But by 1904 it was in Cananea that the largest Chinese colony was found. Located in Arizpe district, in the northeast corner of Sonora near the U.S. border, Cananea was a prototypical company town, a creation of the Greene Consolidated Copper Company. It was exactly the kind of place that attracted Chinese immigrants: of the 1,106 Chinese in Arizpe district, 800 resided in Cananea, which had a total population of about 4,000.

The company town had all the features of a boom town. The vast majority of the population were Mexican workers. Apart from the Chinese, there was another, much smaller foreign colony, composed of the American managers, supervisors, skilled workers, and their families. Some Chinese worked for wages in these American homes as houseboys, cooks, or laundrymen. Some Chinese had truck farms just outside town, where they grew and sold vegetables and fruits that fed the townspeople. Few of them actually worked in the mines as laborers.

Half or more of the Chinese were involved, as owners, partners or employees, in their own small business enterprises, providing essential goods and services to the large Mexican working population. They operated canteens, boarding houses, laundries, groceries, and variety stores—businesses that generally required little capital to start. The big Magdalena firm of Juan Lung Tain opened up two branch stores in the working class barrio of Ronquillo. Although the American copper company had its own *tiendas de raya,* or company stores, including a slaughterhouse and ice plant, these apparently fell far short of meeting all the demands. In fact, evidence suggests that the large number of Chinese *comerciantes* and the American company seldom conflicted and sometimes even worked together. For example, Chinese stores bought meat wholesale from the company's slaughterhouse for retail sale in small amounts. Also, one of the mine's mess halls was operated as a Chinese business.[25]

In other mining towns the Chinese also seized upon new business opportunities with greater alacrity than any other group. As Luis Quon Yui Sen of Magdalena explained: "In my capacity as merchant with a fixed establishment in this town, it is my custom to go periodically to Cerro Prieto on paydays of the mining company there to sell merchandise from my shop and my shoe factory."[26] Minas Prietas in Hermosillo district had 96 Chinese residents, according to the 1904 census of Chinese.

In much of the north, many Chinese were also dedicated to the small enterprise of truck farming—growing and selling fruits and vegetables to an urban population. This was an agricultural activity that, again, did not encroach upon the interests of an established group; Mexican hacendados cultivated mainly cereal crops. Making extensive use of the railroads, these Chinese farmers created a wide distribution network throughout the interior of the state. In its investigation of Chinese truck farmers around Magdalena, the State Treasury noted that "the most important activity to which they are dedicated . . . is the cultivation of potatoes, which they remit in large quantities to Nogales, Guaymas, and this town, and all the population centers in between; according to the records of the railroads, it can be calculated that they send some eight thousand sacks of potatoes each year . . . this without counting the vegetables which they send daily by railroad to Nogales and other parts to retail." Residents of the considerable Chinese colony in the northern border town of Fronteras were almost all farmers, provisioning a number of mining towns, including Cananea. Most of them rented or leased land from Mexicans or North Americans; conforming to common Chinese practices, they worked in partnerships or employed their countrymen.[27]

Mexicans were at first amazed and then resentful that the Chinese were able to live frugally, save money, and start their own businesses. They complained that the Chinese relied heavily on family, relatives, covillagers, and other compatriots for help, and seldom considered hiring Mexicans. If the proprietor and his partners or employees were all single men (usually the case, as most Chinese immigrants were single and the married generally came without their families) they lived on the shop premises, thus saving money on living expenses. Another profitable practice was to keep the store well stocked with a wide variety of items, ranging from fresh produce to luxury goods. So-called groceries, drugstores, hardware stores, and even bakeries sold more than just one type of product. If possible, extra stock was crowded onto the premises, rather than warehoused elsewhere, again to save on overhead expenses. These practices, which their competitors found deplorable, enabled the Chinese to outsell other small businesses by offering lower prices and wider choices.[28]

In addition, as discussed above, the Chinese created their own supply and distribution network, a cooperative system that at the same time helped to open up and integrate the internal market while firmly planting the Chinese at the base of the new petite bourgeoisie. Lacking commercial experience, capital, credit, and international contacts, Mexicans had difficulty competing with any foreign group, including the Chinese.

During the Porfiriato, the largest wholesale-retail, import-export firms remained in the hands of Spaniards and Germans, who had arrived long before the Chinese, and in the hands of a few Mexicans. The European firms would not be dislodged until after World War I, when, among other difficulties, their connections with European suppliers were seriously disrupted. Before the Mexican Revolution, the Chinese did not really encroach upon or compete with these older, established commercial houses, which were located primarily in older towns, such as Guaymas, Hermosillo, and Alamos, and which showed little inclination to expand into the interior. The Europeans, it would seem, left it up to the more recent Chinese arrivals to follow the demographic movements of workers and towns generated by the American mines and railroads under Porfirian development. In this sense it can be said the Chinese immigrants and enterprises followed American investment.

In the new population centers, often located in previously isolated areas, Chinese businesses provided many of the basic goods and services of daily living, for both American bosses and Mexican workers. A relationship of mutual need and benefit developed between American capitalists and Chinese immigrants, one that was rather ironic in view of strong anti-Chinese sentiments in the American West. When persecution against Chinese intensified during and after the Mexican Revolution, individual Americans as well as the U.S. government often came to the aid of these defenseless aliens. Aside from humanitarian concerns, Americans intervened because attacks on Chinese interests afffected them too.

Their close association and identification with the rich, powerful, and much-hated gringos provides one good clue to why the Chinese came under direct fire by xenophobic Mexican nationalists. One oft-cited reason for the outbreak of the Revolution is resentment against the Díaz dictatorship's favoritism toward foreigners. Such sentiment was undoubtedly most intense against North Americans. Yet the Chinese received much of the brunt of overt anti-foreignism because they were widely dispersed and thus highly visible, had a weak government with no consular representation in northern Mexico, and, most importantly, had daily contact with lower- and working-class Mexicans, who were most susceptible to xenophobic nationalism.[29]

The "popular classes" of Mexicans had another reason to fear and decry a growing Chinese presence. Within the ranks of the working class were many potential small businessmen. When the Chinese began arriving during the Porfiriato, they encountered some, but not many, Mexican commercial enterprises, which usually could not compete effectively with foreigners. By the last decade of the dictatorship, lower-class Mexicans began to sense that, if left unchecked, continuous Chinese immigration and the unrestricted demographic and occupational mobility of the Chinese would soon rob Mexicans of their birthright to be the local small business class, a national petite bourgeoisie.

An 1899 editorial in the Guaymas daily *El Tráfico* denounced, in direct and racist terms, the existence in the state of "something terrible that threatens to ruin our small commerce: we refer to the disgusting, despicable and noxious Chinese element. These sons of Confucius, who can be considered a terrible plague, have planted themselves in various towns in the state—we have them in Magdalena, Nogales, Hermosillo, Guaymas, Caborca, etc. etc.—where they have established small stores, adulterating the products and evading taxes whenever possible, thus augmenting their considerable capital . . . These Mongol merchants attract their victims, that is, the consumers, with strategic plans, fictitious promises, with deceit and fraudulent sales of merchandise, and, whenever possible, swindle their good and honest customers." The editorial concluded by lamenting the official protection that the government accorded this "raza abominable."[30]

Significantly, this editorial outburst, which probably represented a good segment of popular sentiment, contrasted sharply with the depiction of the prominent Chinese merchant Guillermo Leytón of Álamos in the official 1905 commerical directory. There Leytón was described as "an excellent Chinese who enjoys popularity in the locality . . . well loved by the working people because he willingly and readily helps them out, especially when a poor harvest or some other cause raises the price of basic necessities." The directory also pointedly noted that Leytón hired a Mexican as chief clerk, as if to counter the widespread accusation, well based in fact, that Chinese employed few Mexicans. Officially, then, it would appear, the Díaz government on the state and federal levels refrained from criticizing the Chinese or their commercial expansion.

Yet a third reaction helps to illuminate the popular sentiment that emerged in the last decade of the Porfiriato toward these ubiquitous, excessively enterprising aliens. If the Díaz regime officially viewed the Chinese and their activities as basically benign and beneficial to development in the state, the Partido Liberal Mexicano (PLM) of the Flores Magón brothers, anarcho-sindicalists who formed the first serious political opposition to the dictatorship and who organized the famous 1906 labor strike in Cananea against the American copper company, specifically called for an end to Chinese immigration in its 1906 party platform, branding it harmful to the welfare of the Mexican working class.[31] It is unlikely that even the PLM believed that the two to three thousand Chinese in Sonora around 1905 seriously threatened the jobs of Mexicans, especially since few Chinese were actually employed as wage laborers in the same capacities as Mexican men.[32] Rather, a combination of nationalism, racism, and fear that growing Chinese economic power would preclude Mexican participation on the local commercial level—precisely the level with which Mexican workers had daily dealings and to which some workers could aspire to enter—probably led the PLM to its early anti-Chinese position.

Conclusions

For the first time since Independence, Mexico became unified as a modern nation under the dictator Porfirio Díaz, whose rule lasted for well over three decades. When the regime finally came apart in 1910, it was largely because this unification did not concurrently bring about central government responsiveness to local needs and interests. In the experience of Sonora, the center's insensitivity to regional sentiments extended to local elite as well as popular classes. Determined to see Mexico develop at all costs—following the typical nineteenth-century notion of rapid, large-scale growth based essentially on heavy foreign investment in extractive industries or commercial agriculture geared for export of primary products—the federal government doggedly pursued pacification of the rebellious Yaqui Indians and facilitated, if not actively encouraged, Chinese immigration to the sparsely populated northwest.

Throughout the Porfiriato, while every Mexican agreed that the Yaqui rebels had to be subjugated, there was always tension surrounding the issue, and every measure taken provoked some controversy. Hacendados and other employers of Yaquis, such as mine and railroad owners, wanted to see the broncos extirpated, but at the same time they insisted that the pacíficos be left undisturbed in their workplaces. Unfortunately for the government, it was apparently the only party to perceive and acknowledge the fact that in a *guerra de comunidad,* or people's war, the entire rebel population must be dealt with as one, with no distinctions possible. In acting accordingly, the Díaz regime eventually arrived at the final solution, that of massive deportation.

The new policy meant that the government would no longer separate the relatively few broncos from the vast popultion of pacíficos, the working Yaquis distributed throughout the state, employed in just about every enterprise in the economy. The problem of Yaqui pacification was complicated precisely by the simple fact that, while resisting total assimilation and acculturation into Mexican society and culture, Yaquis willingly worked in the labor-scarce local economy. Thus the massive deportation of all Yaquis without exception threatened not only the existence of the Yaquis themselves, but also the continued prosperity of local enterprises heavily dependent on Yaqui labor.

Especially vulnerable were Sonoran hacendados producing primarily for the expanded internal market, such as the Maytorenas. These local families, comprising traditional notables as well as more recent arrivals, were early disenfranchised politically by the Díaz regime, their participation in government limited to the municipal level. While it cannot be said that Díaz's Yaqui policy was the proverbial straw that broke the camel's back, it did help to widen the gulf between the center and an important sector of the periphery, deepening the alienation that eventually led to the withdrawal of the regional elite's support from the regime.

Tension between the center and the periphery over the Chinese question was not as pronounced or as persistent as that over the

Yaqui problem, but it definitely grew more pronounced toward the end of the Porfiriato. At the outset of its rule, the Díaz government permitted Chinese immigration to the northwest, as better than nothing. Toward this end it negotiated, in 1893, and then renewed in 1900, a treaty of friendship and commerce with Imperial China, the second time against considerable opposition. But the regime never repudiated its Chinese immigration policy, even in the face of mounting criticism.

The Díaz government believed that the poor, humble Asians would work for low wages in Sonora's burgeoning economy, and probably expected them to fill the void left by the persecuted Yaquis. Contrary to such expectations, however, the Chinese preferred to go into business for themselves, or to work for other Chinese merchants and manufacturers. By the end of the Porfiriato, the form of an incipient petite bourgeoisie, based on these enterprising immigrants, was already taking shape. Yet the government never quite acknowledged this unplanned turn of events, and thus never dealt with it. In the meantime voices in Sonora began to decry the alarming situation of a foreign group taking over control of its local commerce.

Those in Sonora who opposed Chinese participation in the economy overlooked the fact that the numerous and widely dispersed Chinese business community was helping to open up the interior market and to establish a modern distribution network for national and imported products. These Mexicans tended rather to feel robbed by the Chinese of their birthright to be the local *comerciantes*, deprived by them of their claim to prosperity. Consequently they resented the government's protection of what they clearly perceived to be an illegitimate group of foreigners.

Even though the Chinese never did become the massive cheap labor force they were intended to be, ironically labor constituted a source of further tension in regard to the Chinese question. The Partido Liberal Mexicano, anarcho-sindicalist champion of the Mexican proletariat, accused the Díaz regime of failure to protect Mexican workers from unfair competition from the Chinese, and called for the prohibition of Chinese immigration in its 1906 political program. The party's manifesto best sums up this sentiment: "The prohibition of Chinese immigration is, above all, a means to protect workers of other nationalities, especially the Mexicans. The Chinese, disposed in general to work for the lowest wages, submissive, avaricious in their aspirations, are a great obstacle for the prosperity of other workers. Their competition is lamentable and must be avoided in Mexico. In general, Chinese immigration to Mexico has not produced the least benefit."[33]

Significantly, and in contrast to the Yaqui situation, those Sonorans who protested the strong Chinese presence in local commerce (a visible fact), or the Chinese threat to Mexican workers (still more potential than real), came essentially from the lower classes—workers and small businessmen. These sectors of society were never much committed to the Díaz dictatorship, although in the north, because of the predominance of mines and railroads in a sparsely populated environment, work was more available and wages higher. Yet it was also in the north that some of the earliest and most serious strikes took place during the last decade of the Porfiriato. The Mexican mine workers who struck in Cananea in 1906, under anarcho-sindicalist leadership, directed their rancor at the company's practice of predominantly hiring North Americans for the better paid skilled jobs and of paying North Americans higher wages than Mexicans received for similar jobs. During the actual strike, Chinese merchants or Chinese workers were never even an issue, despite the specific reference to Chinese immigration in the PLM's manifesto. It can be argued in fact that the Chinese were scapegoats for a problem created by other foreigners. The failure of the center to take seriously northern workers' growing frustration at their inability to compete effectively for jobs with foreigners—North Americans and Chinese—alienated them further from a regime to which they owed little allegiance in the first place. If the Díaz government understood the contradiction of its Yaqui policy—that in solving the rebel problem it exacerbated the labor problem—it certainly did not fully appreciate the irony of the Chinese experience that unfolded in Sonora—an immigrant group that was criticized locally both for what it did and what it did not do. In any case, the center's response to and handling of what on the northwest periphery were perceived to be serious conflicts intensified, rather than defused, the tensions that were later released in the Revolution.

NOTES

1. In recent years a number of historians of Mexico have discussed the so-called peculiarities and traditions of Sonora. They include the following: Stuart Voss, "Towns and Enterprises in Northwestern Mexico— A History of Urban Elites in Sonora and Sinaloa, 1830–1910," Ph.D. diss. (Harvard University, 1972); Barry Carr, "Las peculiaridades del norte México, 1880–1927: Ensayo de interpretación," *Historia Mexicana* 22 (Jan.–March 1972): 320–45; Hector Aguilar Camín, "The Relevant Tradition: Sonoran Leaders in the Revolution," in D. A. Brading, ed., *Caudillo and Peasant in the Mexican Revolution,* ed. D. A. Brading (Cambridge, 1980), 92–123.

2. For the church-state conflict, see David C. Bailey, *Viva Cristo Rey: The Cristero Rebellion and the Church-State Conflict in Mexico* (Austin, 1974). Perhaps more than any truly socially based radicalism, Calles's anticlericalism earned him the epithets of Red and Bolshevik. See Evelyn HuDeHart, *Missionaries, Miners and Indians* (Tucson, 1981) for a detailed study of Jesuit-Yaqui relations during the colonial period.

3. David M. Pletcher, "The Development of Railroads in Sonora," *Inter-American Economic Affairs* 1 (1948): 3–44; Daniel Cosío Vellegas, ed., *Historia Moderna de México, Vol. 8: El Porfiriato; La vida económica,* Nicolau d'Olwer et al. (Mexico, 1965), pt. 2, 1103–34; Andrew D. Barlow (Consul General of Mexico City), "Mexico: United States Enterprises in Mexico," in *Commercial Relations of the United States with Foreign Countries During the Year 1902,* Bureau of Foreign Commerce, Department of State (Washington, 1903), vol. 1, 433–503.

4. Walter S. Logan, *Yaqui: Land of Sunshine and Health* (New York, 1894); Compañía Constructora Richardson Papers, 1904–1927, Special Collections, University of Arizona Library, Tucson.

5. Claudio Dabdoub, *Historia de El Valle del Yaqui* (Mexico, 1964), 210; Antonio G. Rivera, *La revolución en Sonora* (Mexico, 1969), 111–16; Stuart Voss, "Porfirian Sonora: Economic Collegiality," unpub. paper presented at the American Historical Association Meetings (San Francisco, Cal., 28 Dec. 1979).

6. Justo Sierra, *Evolución política del pueblo mexicano,* ed. by Edmundo O'Gorman, *Obras completas del maestro Justo Sierra,* ed. Edmundo O'Gorman, vol. 12 (Mexico, 1948), 398.

7. Logan, *Yaqui,* 10.

8. Francisco P. Troncoso, *Las guerras con las tribus Yaquis y Mayo del estado de Sonora* (Mexico, 1905), 235, 261, 269–72; Daniel Cosío Villegas,

ed., *Historia moderna, Vol. 4: El Porfiriato; La vida social,* Moisés González Navarro, 252.

9. Dabdoub, *Historia,* 210; Troncoso, *Guerras,* 266–67; Telegram, F. Sánchez to F. Muñóz, Moctezuma, 5 July 1902, and lists of women and children apprehended, in Patronato de la Historia de Sonora (private collection of documents bound in one hundred volumes, hereafter cited as PHS), 14: 215; 15: 140–41.

10. List of Yaquis "justified as rebels," Tórin, 26 Sept. 1904, PHS 18: 196; list of Yaquis "who are not justified as pacíficos," Hermosillo, 30 Sept. 1904, PHS 18: 207; Governor to Prefect of Arizpe District, 29 Aug. 1905, PHS 20: 210.

11. Sentences given to arrested Yaquis, March 1904, PHS 17: 172–78; on Carlos Johnson's complaints, PHS 18: 179–88; on other hacendados' complaints, PHS 22: 120–21, PHS 20: 128, PHS 21: 287–90; "Mexico's Indian Policy," *The Arizona Star,* 27 April 1904, PHS 17: 262–63. Meanwhile, Izábal made sure to send necessary workers to his own estates; see lists of workers sent to Izábal haciendas, PHS 21: 69. Moreover, he had a reputation as a cruel hacendado; after the Revolution a great variety of punitive and torture instruments were allegedly found on his hacienda *La Europa;* see Dabdoub, *Historia,* 210.

12. Governor Izábal report to State Congress, 1903–7, PHS 17: 155–56; "Memoria presentado al Congreso de la Unión por el Secretario de Estado y del Despacho de Fomento, Colonización e Industria de la República Mexicana, Lic. Olegario Molina," January 1905–June 1907, PHS 19: 85–87; Moisés González Navarro, *Raza y tierra: La guerra de casta y el henequén* (Mexico, 1970), 183–88; Cosío Villegas, *Porfiriato; vida social,* 259.

13. Article in *The Tucson Post,* 24 Aug. 1906, PHS 18: 48–49; Archivo de la Defensa Nacional, Archivo Histórico, Mexico City (hereafter cited as ADN), expediente 14708; orders to round up Yaquis in the northern districts, scattered in PHS 47; report of the Ferrocarril de Sonora, 2 Oct. 1907, PHS 46: 237; Prefect of Arizpe to State Secretary, Arizpe, 11 Feb. 1908, PHS 47: 250.

14. Lorenzo Torres to Chief Bule, 9 June 1908, PHS 48: 124; CONDUMEX, S.A., Centro de Estudios de Historia Mexicana, Ramón Corral Papers, expediente 30; telegram, Corral to Lorenzo Torres, 28 June 1908, PHS 49: 198.

15. John Kenneth Turner, *Barbarous Mexico* (Austin, 1969 [1909]), 76; Cosío Villegas, *Porfiriato; vida social,* 258–59.

16. Lorenzo Torres to A. Cubillas, 4 July 1908, PHS 48: 234; ADN, 14709, no. 658.

17. Antonio Manero, *El antiguo regimen y la revolución* (México, 1911), 209–29.

18. Lorenzo Torres on activities of the Maytorenas, July 1908, PHS 49: 384; see also PHS 48: 223, 277–78.

19. *Estadísticas económicas del Porfiriato: Fuerza de trabajo y actividad económica por sectores* (México, 1964), 26–28.

20. Numerous reports from Consul A. Willard of Guaymas to State Department on entry and movements of Chinese in the state, 1886–90, in "Dispatches from U.S. Consuls in Guaymas, 1832–1896," U.S. National Archives, General Records of the Department of State, Record Group 59, M284, reel 5.

21. Ibid. Ramón Corral, *Memoria de la administración pública del Estado de Sonora* (Guaymas, 1891), 1: 586–602.

22. Leo M. D. Jacques, "The Anti-Chinese Campaign in Sonora, Mexico, 1900–1931," Ph.D. diss. (University of Arizona, 1974), 50–51, citing U.S. Department of Commerce figures. Prefects' report to Governor on industries in their districts, 1902, Archivo Histórico del Gobierno e Estado de Sonora (AHGES; located in Hermosillo, Sonora), tomo 1739, exp. 9.

23. Federico García y Alva, *México y sus progresos,* "*Album-directorio del Estado de Sonora*" (Hermosillo, 1905–7). Vice-consul Josiah Stone of Nogales to State Department, report on Lau Chi, principal partner of Juan Lung Tain and Company, 11 Feb. 1892; and Consul Darnall of Nogales to State Department, report on Lau Chi and Juan Lung Tain, 31 Oct. 1898, in U.S. National Archives, Consular reports from Nogales, Mexico, Record Group 59, M283, reel 1, no. 110, reel 3, no. 32. Fo Chi Chong Hermanos of Guaymas to Governor, 27 March 1909, AHGES, tomo 2349; State Treasurer to Secretary of State Government, on transactions between Chinese merchants and Mexican hacendados, 4 July 1910, AHGES, tomo 2556; Fon Qui (another large Chinese commercial house, with headquarters in Magdalena and various branch stores) to State Government, protesting a fine, 5 April 1900, AHGES, tomo 1566.

24. John R. Southworth, *El estado de Sonora, México: Sus industrias comerciales, minerías, y manufacturas* (Nogales, 1897), bilingual test. By oversight or prejudice, Southworth failed to take note of at least two other Chinese commercial houses already well established by 1897: Fon Qui and Juan Lung Tain (see García y Alva, *"Album-directorio"*).

25. The definitive history of this important frontier, mining, and company town has yet to be written. A popular history of Cananea, actually of the personality and career of Colonel Greene, founder of the copper company, is C. L. Sonnichsen, *Colonel Greene and the Copper Skyrocket*

(Tucson, 1974). By 1912 the Chinese colony in Cananea had grown to between fifteen hundred and two thousand people, with half or more of them (eight hundred to nine hundred, according to U.S consular agent George Wiswall) working as merchants; see George Wiswall to Alexander Dye, consul of Nogales, 27 April 1912, in a special collection of documents from the National Archives, entitled "Records of the Department of State Relating to the Chinese Question in Mexico, 1910–1929," Microfilm Collection, University of Arizona, Tucson, Arizona (hereafter cited as NA "Chinese"). Hum Fook (Chinese merchant with stores in Cananea and Santa Cruz) to Governor, 24 Sept. 1912, AHGES, tomo 2802.

A kind of American-Chinese partnership is suggested by the example of Fong Sing, who operated a restaurant, or canteen, within the territory of the American-owned Mazapil Copper Company, near Saltillo, Coahuila. Fong Sing and the American company each owned half the restaurant; it appeared to be a case of the Americans investing in a Chinese business to help it get started, because it provided a necessary service for the company's workers; see Vice-Consul Silliman to State Department, 19 Jan. 1914, in NA "Chinese."

26. Luis Quon Yui Sen to State Government, 12 June 1908, AHGES, tomo 2336.

27. State Treasurer to Secretary of State Government, report on Chinese farmers in Magdalena district, Hermosillo, 12 Oct. 1909, including testimony of some of these farmers, 10 Sept. 1909, that Mexican landowners leased them poor land not suitable for wheat cultivation, and that none of the Chinese themselves are "propietarios de fincas de labranzas," AHGES, tomo 2440.

28. José Ángel Espinosa, *El ejemplo de Sonora* (Mexico, 1923), 22–25. This leading anti-Chinese propagandist, though exaggerating his points at every turn, nevertheless provides much insight into Chinese business operations. Chinese store advertisements persistently called attention to their competitiveness. For example, "La Estrella," owned by Tac Fo Lung y Cía. of Guaymas, announced "prices without competition"; "El Nuevo Mundo," owned by Man Lung y Cía. of Guaymas, boasted "the lowest prices in the plaza"; both in *El Noticioso* (Guaymas), 27 July 1910, AHGES, tomo 2645.

29. This is essentially the interpretation of Charles Cumberland in his pioneering study of the Chinese in Mexico, "The Sonoran Chinese and the Mexican Revolution," *Hispanic American Historical Review* 40 (1960): 191–211.

30. *El Tráfico*, 5 April 1899, Hemeroteca Nacional, México.

31. The PLM political program can be found in the appendix of James

Cockcroft, *Intellectual Precursors of the Mexican Revolution, 1700–1913* (Austin, 1968).

32. The argument that Chinese men working as cooks, laundrymen, peddlers, street hawkers, and domestic servants took jobs away from Mexican *women* has greater validity. Indeed, after 1910, working-class women, such as the mineworkers' wives in Cananea, often led anti-Chinese demonstrations and formed women's branches of anti-Chinese leagues. See Consul Frederick Simpich of Nogales to State Department, 26 Feb. 1914, in NA in "Chinese."

33. Isidro Fabela, *Documentos históricos de la Revolución Mexicana* (México, 1966), 10: 46.

8
Yucatán:
Violence and Social Control
on Henequen Plantations

Allen Wells

The swift rise of Yucatán's henequen economy during the Porfiriato was an integral part of Mexico's stunning economic transformation. The industrial growth of Western Europe and the United States tied much of Mexico, including the Yucatán peninsula, to the global economy. Foreign investors—who needed markets, raw materials, and investment opportunities—cooperated with local elites—who welcomed foreign capital, railroads, technology, and sundry consumer goods—to spur the modernization of Mexico during the rule of the dictatorial Porfirio Díaz.[1]

In Yucatán the growth of the export sector was the direct result of increasing foreign demand for henequen (sisal). Encouraged by North American markets, local landowners turned the northwest portion of the state of Yucatán into commercial henequen plantations. Production increased from 41,864 bales (one bale weighs 350 pounds) in 1876 to more than 680,000 bales in 1911, as entrepreneurs restructured the local economy and geared production toward the export sector. By the end of the Porfiriato, the peninsula's colonial-style haciendas had been transformed into modern henequen plantations. The final destination of this raw fiber, or hemp, was the cordage factories of the United States, where manufacturers converted it into binder twine for grain farmers throughout North America.[2]

The rise of the monocrop economy affected the lives of thousands of Maya Indians who worked on the henequen estates. The changeover dramatically transformed the role of the Yucatecan field worker (*jornalero de campo*), as the *hacendado* used a variety of methods to assure himself an effective, dependent labor force during the henequen boom (*auge*). Unfortunately the entire subject of working conditions on henequen plantations during the Porfiriato has been the subject of much acrimonious debate ever since the muckraking journalist John Kenneth Turner visited the region in 1909. Apologists for, and critics of, the plantation system have disputed the precise nature of working conditions for Maya campesinos on henequen estates.[3] These divergent schools of thought dramatize the emotionally charged issue, leaving little room for compromise.

Apologists, generally ex-hacendados, foreign investors with a stake in the export trade, and descendants of the planter elite, stressed the symbiotic relationship between master (*amo*) and servant (*sirviente*). They point to the sense of security that the worker felt toward his place in the hacienda community and to the conditions of labor scarcity which inflated the value of the plantation work force and precluded a martial regimen on the estate.[4] Visiting observers, like Turner and the British travelers Arnold and Frost, depicted a repressive labor system predicated on the unceasing exploitation of a downtrodden Indian majority.[5]

One factor which both supporters and critics of the plantation society agreed on was the dependent status and docility of the campesinos. Yet even if both schools of thought concurred on the Indians' character, they offered differing views on the reasons for workers' meek acceptance of their status. For outspoken critics, Maya passivity toward the regime confirmed planter oppression and exploitation. Spokesmen for hacendados, on the other hand, argued that the absence of singular and collective acts of resistance by the

Yucatán, 1910

indolent campesinos demonstrated the existence of a paternalistic ethos which insulated and protected the worker from a dangerous world outside the boundaries of the plantation.

This view of worker dependence and docility demands revision. Recent work by Mexican historians has documented widespread campesino dissatisfaction throughout the nineteenth century.[6] One agrarian historian argues that Mexico was in a "permanent state of rebellion" throughout the period.[7] One aim of this chapter will be to discuss the nature of violent protest in the henequen zone (*zona henequenera*) during the dictatorship of Porfirio Díaz and to correct the exaggerated misperceptions of both apologists and critics.[8]

Given the nature of the debate, it is not surprising that little attention has been paid to the mechanisms of social control which planters and civil authorities utilized to ensure peace and tranquility on the plantations. Nor has an analysis been made of work disturbances and demonstrations of collective resistance within the region. The purpose of this chapter will therefore be three-fold: to contribute to, and clarify, the ongoing debate on working conditions through a systematic investigation of the coerced labor system used on the henequen plantations; to study the forms and nature of violence that periodically erupted in the countryside, together with the state's mechanisms of social control designed to counter such hostilities; and to demonstrate the degree to which labor patterns changed as a function of the Porfirian policy of economic modernization.

Life on the Henequen Plantations

Prior to the henequen boom, local hacendados had successfully dictated local labor patterns to suit their own specific manpower needs. Labor requirements for the pre-boom livestock economy demanded only a skeleton work force. A majority of the Maya population lived in villages and worked on common lands. With the rise of the commercial henequen economy, after 1850, landowners needed an organized, mobile, albeit unskilled labor force. Any villager, therefore, became a potential asset for the labor-starved estate. A planter's success was measured by his ability to snare, entrap, or coax villagers to join the plantation work force. Whereas a condition of labor surplus had existed prior to the boom, chronic labor shortages became the order of the day during the height of the henequen boom. Such a radical transformation, while permanently changing the campesinos' responsibilities, failed to improve their input into the decision-making process. In fact, the new monocrop economy limited laborers' options and curtailed their ability to maintain any degree of independence from the encroaching haciendas. The process of modernization demanded that the jornalero work on the estate; hacendados could no longer afford to allow the tenant/sharecropping arrangements which had characterized the earlier period.

The boom necessitated constraints on the Indians' freedom of movement, on their ability to provide for themselves and their families and on their perception of their own role in society. The planters' success in altering past labor patterns demanded a geographic and demographic change in regional distribution patterns, forcing a contraction in the size of villages and inducing a migration from the marginal southeast to the henequen zone in the northwest. In short, the rise of the henequen plantation effected a revolution of sorts, transforming local labor arrangements and upsetting the regional economic framework. Most importantly, the peasants reacted to the transformation with random acts of violence, periodic escapes, and chronic alcoholism, all of which indicate that many did not accept their fate lightly.

In order to accommodate such a sweeping transformation, henequen planters had to make wholesale changes in the preexisting mode of utilizing laborers. Prior to the growth of the monocrop economy, a labor surplus had enabled hacendados and workers jointly to fix contractual arrangements for labor services. The livestock economy demanded a minimal work force, which meant a low degree of friction between landowner and peasant and allowed for greater flexibility in labor-management relations. Those villagers that wanted to work or rent parcels of land from the hacendado contracted directly with the landowner or through an intermediary, usually the village chief (*cacique*). Since the arrangements varied with the respective worker and landowner, it is difficult to categorize general labor patterns. Nevertheless, three distinctive types were prevalent in the pre-boom era: the resident servant (*peón acasillado*); the renter/sharecropper; and the *lunero*, a combination of the first two types.[9]

The peón acasillado lived and worked on the cattle hacienda and received either a fixed monthly wage or an adjusted weekly wage for tasks completed. In exchange for the peón's labor, the owner provided the worker with a small plot of land (corn cultivation was strictly prohibited), a house, firewood, water, and the right to graze livestock on hacienda lands. The resident had a running account with the owner and in this fashion fell inextricably in debt. The servant became tied to the estate by his debt, which generally increased throughout his lifetime, due in large measure to meager wages and the cash requirements for ceremonial functions (births, deaths, weddings, baptisms, etc.). From colonial times on, hacendados paid their servants in tokens or script; "on a sheet of paper various markings were made intersecting a horizontal line, these represented his purchases . . . At the time the *peón* made a purchase he produced his papers and the entry was made in his presence regardless of the book accounting at the store . . ."[10]

Renters, who managed to avoid the clutches of debt, could live on the hacienda or in the nearby town. Terms of the sharecropping agreement were worked out in conjunction with the hacendado, although from 10 to 15 percent of the tenant's crop was the accepted standard of payment. A typical agreement is that of 1856 by which the prominent hacendado Manuel José Peón y Maldonado rented out a portion of his hacienda, Cheuman. Four Indians from nearby Caucel rented some of Cheuman's forests (*montes*), agreeing to pay ten *cargas* (one carga equals one hundred pounds) for each hundred cargas cut, a 10 percent rental. The same 10 percent rental was extended to crop cultivation. Unlike residents, renters possessed freedom of movement throughout the year and could hire out their services at their own discretion.[11]

The third category, that of luneros, underwent significant changes during the nineteenth century. Originally the contractual arrangement was created to enable local inhabitants to obtain drinking water, a precious commodity throughout the arid northwest quadrant of the peninsula. As the arrangement evolved, luneros came to live on the hacienda like the peones acasillados, receiving the same rights to a house, water, firewood, and grazing land. In addition, luneros received a plot to use for a *milpa* as did tenants. In return luneros were obliged to work one day a week for the hacendado; hence the name lunero, literally Monday man. Luneros also cultivated twenty *mecates* of corn (ten mecates of first-year corn and ten mecates of second-year corn) for the landowner.[12] In theory any additional work load would be at the luneros' discretion. In practice however, like the resident peones, they fell into debt, thereby limiting their potential mobility.[13]

These pre-auge labor patterns suggest some flexibility in contractual arrangements between landowners and laborers. Only the residents, theoretically, were tied to the hacienda. Luneros, renters, and village work teams, comprising the great majority of the rural work force, contracted with hacendados in a relatively open labor market. It must be emphasized that these flexible agreements were in the landowners' best interests; the labor requirements of a livestock economy hardly demanded a fixed work force. That is to say, while laborers did have options, landowners contracted from a position of strength. Research has confirmed this notion of an open labor market in the years preceding the destructive Caste War, which rocked the peninsula in 1847. Coaxed by the expansion of the sugar industry in the southeast, peasants left the northwest in droves, attracted by the possibilities for employment in the cane districts of Tekax, Peto, and Valladolid. Given this extensive demographic shift, northwestern contractual arrangements must have allowed peasants freedom of movement.[14]

The divisive Caste War not only reversed this demographic flow, but also benefited the expanding henequen industry. As rebel Maya overran southeastern sugar *ingenios* and razed frontier settlements, the available labor supply fled to the northwest, the only sector safe from Maya attacks. If the war itself did not spur the dynamic growth of the monocrop economy in the northwest, it did provide northwestern landowners with the necessary labor force to transform their haciendas into commercial henequen plantations. Hacendados, welcoming the new recruits, soon came to realize, however, that past contractual arrangements could no longer accommodate the new style of plantation agriculture; the henequen economy forced significant changes in the utilization of the labor force. Unlike many monocrops, such as sugar or cotton, henequen can be harvested throughout the year, necessitating a permanent labor supply. Henequen plantations needed workers for all phases of production: clearing lands, cultivation, weeding (*chapeo*), harvesting, processing, and transport. Although technological advances had increased production capabilities, a large number of skilled workers were not required: rather, a sizable, mobile labor force was needed to work effectively during all aspects of the plantation production cycle, as the situation demanded. Finally, the dynamic growth of world market demand for the fiber meant, from a purely numerical standpoint, a radical change in northwest labor patterns.[15]

Casual agreements had to be replaced with concrete restraints on the open-market labor system. Freedom of movement had to be limited if the resident hacienda population was to be increased. Servants, who previously had comprised the smallest group of laborers, soon found their numbers increasing. Luneros and renters, who before had exhibited a degree of independence in their relationship with local landowners, found themselves mired in debt, the single most important factor enforcing labor immobility. Luneros were compelled to work more than the traditional one day a week, in order to keep up with their increasing indebtedness. The only factor which now distinguished them from peones acasillados was the continued cultivation of their own plots (*sementeras*).

Local political authorities, who had officially sanctioned debt peonage in 1843, reiterated their support for the institution in 1882 by promulgating the *Ley agrícola industrial del estado de Yucatán*.[16] Article 5 stipulated that peones who left work without paying sums owed would be prosecuted before the courts. In addition if an indebted servant escaped and took refuge on another estate, the landowner hiding the servant could also be arrested. While the state refused to implement an overt system of servitude, it did tacitly allow its existence under another name.[17]

Although debt peonage had existed prior to the boom, the institution took on a greater significance as the value of the plantations increased. Peones increasingly became tied to the estate, not to the individual landowner. If and when the hacendado sold his estate, and this occurred all too frequently in the unstable Yucatecan economy, peones' debts were included in the bill of sale. Workers were tied to the estate by their debts; unless they repaid those debts, they were likely to live out their lives on the estate.[18] In fact, debt peonage was so ingrained in local labor practices that Yucatecan railway entrepreneurs utilized the institution to limit mobility of their own scarce labor force. Records of the Mérida-Peto railway confirm that railway jornaleros accumulated substantial debts over a ten-year span (1899–1908).[19]

Debts were further reinforced by the institution of the *tienda de raya*, or hacienda store. Due to the relative lack of data available on the store's day-to-day accounting, Mexican historians have disagreed considerably on the impact of the tienda de raya on peón indebtedness. Were prices higher or lower at the tienda than at nearby local markets? Did the hacendado utilize the store as a means of procuring a supplementary margin of profit or were store prices kept low (or at least consistent), in order to entice nearby villagers to join the estate work force? Whether the hacendado or the local merchant, who often leased the concession from the planter, took advantage of the immobile residents still remains unclear. These concerns tend to beg the question of peón indebtedness and to obscure the important role of the tienda in limiting peasant mobility. Whether the tienda overcharged its customers or not, it did provide a significant mechanism whereby hacendados could increase peón debts. Since campensinos did in fact purchase their goods at the store, either because of the available credit facilities or simply for convenience, the tienda was instrumental in reinforcing debt peonage and in diminishing campesino freedom of movement.[20]

If debt peonage was the linchpin of the new closed labor system, several complementary factors aided planter attempts to enforce stricter contractual arrangements. Changing land tenure patterns broke up village common lands (*ejidos*), enabling planters to increase the size of their landholdings while simultaneously bolstering their estate work force. Liberal reform laws of 1856 and 1857 had decreed the breakup of all corporate forms of landownership, including village common lands. The Liberal ideal of private property was quickly abused by wealthy land speculators, surveying companies, and hacendados, with an eye toward expanding their own properties. According to the laws, village lands were to be parceled out in small allotments to all village heads of family. Nearby hacendados could and did buy out individual allotments, negotiating directly with the respective heads of families. The result was a contraction in the physical size of villages; sixty-six ejidos were broken up in Yucatán alone from 1878 to 1912.[21] Villagers stripped of lands heretofore used for subsistence plots had little choice but to move to the nearby hacienda. The hacendado's ample supply of corn, water, and firewood furnished the campesinos with three commodities needed for survival. The villages, which since early colonial days had held the land in usufruct and had thereby maintained a degree of independence from the private sector, soon lost their basis of existence, the village commons. By the end of the Porfiriato, landowners had demonstrably expanded their estates at the expense of villagers and had secured a steady labor supply at the same time. Even those villagers who managed to remain on their land found themselves working at least occasionally on hacienda lands.[22]

This trend was accentuated whenever ecological disaster occurred in the region. While insufficient rains regularly limited corn production throughout the area, necessitating heavy importations of foreign and central Mexican cereals, serious locust plagues often induced famine, accompanied by rioting and other violent acts. One particularly devastating plague hit the peninsula in 1881 and recurred for five consecutive years, laying waste each year's corn crop. State authorities were forced to import huge grain shipments to feed the starving populace. Many villagers, particularly those in the corn-growing regions of Ticul and Sotutá, were forced to leave their lands and accept employment on henequen haciendas in the northwest. Planters eagerly accepted this influx of labor just as demand for the fiber soared in North American cordage markets. Although exact figures are not available, the hacendado's supply of imported corn must have persuaded a sizable number of campesinos to join the plantation labor force during the years of the plague (1881–87). Once the peasants were firmly esconced on the estate, the institution of debt peonage conspired to hold them there.

Another factor which inhibited campesino independence was the specter of required military service. Since the Caste War continued for fifty years after the initial uprisings of 1847, the state needed a permanent army to protect the border settlements of the southeast from Indian attacks and a mobile national guard force with the flexibility to act as a support column to the southeastern army (*colonías del sur*) and to maintain law and order on the local level. Conscription for the colonías was uniformly abhorred by all recruits; many fled at the sight of local *jefes políticos,* who were charged with fulfilling the draft quotas. Males between the ages of fifteen and sixty were required to serve annually. Exemptions could be secured in three cases: if the individual could pay a set fee (*cuota*) or find a replacement to serve for him; if a peasant was classified as a permanent resident laborer (jornalero de campo) attached (which came to mean indebted) to a hacienda; or if one had a debilitating illness (an affidavit from a doctor was required for proof). Since day workers or villagers who only worked on the haciendas could not frequently qualify for the jornalero de campo exemption from military service, many villagers found it more attractive to move to the plantation in order to escape conscription. One need only read through the hundreds of petitions found in the Ramo del Poder Ejecutivo of the Archivo General del Estado de Yucatán requesting exemption from guard service to understand local dissatisfaction with conscription. Case after case of military desertions, medical affidavits, jefes políticos dragging recalcitrant recruits from the countryside and imprisoning villages who had harbored deserters, all underscore the great lengths to which local resident would go to avoid service. Despite the fact that jefes políticos were required to keep up-to-date lists of each hacendado's resident jornaleros de campo, letters from planters abound in the *legajos* of the Archivo General, imploring local jefes to release their unjustly conscripted peones acasillados.[23]

If fear of national guard service was not enough to entice villagers to take up permanent residence on nearby haciendas, there was also the road work contributions (*fajinas*), which required all Yucatecan males between the ages of fifteen and sixty to work on road gangs twice a year. Although this requirement, abolished in 1891 because railways had replaced roads as the primary mode of transport, failed to evoke the universal antipathy that national guard services aroused, road fajinas were nevertheless subject to various abuses. The most common complaint registered was that local políticos exploited road gangs by forcing them to work on their private property. In one instance Demetrio Montejo, justice of the peace (*comisario*) of the municipality of Cantamayec, was accused of forcing nine workers from a nearby hacienda to work as slaves on his own milpa, under the pretext of carrying out prescribed road fajinas. Twenty-one petitioners signed the complaint requesting the removal of Montejo: "We are treated as if we were slaves or better said as they unfortunately treat crazed animals in our country. We are forced by Sr. Montejo to perform all these works without compensation and against our will in the milpas of the jefe político . . . We are beaten and jailed in the worst possible fashion."[24] With the same exemptions facing road contributors as national guardsmen, villagers, luneros, and renters had to think seriously of the benefits of resident peón status. The state, the weather, locust plagues, and changes in local land tenure patterns had all conspired to limit the flexibility and independence of local laborers. Even so, many resident peones found working conditions on henequen plantations so abominable that escapes were commonplace. Planters were forced to tighten hacienda security and to enlist state aid in capturing wayward jornaleros de campo.

One method of returning escaped servants was to employ bounty hunters. José Encarnación Cámara Peón, who operated Hacienda Yaxnic, near Mérida, for his mother, Bibiana Peón, had a running account especially for extraordinary expenses such as payments to bounty hunters. In 1860 Secundario Callí, José Sulú, and Hilario Noh all fled Yaxnic. Cámara Peón had to pay almost twenty pesos for the return of the three escapees.[25] The employment of bounty hunters intimates that the state apparatus for preventing or returning escaped resident peones early on was not very successful. The use of bounty hunters continued into the twentieth century, despite improvements in social control. In 1905 *El Peninsular*, a local independent daily newspaper published by José María Pino Suárez, who later became governor of the state and vice-president of Mexico, documented the existence of special agents who were generally paid fifty pesos to capture runaway servants. While the term special agent had replaced bounty hunter and inflation had increased their asking price, these private enforcers played an important role in limiting the resident peón's freedom of movement.[26]

Another method of social control utilized by hacendados was to print notices in local newspapers alerting the public that their servants had escaped from the estate. Usually the notice stipulated the amount of debt and invariably asked for the servants' whereabouts. Sometimes a rider was included, stressing that the escaped servant would be prosecuted to the fullest extent of the law. In an

1886 notice, José E. Maldonado listed more than a dozen escaped servants from the *finca* Piste in Mamá, their debts, marital status, dependents, and age. Maldonado, the lawyer handling the affair, informed the public that the owners of Piste were in a position to accept payment for the debts of the servants. One celebrated instance involved Juan N. Durán, a servant of Hacienda Chacabal, in Yaxkukul, twenty kilometers northeast of Mérida, owned by Servula Conde de Peniche. The owner's lawyer printed the notice in 1891, and news of the incident quickly spread to Mexico City. The capital press condemned the practice of advertising for escaped servants and characterized Yucatecan hacendados as slaveholders. Local reaction indicated a decided sensitivity toward this nefarious image. *El Eco del Comercio* recommended that notices of this type should not be printed. They did in fact disappear, as local planters began to rely more heavily on the state as primary agent in limiting labor mobility.[27]

Since the state conducted national guard and road fajina conscription, the apparatus for maintaining control over the local labor force already existed. Jefes políticos had only to adapt their operations slightly to keep track of wayward residents. Under the pretext of checking a jornalero de campo's national guard exemption, local political authorities could determine whether or not the worker had left an estate. Once an escaped servant was located, jefes dragged the servant into the national guard if quotas were low, or returned the peón to the estate, where the jefe would more than likely be properly rewarded by the hacendado. Identification papers soon became necessary for residents leaving the estate even for a short time. John Kenneth Turner stressed the harsh climatic conditions, particularly the scarcity of water, which invariably forced an escapee to find his way to a plantation or a village. Once visible the newcomer was quickly caught and held for identification. "A free laborer who does not carry papers to prove that he is free, is always liable to be locked up and put to much trouble to prove that he is not a runaway . . ."[28] By then henequen planters had successfully enlisted the aid of the state in limiting mobility. Given all the factors which lured laborers to the hacienda and all the coercive techniques which prevented their departure, it is understandable that henequen planters were able to augment and control their labor force. With the chronic labor scarcity along with the increasing demands for production, a reliable labor contingent became an indispensable tool in the day-to-day running of the henequen plantation.

As early as 1881, Yucatecan hacendados had begun to look outside the peninsula for potential sources of plantation labor. The policy of importing indentured workers, euphemistically called colonization, continued throughout the boom as local elites desperately sought to meet their expanding labor requirements. Eulalio Casares, proprietor of Xcuyum, was determined to supplement his work force with oriental indentured servants. In 1901, in conjunction with several other henequen hacendados, Casares signed a contract with a Mexico City agent, Francisco Cacho Alonzo, for twenty Asiatic field workers between the ages of twenty and thirty-five. The terms of the contract specified that Cacho Alonzo had three months to bring the workers to Yucatán. Casares and the other interested planters had to deposit twenty pesos per worker in the account of Olegario Molina y Compañía, the merchant firm handling the transport arrangements. Casares also had to pay extra for a foreman who would act as liaison between the hacendado and the new indentured servants. Cacho Alonzo received one hundred pesos per worker. The indentured servants' wages were specified in the agreement: 37.50 *centavos* per 1000 leaves cut; 25 centavos per mecate cleared and weeded; and 37.50 centavos for a lot of firewood. These salaries were representative of prevailing wages paid to local Maya henequen workers. The Asiatic indentured servants signed a contract for a period of two years from their arrival in the principal port. If the workers left before the requisite period, they had to repay the expense of their passage across the Pacific.[29]

Intrigued by the results of his first venture into so-called colonization, Casares participated as a board member of a state-government-sponsored Junta Directiva de Colonización Agrícola, in 1902. The group, formed at the behest of Governor Olegario Molina, was determined to organize a large-scale expedition. Planters had to pay 375 pesos per family, with discounts available if an order were placed for more than six hundred families. Hacendados had to pay 10 percent of the passage in advance and the rest in full upon the workers' arrival in Progreso. The junta was responsible for fulfilling several contracts, but the number of indentured servants never quite met expectations. Casares had several Chinese, Korean, and Japanese families on Xcuyum.[30]

Perhaps the most notorious use of coerced labor was the importation of thousands of Yaqui Indians into the Yucatán peninsula during the first decade of the century (see chapter 7). Turner's description of the march of the Yaquis from the northwest state of Sonora to Yucatán created quite a stir both inside and outside Mexico.[31] Federal authorities during the Porfiriato felt that the only way to deal with the rebellious Indians was to forcibly evict them from their traditional home, the Mayo and Yaqui river valleys in Sonora. What better place to relocate the nettlesome Indians than Yucatán's henequen plantations.[32]

The horrors of the long march aside, the captured prisoners of war found themselves completely disoriented when they arrived in Yucatán. The Yaquis had to adapt to a different and brutal climate, a new language (almost all workers on henequen plantations conversed in Maya), separation from friends and family, and the devastating realization that they would never return to their ancestral homeland. In one striking case, the Mérida press reported that 250 women and children were brought from Sonora in 1900 (by boat to Salina Cruz, over the isthmus by forced march, and then by boat to Progreso). The women were almost all widows, since federal authorities had annihilated Yaqui rebel warriors at the battle of Mazacoba. Henequeneros, eternally optimistic about new sources of labor, intimated that for certain jobs on the hacienda the Yaqui women "were just as strong as the men." Some performed twice as much weeding per day as the men traditionally did.[33]

In a sense the Yaquis were slaves on the henequen plantations.[34] Bereft of cultural identity and loved ones in most cases, they were prisoners of war—their death sentence had been commuted in return for the arduous task of cutting henequen leaves under the torrid tropical sun. Many simply did not survive. Whether they died of psychological shock, the harsh new climate, or the strenuous working conditions, the Yaqui failed to be the solution henequeneros were seeking to their labor problems. Although it is difficult to ascertain exactly how many found their way to Yucatán, their numbers never altered the traditional balance on the estates. The geographer Chardon estimates that all the contract groups together never amounted to more than 10 percent of the work force.[35] One newspaper account estimated that by 1911 only four thousand Yaquis were working on henequen haciendas.[36] The local Maya were and remained the overwhelming majority throughout the Porfiriato, despite numerous attempts by hacendados to increase the labor force from outside the area.

Whether speaking of Yaqui prisoners of war, Korean contract laborers, or Maya peones, the continuous battle with the tropical elements made working conditions on the plantation less than inviting. Harvesting and weeding, exceedingly difficult under any climatic conditions, became nearly impossible under the broiling tropical sun. Cutting leaves (*pencas*), which took place all year long, was made particularly onerous by the brutal climate. The cutting consisted of lopping off the sharp spine at the end of each penca and then removing the leaf itself by drawing the *coa* blade (a curved iron blade set on a wooden shaft about two feet long) directly across its base while holding the leaf steady. Once cut, the leaves were bound in bundles of fifty and carried to the foot of the row of the field (*plantel*), where they were picked up and transported by tramway (*tranvía*) to the processing plant.[37] An average day's harvesting was one thousand leaves cut and bound, but often jornaleros de campo cut fifteen hundred or two thousand leaves in a day, depending upon the demands of the plantation administrator. Fernando Benítez, in his novel *Ki,* which describes life in the henequen zone, gave this graphic picture of the henequen cutter's condition: "I saw his hands; filled with thorns, pierced by prickly spines, bloody, seeming to exist independently from his body and contorted like the agonizing Christs of Grünewald."[38]

While harvesting transformed the jornaleros' hands, chapeo and *tumba,* the clearing of old henequen fields (*henequenales*) abused their backs. For Benítez, tumba was the most arduous task of the entire henequen cycle, particularly the clearing of a thirty-year-old field. "He worked covered with leaves, twigs, insects, covered with sweat, his hair matted, filled with dust, almost transformed into a tree . . ."[39]

Work had to begin early, shortly after dawn, to take advantage of the relatively cooler hours. Henequen workes reported to the work-gang chief (*mayacol*) for assignment. Certain workers had specific occupations, such as carpenter or livestock herder (*vaquero*); the great majority of the work force, however, was a flexible group performing tasks in all phases of the henequen production cycle. One week the work force might have to weed a certain plantel. The following week harvesting might be the order of the day. During periods of low henequen prices, harvesting and processing might be forsaken in favor of the clearing of new fields or the weeding of young henequenales. Table 1 illustrates the variety of tasks around the estate.

Several examples from the administrative account books of Hacienda San José Kuché in Tixkokob *partido* will demonstrate the internal mobility and flexibility of the henequen labor force. During a typical week in August 1897, one *jornalero*, Bernardo Tec, performed chapeo on Monday, cut one thousand leaves on Tuesday and Wednesday, weeded two mecates on Thursday, and worked with the hydraulic press on Friday and Saturday as well as pressing five bales those last two days. Tec received some two and a half pesos for his week's work. Mariano Euan, on the other hand, performed chapeo all that week, for one and a half pesos. The week before, Euan cut leaves four days a week and weeded the other two days, for the same wage. From one day to the next, the henequen worker's chores varied, depending on the specific needs of the plantation.[40]

Table 1 does suggest a specific hierarchy, but outside of the administrator, the overseer, the work-gang leader, and several specialists—all of whom received set wages—work and salaries varied as the situation demanded. Wages, of course, were according to tasks completed—the more firewood a peón cut for the boiler house, the more pay he would receive. Certain jobs, however, received a fixed wage: the mule driver at Kuché was paid fifty centavos per day; the gardener, thirty-seven centavos. Salaried workers were generally better paid than the majority of the work force. A henequen cutter at Kuché had to cut two thousand leaves a day, twice the normal amount, to equal the salaries of the carpenter, stoker, or mule driver. The division of labor on the plantation, based on this dual system of salary and piecework payment might suggest a certain amount of flexibility in laborer decision making; a peón might cut as many or as few leaves as he desired. In practice, however, particularly during boom years when production fell far behind demand, labor scarcity inhibited a worker's choices.[41]

Table 1. Chores and Daily Wages on San José Kuché, August 1897

Administrative:	
Encargado—Administrator	40 pesos/month and 3 cargas (300 pounds) of corn
Mayordomo—Overseer	22 pesos/month
Mayacol—Work-Gang Chief	.05 peso/day
Agricultural:	
Chapeo	.25 peso/*mecate*
Cutting	.25 peso/1000 leaves
Cutting	.37 peso/1500 leaves
Transport:	
Platform driver	.50 peso/day
Tramway driver	.50 peso/day
Industrial:	
Rasper	.50 peso/day
Waste Hauler	.37–.50 peso/day
Machinist	.75 peso/day
Stoker	.50 peso/day
Packer	.62 peso/5 bales
Fiber Dryer	.18–.25 peso/day
Miscellaneous:	
Carpenter	.50 peso/day
Gardener	.37 peso/day
Beekeeper	.50 peso/day
Ropemaker	.50 peso/day
Firewood Cutter	.50 peso/day

Note: Wages were low in 1897 due to a low world market price for henequen.

Source: AGEY, Ramo de Justicia, "Cuenta de administración de la finca San José Kuché y su anexa San Francisco correspondiente a un més corrido de 25 de julio a hoy agosto 25 de 1897."

World market demand, high henequen prices, debts, and poor wages all conspired to keep jornaleros from extricating themselves from debt. Although the average wage in Yucatán increased from twenty centavos per day in 1870 to one peso per day in 1910, rampant inflation which the auge precipitated more than counterbalanced periodic salary increments.[42] Friedrich Katz estimates that real wages declined by 20 percent throughout Mexico during the dictator's rule.[43] In Yucatán monocrop cultivation necessitated the import of large quantities of foreign and Mexican foodstuffs, driving up the cost of basic commodities and thereby diminishing real wages even further. A circular from the Secretaría de Fomento, in 1902, reported that food prices in Yucatán were well above the national average.[44] Yucatán's meat, beans, and corn prices were well above the national average, particularly after the 1898 boom in henequen prices. These increases were naturally passed along to the resident peones through the institution of the tienda de raya.

The henequen worker's diet, primarily corn, beans, and an occasional sampling of meat, provoked considerable health problems as well. Chronic intestinal disorders, brought on by unsanitary conditions in the countryside, were particularly common among the young. Diarrhea was the principal cause of mortality. Pellagra, a vitamin B-12 deficiency brought on by the poor diet, induced scaling, itching, and inflammation of the skin and finally serious personality disorders, often culminating in suicide. Yucatecans blamed the disease on rancid corn imported from the United States.[45]

Wages as well as food prices were tied to the fluctuations in the world market price of henequen. The peones' livelihood depended closely on the vicissitudes of the world market; jornaleros were forced to take pay cuts when henequen prices decreased. During the 1907 panic, when fiber prices dropped to three cents per pound, landowners lowered wages across the board. Salaries, therefore, were not a fixed expenditure; planters could adjust them to meet their expectations of profits. Peones did not outwardly complain about the salary cuts, perhaps because their wages were little more than credits toward their increasing debts. They were fixtures on the plantations, tied by their debts and dependent on increases in the world market price of the fiber for their own limited wage hikes.[46]

If wages fluctuated with demand for fiber, debts went only in one direction. Jornaleros had two running debts, *chichan cuenta* and *no hoch cuenta:* the former was a small debt for daily purchases and weekly wages; the latter was a large account from which servants rarely extricated themselves (for marriages, fiestas, etc.).[47] Hacendados kept detailed records of the no hoch cuenta.

Plantation Social Relations Revised

The henequen boom lowered campesinos' mobility and real wages and worsened day-to-day working conditions. Yet apologists have lauded the patron-client relationship as the key humanizing factor in the operation of the plantation. They have stressed the sense of security the workers felt toward their place in the hacienda community and the special relationship they enjoyed with the planter.

Unfortunately the image of the Yucatecan planter aiding an infirm servant or personally overseeing a gala fiesta of the hacienda's patron saint must undergo some modification. Yucatecan hacendados were for the most part absentee landlords, leaving the daily operation of the hacienda to an *encargado* or *personero*. Jornaleros directed their problems, complaints, and requests to a hired employee. Conscientious planters may have visited their estates on weekends, preferring to spend the rest of their time in Mérida, where they could keep a watchful eye on their myriad investments. For example, the owner of Hacienda Polabán, in Tecoh, averaged three weekend trips to the finca over a one-year period.[48] Certainly the prototypical planter-servant relationship must be scrutinized. Unlike antebellum southern cotton planters, who for the most part resided on the plantation and in so doing encouraged a different type of paternalism, brought about by the close proximity of masters and slaves, the Yucatecan model necessarily diminished the possibilities for an integrated working relationship between amo and sirviente.

This is not to say that certain Yucatecan hacendados did not take a special interest in their peones or that that paternalistic relationships based on mutual obligations and responsibilities did not exist in Porfirian Yucatán. Paternalism did exist in the henequen zone, but it could never reach the level of sophistication that prevailed in the United States, simply because henequen planters on the whole never invested the time and effort required to nurture the complex relationship. Planters regarded their estates as business investments, and speculation in rural real estate, particularly during bust cycles in the regional economy, forced entrepreneurs to consider henequen haciendas as liquid assets.[49] The Peón Casares family, for example, swapped fincas with Ricardo Molina Hübbe in 1907. Hacienda Ticopó, a Peón hacienda for fifty years and arguably the largest henequen plantation in Yucatán, was traded for San Lorenzo Aké and several adjoining fincas in Tixkokob *municipio*. How could Ticopó's servants enjoy a sense of security, a working relationship with an absentee landlord, who at any moment might sell, trade, or gamble away his own birthright? Speculators, like the Peón family, bought haciendas on advisement during bust periods and then sold them for a profit when the economy turned around. Surely local models of paternalism must be reexamined in the light of the fluidity of the monocrop economy.[50]

For the planters paternalism not only had to define the peasant's labor as a legitimate return for protection and direction, but also had to ensure a complaint, manageable work force to carry out the daily tasks on the estate. As Eugene Genovese points out, "it [paternalism] grew out of the necessity to discipline and morally justify a system of exploitation . . . wherever paternalism exists, it undermines solidarity among the oppressed by linking them as individuals to their oppressors . . ."[51] The Yucatecan campesinos' definition of their condition had to rationalize their own dependent status in the hacienda community. Yet while the slaves of the American South forged a religion which "taught them to love and value each other, to take a critical view of their masters, and to reject the ideological rationale for their own enslavement," the Yucatecan campesinos, who did not have as intricate a relationship with their white masters, lashed back at the cruel, exploitative system, usually at the closest symbol of authority—the planter's paid hireling, the encargado.[52]

The notion that Yucatecan campesinos meekly accepted their dependent status also deserves revision. It rests on a false premise: that the jornaleros accepted their condition as a fait accompli; that they eagerly accepted what meager morsels of kindness and benevolence the planters tossed their way; and that they could only display a sense of wretched inferiority. This docile, so-called sambo image has been utilized by muckrakers and apologists alike, to reinforce their own diametrically opposed views.[53] For instance, "The average Indian is as submissive as a well whipped hound creeping up after a thrashing to kiss his master's hand . . ."[54] Similarly, "As a rule the Yucatecan Indians are regarded as being meek, humble and not easily stirred to ire and cruelty basing such an opinion on the fact that the most customary punishment among them was a whipping applied with moderation. This kind of punishment did not offend them, if they were informed of the reason why it was meted out to them, nor did they consider it degrading . . ."[55] The first statement was issued by the British journalists Channing Arnold and Frederick J. Tabor Frost, in 1909; the second statement, made by an ex-governor of Yucatán, Santiago Méndez, in 1870, expresses the same sentiment. Méndez, however, would have argued with Arnold and Frost about working conditions on the plantations. In a sense the peasant's docile status in henequen plantation society became a double-edged sword. For outspoken critics of the planter-servant relationship, Indian docility served to confirm white exploitation. For ex-hacendados and erstwhile supporters of the plantation regime, the sambo image repudiated the notion of planter mistreatment and implicitly recognized the mutual obligations of the paternalistic system.

The image of the indolent, docile peasant is a pure fabrication, created to serve the ends of both supporters and critics of the auge economy. In reality the system fostered a large degree of social violence. Planters and political authorities were forced to resort to such repressive mechanisms as bounty hunters, secret police, and the ever-present jefes políticos to contain peasant dissatisfaction. The white ruling class lived in constant fear of large-scale uprisings.

Any instance of hacienda violence, therefore, had to be countered with excessive force by the white elite. The state was careful to isolate instances of upheaval, generally sending an overwhelming number of national guard troops to the trouble spot. As a rule social violence erupted as a reaction to local stimuli. Sometimes a repressive jefe político might engender peasant outrage. In 1910 the celebrated Valladolid uprising, which touched off the Mexican Revolution, was caused by local hatred for a newly appointed jefe político. However, for most henequen workers, the chief focus of dissatisfaction was the administrator of the plantation. A typical incident took place on Hacienda Eknakán, owned by Luisa Hübbe de Molina. In 1909 an encargado cut the wages of four platform drivers who had refused to work on a Sunday, claiming it was their day off. When violence erupted the national guard was sent in to restore order. The captain of the force was forced to withdraw with contusions of the right shoulder. One servant was killed in the uprising and eight were injured. Reinforcements from Mérida had to be rushed in to quell the disturbance. The ruling class refused to countenance large-scale revolts; their fear of a spreading contagion impelled them to limit these sporadic outbreaks before they could spread.[56]

Abuses by overseers were not the only reason for local violence. Often jornaleros felt that punishment meted out did not fit the infraction. On Hacienda Oxcum, near Umán, owned by the prominent henequen exporter Avelino Montes, 110 peones marched from the hacienda to the *palacio municipal* of Umán, to protest the imprisonment of three co-workers. National guard troops were dispatched from Mérida, six kilometers away. Despite the show of force, violence reappeared at Oxcum when 6 servants beat up the personero. The national guard had to be called out again, this time to arrest the 6 offenders.[57]

It is difficult to determine whether violence increased as a function of the growth of the exploitative henequen economy, or whether newspaper coverage of random plantation uprisings improved during the last years of the Porfiriato. For whatever reason, during the period between 1907 and 1911, newspapers were filled with stories of violent disputes between village ejidos and encroaching haciendas, arguments over salary cuts brought on by the decline in the world market price of henequen, and objections raised by peasants who refused to serve in the national guard. These small-scale revolts at first appeared to be of minor significance. Yet their marked increase over the last years of the Porfiriato suggests that social violence in Yucatán became the peasants' principal manner of protest. By 1911 the situation had so degenerated that every day brought new reports of violence, both in the henequen zone and in the southeast. General Curiel, appointed governor by President Díaz in 1911, to stem the rising tide of violence, refused to detain the so-called guilty ones at the risk of provoking a general uprising. A commission reported that "the peasants who have left their work on the hacienda are in short, a threat against security and the public order."[58] During the last years of the Porfiriato, Yucatán witnessed a breakdown of the social control mechanisms of the state: it could no longer isolate the sporadic outbreaks of violence. And while "Viva Madero" may have been heard on various occasions during the fighting, political ideology played a very minor role in sparking local unrest. In nearly every documented case of violence, the reaction was aimed at local authority figures, whether they were a local jefe político (Valladolid, 1910), an hacendado (the Cirerol brothers, Hacienda Catmis, Peto partido, 1910), or a plantation administrator.

Conclusions

The ability of state authorities to restore order to the inflamed countryside by 1912 must be attributed to the repressive mechanisms developed by the plantation society and to the obvious lack of unity among the rural proletariat. While encargados and besieged jefes could no longer contain sporadic outbreaks, federal and state authorities were able to isolate local violence and deter an organized revolt. The same factors which prevented the campesinos from leaving the estate also served to diminish the potential for revolution. The late Porfiriato was characterized by a succession of isolated violent episodes of campesino protest. The products of frustration and limited options, they flared up and died, without long-term consequence except perhaps to scare the local planters and authorities into excessive overreaction and a tightening of control mechanisms which only further isolated the campesinos on the estates. It was this isolation—of the peones from each other on the plantation, the plantations' isolation from potentially meddlesome outsiders, and Yucatán's geographic and cultural distance from the rest of Mexico— which characterized the henequen economy and argued for the harshness of its labor regime. The result was slave-like conditions in Yucatán, at a time when slaveholding was being legally abolished in the Americas.[59] Yucatecan campesinos also lacked a dynamic, charismatic leader, on the order of a Zapata or a Villa, who could effectively organize and channel their frustrations.

Once the brief moment of sustained violence in 1911 had passed, state and federal authorities regained control of the countryside and Yucatán was denied the throes of revolutionary upheaval which spread throughout most of the rest of Mexico. But the repeated instances of sporadic violence should put to rest once and for all the notion that the Yucatecan peasantry blindly accepted their fate during the so-called golden age. On the whole peasants rejected the weak paternalistic ethos presented to them by the white ruling class. Plantation life was a cruel, exploitative system and the peasants demonstrated their widespread dissatisfaction by striking out at the symbols of their oppression. The historical legacy of the Caste War and the devastating demographic and geographical dislocation of traditional peasant society which followed greatly assisted the expanding planter class as it sought to control the peasants and to mobilize their labor. Only fifty years after the bloodiest battles of the Caste War, Yucatán's oligarchy had instituted a thorough system of defense and repression, a system to guarantee against a repeat of that great rebellion.[60] Although random violence continued throughout the last years of the Porfiriato and the early years of the Revolution, the chance for united peasant reaction was lost.

NOTES

1. For a thorough discussion of foreign penetration in Yucatán's economy, see Allen Wells and Gilbert M. Joseph, "Corporate Control of a Monocrop Economy: International Harvester and Yucatán's Henequen Industry during the Porfiriato," *Latin American Research Review* 17, no. 1 (Spring 1982): 69–99.

2. Production statistics from Siegfried Askinazy, *El problema agrario de Yucatán* (Mexico, 1936), 100–101.

3. Throughout this study I use the terms *campesino, peón, jornalero de campo*, and laborer interchangeably. Although many of the workers on the henequen estates were peones tied to the plantation through the institution of debt peonage, others were villagers who hired themselves out on an irregular basis. The result was that a large part of the work force was a rural proletariat tied to the plantation, but a considerable number were still independent actors, or so-called campesinos, who exercised some choice. As the boom years continued, fewer and fewer campesinos maintained their independence from the encroaching estates. Given the general

definition of the term campesino, for the purpose of this study I have used the word to mean henequen worker in a general sense.

4. Alberto García Cantón, *Memorias de un ex-hacendado henequenero* (Mérida, 1965); International Harvester Company, *The Binder Twine Industry* (Chicago, 1912); and Gustavo Molina Font, *La tragedia de Yucatán* (México, 1941).

5. John Kenneth Turner, *Barbarous Mexico* (Austin, 1969); Channing Arnold and Frederick J. Tabor Frost, *An American Egypt* (London, 1909); and Henry Baerlein, *Mexico, Land of Unrest* (London, 1914).

6. Jean Meyer, *Problemas campesinos y revueltas agrarias 1821–1910* (México, 1971); Gastón García Cantú, *El socialismo en México, siglo XIX* (México, 1969); Leticia Reina, *Las rebeliones campesinas en México* (México, 1980); and Miguel Mejía Fernández, *Política agraria en México en el siglo XIX* (México, 1979).

7. Mejía Fernández, p. 71.

8. Moisés González Navarro has recently upgraded the quality of the debate by undertaking a comprehensive review of labor conditions in the peninsula from colonial times to the present. González Navarro's *Raza y tierra: La guerra de castas y el henequen* (México, 1970) delineates the changing roles of the Yucatecan peasant over time. *Raza y tierra* effectively synthesizes several trends during this changeover. It highlights the breakup of village lands, the determination by local authorities to override institutional safeguards of labor freedoms, and local attempts to supplement the local Maya work force with indentured servants from the Caribbean, the Orient, and other parts of Mexico. Yet despite the work's balanced portrayal, the scope of the study allows for only a summary of working conditions in the henequen zone during the Porfiriato. The author dwells on the all-too-familiar sensational accounts, such as President Díaz's trip to Yucatán in 1906, Turner's protestations several years after the dictator's visit, and the celebrated Xcumpich affair, all of which scandalize the benevolent *patrón* image of the Yucatecan planter, specifically indicting the wealthy landowner Audomaro Molina, brother of Governor Olegario Molina. Succumbing to the same temptation which has marred past attempts to understand the sensational subject matter, González Navarro concentrates on the obvious at the expense of a painstaking evaluation of the evidence.

9. These three types were initially distinguished in Tomás Aznar Barbachano, *Las mejoras materiales* (Campeche, 1859) 1: 7.

10. Aznar Barbachano, *Las mejoras;* on payment by token or script, Edwin C. Leslie and A. F. Pradeau, *Henequen Plantation Tokens of the Yucatan Peninsula* (Washington, 1972).

11. Aznar Barbachano, *Las mejoras,* 1: 7.
12. A mecate equals 400 square meters.
13. Antonio Betancourt Pérez, *Revoluciones y crisis en la economía de Yucatán* (Mérida, 1953), 28–31.
14. I am grateful to Lawrence Remmers for sharing with me a draft of the opening chapters of his dissertation, "Henequen, the Caste War, and Economy of Yucatan, 1846–1883: The Roots of Dependence in a Mexican Region," University of California, Los Angeles, 1981.
15. González Navarro, *Raza y tierra,* 60–62.
16. Ibid., 62.
17. *La Unión Yucateca,* 11 Oct. 1882.
18. On the frequency of estate sales, see Allen Wells, "Henequen and Yucatan: An Analysis in Regional Economic Development, 1876–1915," Ph.D. diss. (State University of New York at Stony Brook, 1979), chapter 3.
19. Archivo Notorial del Estado de Yucatán (hereafter cited as ANEY), ed. Tomás Aznar Rivas, vol. 1, book A, 16 Jan. 1909, 16–99; Archivo General del Estado de Yucatán (hereafter cited as AGEY), Ramo del Poder Ejecutivo, "Relación de empleados de Acancéh, Tecoh, Ticul y Tekax," 1899.
20. Friedrich Katz, "Labor Conditions on Haciendas in Porfirian Mexico: Some Trends and Tendencies," *Hispanic American Historical Review* (hereafter cited as *HAHR*) 54, no. 1 (Feb. 1974): 1–49.
21. Keith Hartman, "The Henequen Empire in Yucatan: 1870–1910," master's thesis (University of Iowa, 1966), 156.
22. This phenomenon was not limited to Yucatán alone; Porfirian land policy was a significant catalyst for regional dissatisfaction throughout Mexico.
23. AGEY, Ramo del Poder Ejecutivo.
24. On road fajina abuses, see AGEY, Ramo del Poder Ejecutivo, Sección de Peticiones, 29 Nov. 1886.
25. One Mexican peso equalled one U.S. dollar before 1905. After 1905 the ratio changed to two pesos per dollar.
26. Personal papers of Licenciado Carlos Peniche Escalante, "Papers of Hacienda Yaxnic." For 1905 mention of security agents, *El Peninsular,* 31 March 1905.
27. *La Revista de Mérida,* 13 Feb. 1886; *El Eco del Comercio,* 11 July 1891.
28. Numerous complaints directed at jefes políticos who dragged jornaleros into the national guard fill the Ramo del Poder Ejecutivo of the AGEY. Complaints came both from irate hacendados, who opposed the

depletion of their work force, and from wives and relations of the forced conscripts. On identification papers, see Turner, *Barbarous Mexico,* 12.

29. ANEY, Maximiliano Canto, Cuarto Bimestre, 29 Nov. 1901.

30. *El Eco del Comercio,* 20 March 1902.

31. See Turner, *Barbarous Mexico,* chapter 1.

32. Evelyn Hu-DeHart, "Pacification of the Yaquis in the Late Porfiriato: Development and Implications," *HAHR,* 54, no. 1 (Feb. 1974): 72–93; see also chapter 7 above.

33. *La Revista de Mérida,* 20 June 1900.

34. In defining the Yaquis as slaves I am drawing on a definition developed by Orlando Patterson, "On Slavery and Slave Formation," *New Left Review* 117 (1979): 31–41.

35. Hartman, "The Henequen Empire," 108.

36. *El Imparcial,* 28 July 1911.

37. Malcolm K. Shuman, "The Town Where Luck Fell: The Economics of Life in a Henequen Zone Pueblo," Ph.D. diss. (Tulane University, 1974), 49–51.

38. Fernando Benítez, *Ki: El drama de un pueblo y de una planta* (México, 1956), 51.

39. Ibid., 49.

40. AGEY, Ramo de Justicia, "Cuenta de administración de la finca San José Kuché y su anexa San Francisco correspondiente a un mes corrido de 25 de julio a hoy agosto 25 de 1897."

41. Ibid.

42. Wages varied by task completed, but on the average I would concur with Hartman's figures, "The Henequen Empire," 118.

43. Katz, "Labor Conditions," 1. Katz's figures are taken from *Estadísticas económicas del Porfiriato; Fuerza de trabajo y actividad económica por sectores* (México, 1964), 147–48.

44. AGEY, Ramo del Poder Ejecutivo, "Circular de la Secretaría de Fomento," 25 March 1902.

45. Fernando Arjona, *Breves apuntes sobre la pelagra* (Mérida, 1898).

46. Consider the case of one of Ricardo Molina Hübbe's haciendas: several overseers were killed and eleven people were injured as a direct result of the hacendado's order to lower peón salaries. One hundred national guard troops were brought in to quell the disturbance (*El Imparcial,* 24 Sept. 1909). Further data is available to support the notion that wages of henequen jornaleros were also reduced during the 1890–97 decline in henequen prices; see *El Eco del Comercio,* 8 April 1890.

47. I am grateful to Shubert Peniche Peniche for taking the time to explain the concepts of *chichan* and *no hoch cuenta.*

48. AGEY, Ramo de Justica, "Intestado de José Clotilde Baquéiro," 1899.
49. See Allen Wells, "Family Elites in a Boom and Bust Economy: The Molinas and Peóns of Porfirian Yucatán," *HAHR*, 62, no. 2 (May 1982): 224–53.
50. On the Ticopó swap see ANEY, Patricio Sabido, oficio 17, vol. 16, 4 May 1907, 944–55.
51. Eugene Genovese, *Roll Jordan Roll* (New York, 1972), 4–5.
52. Ibid., 3–7.
53. The sambo thesis was first advanced by Stanley Elkins in *Slavery* (Chicago, 1959), who first compared ante-bellum slave attitudes with those of World War II concentration camp victims.
54. Arnold and Frost, *An American Egypt*, 76.
55. Santiago Méndez, Antonio García Cuevas, Pedro Sánchez de Aguilar, and Francisco Hernández, *Report on the Maya Indians of Yucatan*, ed. and trans. Marshall H. Saville (New York, 1921), 158.
56. *La Revista de Mérida*, 20 Sept. 1909.
57. *La Revista de Mérida*, 5 Sept. 1907; and *El Imparcial*, 6 Sept. 1907.
58. *El Agricultor*, July 1911, 306.
59. Unpublished critique by Gilbert M. Joseph of Allen Wells's paper "Debt Peonage and Mechanisms of Social Control on Yucatán's Henequen Plantations during the Porfiriato," presented at the 1981 meeting of the Southeastern Council of Latin American Studies, Tuscaloosa, Alabama, 16 April 1981.
60. Ibid.

9
La Comarca Lagunera: Work, Protest, and Popular Mobilization in North Central Mexico

William K. Meyers

The revolution which enveloped Mexico after 1910 provided graphic proof of the social tensions generated during the thirty-four years of the so-called *pax Porfiriana*. Popular unrest in the rural areas also demonstrated the acuteness of unrest in the countryside. Nonetheless, after more than sixty years of study, we are still debating the origin and character of popular protest at the local and regional levels. Studies of popular mobilization have tended to focus upon the revolutionary period, while largely neglecting the Porfiriato. Research on discontent during the Díaz regime has generally concentrated upon such topics as mechanisms of social control utilized by authorities to maintain peace; the breakdown of that system with major uprisings such as the Yaqui revolt and the strikes at Cananea, Río Blanco, and Orizaba; or the careers of men who emerged as leaders during the Revolution. But what about the neglected popular classes, the workers and peasants who formed the social basis of the Revolution? What prompted them to revolt in 1910? They were clearly not quiescent prior to this time, but what were the causes, forms, and frequency of their protest and mobilization during the Porfiriato? These questions are critical for our appreciation of the social origins of the Mexican Revolution as well as of the direction, successes, and failures of the popular movement after 1910.[1]

Toward a better understanding of the source and character of popular protest and social mobilization during the Porfiriato, this essay examines the evolution of agrarian unrest in one area: the Laguna region of north central Mexico. Between 1876 and 1910 the region was transformed from barren desert into one of the nation's major agricultural, mining, and industrial zones. In the same period, the area also emerged as a center of peasant radicalism. The Laguna's agricultural workers provided an important source of prerevolutionary discontent, especially between 1900 and 1910. They were also among the first groups to revolt against the Díaz government and subsequently formed a key element in the armies of Madero, Huerta, Villa, and Carranza. Popular protest did not end with the Revolution; throughout the 1920s and early 1930s the Laguna remained the site of widespread agrarian protest. This culminated in 1936 with a general strike and Cárdenas's intervention to nationalize the cotton plantations and settle the agricultural workers on collective farms throughout the region.

Why was this rural population so militant? Was the Laguna's revolutionary movement a spontaneous popular outburst in response to Madero's call to revolt? Or was there an evolutionary pattern indicating a long tradition of protest among the region's agricultural work force against specific local conditions? Moreover, what were the different rural groups involved, and did their pattern of protest and social mobilization change during the Porfiriato?

To answer these questions, this essay first briefly examines the frequency of rural protest in the region and identifies the groups that mobilized, together with the different sources of their discontent and the forms the protest took. The second section places the growth of the rural work force in the general context of the Laguna's economic growth, examining the uniqueness of the region's development as well as the factors which make it a microcosm for un-

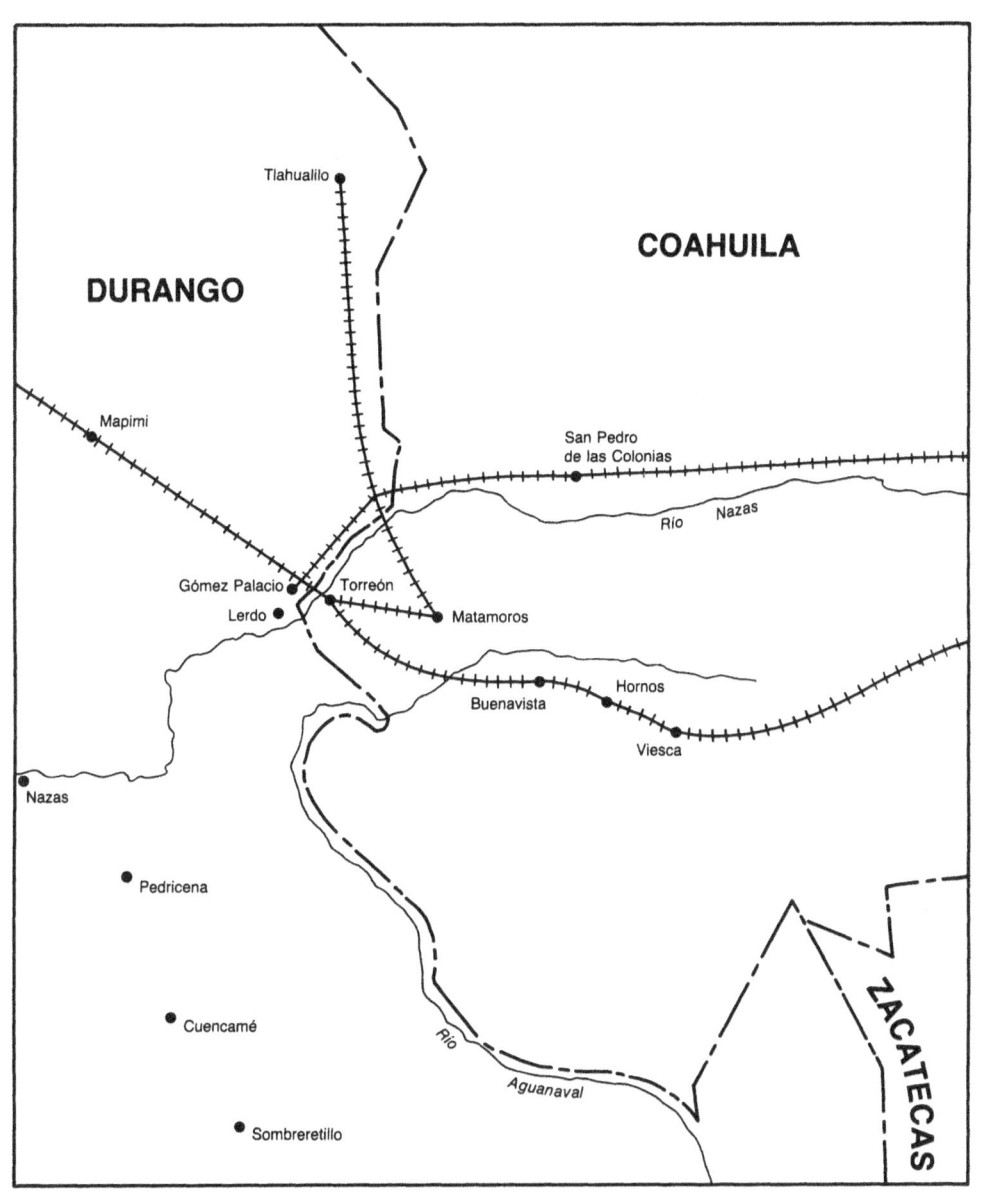

La Comarca Lagunera, 1910

derstanding the broader tensions generated by Mexico's rapid economic growth and social change between 1876 and 1911. Finally, the essay focuses specifically upon the pattern and character which rural protest assumed during this period, tracing its evolution from isolated and sporadic incidents of dissent to a general social rebellion.

Rural Protest: Source and Character

To consider the Porfiriato a time of peace in the Laguna countryside greatly underestimates the dynamic of social change in the region's development. Throughout most of the period, rural unrest appears commonplace. In twenty-three of the thirty-four years between 1876 and 1911, serious incidences of popular discontent and violence disrupted the countryside. This protest came from two groups: small landowners and Indian villagers maintaining a marginal existence in independent communities. These settlements consistently and actively resisted attempts by large landowners to usurp their land and water. Landless agricultural workers constituted the second major source of rural discontent, as they rebelled against the insecurity of their work situation, low wages, high prices of basic foodstuffs, and poor working conditions. While the small landowners' form of protest involved pitched battles against the armed retainers of the large plantations, the landless wageworkers expressed their discontent through a variety of means, including banditry, food riots, demands for higher wages, and armed attacks on landowners.

Significantly, the protests and mobilization of both groups were directly linked to the region's development and yearly economic cycle. The complaints of the smallholders involved specific and long-standing disputes over water and land, but they intensified with the expansion of large-scale agriculture. The protests of the agricultural workers generally resulted from unemployment caused by short water supply, low cotton production, or seasonal fluctuations in labor demand. As the population of landless wageworkers grew, however, the social and political implications of these economic fluctuations and the resultant protest increased. While rural unrest was initially sporadic, with little organization or political consciousness, its potential for igniting a mass revolt increased as the region's development made the population more dependent upon the national and world economic systems and more aware of their position within that larger structure.

The Laguna: Social and Economic Development

An understanding of the interrelation of work, protest, and popular mobilization in the Laguna's development must begin with an overview of the region's dramatic economic and social transformation. Located midway between Mexico City and the United States border, the Laguna is a large alluvial basin of over two thousand square miles, the larger portion of which is located in southwestern Coahuila, with a smaller section in northeastern Durango. When Díaz took office in 1876, the Laguna was underdeveloped and largely uninhabited, known for little more than its location, barren desert, and erratic water supply. Until 1880 the Laguna's real agricultural potential remained untapped because of extreme variations in water and climate as well as because of Mexico's general lack of economic infrastructure and investment capital.

Between 1880 and 1910, however, Porfirian economic policies attracted domestic and foreign capital to the region and transformed it into Mexico's newest and fastest-growing area. Díaz's program of railroad building solved the major problem of transportation and converted the Laguna into the major rail center of north central Mexico. Mining revived along the region's western border, while the central location and rail facilities of Torreón and Gómez Palacio made this zone the most rapidly expanding urban and industrial area in Mexico. The region's diversified economic base conformed to the Porfirian ideal of coordinating Mexico's agricultural and industrial potential to overcome its economic backwardness.

Cotton furnished the key to this phenomenal growth. Through the expansion of irrigation systems, large, highly capitalized commercial estates overcame the factors which had previously limited agricultural development. Between 1880 and 1900, these plantations spread along the floodplain of the Río Nazas, extending fifty miles from the upper river zone, in Durango, to the lower river zone, in Coahila. They absorbed the bulk of investment capital in the region, generated the largest profits, employed the majority of the population, and by 1910, produced most of the cotton grown in Mexico. The rubber-producing shrub *guayule* provided an additional source of agricultural wealth; by 1908 rubber in fact rivaled cotton as the area's most valuable export. The gathering of guayule from large expanses of barren land made previously worthless areas valuable and provided an alternative source of income for agricultural workers and smallholders.

As the basic unit of production, the cotton plantation determined the structure of rural society. As is typical of recently settled frontier areas, social groupings were less bound by traditional social and economic ties than was true of the rest of Mexico. Rather, the Laguna's plantations constituted occupational communities, where social relations reflected the organization for production. The landowning elite was less a traditional landed gentry than a market- and profit-oriented business class. It clung tenaciously to its monopoly over land and water. The only groups that existed in the great social gulf between owners and workers was a small rural managerial class and an urban middle class who served the administrative, commercial, legal, and financial needs of the cotton planters.

Workers formed the largest and most visible element in the social structure. To guarantee a steady and flexible labor force, employers offered the highest wages available in Mexico to unskilled workers. As a result between 1880 and 1910, a mass of landless peasants poured into the Laguna from throughout Mexico, expanding the rural population from less than twenty thousand to over two hundred thousand and creating an industrial labor force of over thirty thousand.[2]

Despite this spectacular growth and great promise, problems arose. Although it was expanding, the economy experienced wild fluctuations as each year's situation depended upon erratic forces outside regional control: the price of local commodities on the world market, the supply of credit, and the availability of sufficient wage labor to plant and harvest the crop. But the most critical and unpredictable variable was water. Two torrential rivers supplied the Laguna's water—the Río Nazas and the smaller Río Aguanaval. The Nazas's course and yearly volume determined both the pattern of settlement and the economic fortune of the region. The wide variations in water supply, coupled with erratic weather conditions, created boom-and-bust cycles that annually affected the health of the agricultural sector and, consequently, the economic life of the entire region.³ The social costs of rapid development, exacerbated by yearly variations in the region's economy, generated the tensions that formed the basis for discontent and conflict among various sectors of the region's population. An examination of the composition and character of the region's smallholders and agricultural working class demonstrates that they bore the brunt of the contradictions and uncertainty inherent in the region's phenomenal growth and prosperity. It also helps explain the subsequent behavior of these groups in the events leading up to the Revolution.

Prior to the arrival of the railroad, in the 1880s, only five major settlements existed outside the large estates: Lerdo, an urban residence for large plantation owners of the upper river zone; Mapimí, the region's oldest mining center; and the free settlements of Cuencamé, San Pedro de las Colonias, and Matamoros de la Laguna. Around Cuencamé, in the upper river zone, a population of Ocuilán Indians and mestizo smallholders farmed small plots to meet their own basic needs and to supply nearby mining communities. In the middle river zone, independent settlers founded the community of Matamoros de la Laguna in 1836 and began cultivating small sections of land between the Río Nazas and the Río Aguanaval. In the center of the lower river zone, the town of San Pedro de las Colonias began in 1869 as a colony of former soldiers of the Republican Army, who opened small cotton *ranchos* along the lower floodplain of the Nazas. Although self-sufficient, these settlements remained small and isolated from state and national affairs throughout the nineteenth century, scarcely providing enough labor to satisfy the demands of their own limited agricultural operations.⁴

Economic development, therefore, depended upon labor migration. The majority of workers arrived landless, unskilled, and entirely dependent on cash wages. First they came to construct the railroads, clear the lands, dig the irrigation canals, and lay out the vast cotton plantations. Many of these migrants eventually became resident workers on these properties. Each hundred hectares of cotton cultivation required eight permanent workers; with estates ranging from five thousand to one hundred thousand hectares in size, resident workers formed a population numbering more than one hundred thousand by 1910.⁵

In addition to this resident work force, the cotton planters depended upon two other sources of labor: temporary workers from within the region and migrant cotton pickers from outside. Each year from mid-summer to late fall, between ten thousand and fifty thousand migrants came to the Laguna to pick the crop. Their total number and their arrival and departure dates depended upon the size of the crop and weather conditions. Plantations relied upon labor agents to attract these workers in the summer, and called in the hacienda guards to move them out in the late fall.

Temporary workers, *trabajadores eventuales*, played a critical role in the region's economy, since cotton cultivation, especially in the Laguna's varying environment, required a large, mobile labor pool for temporary and emergency tasks. To supply this need, landowners sent labor agents to recruit workers from towns such as Matamoros, Hornos, Cuencamé, Nazas, Viesca, and the small railroad stations, which became the collecting point for this temporary labor. Without secure employment, these trabajadores eventuales took whatever jobs were available. Consequently their wages and employment fluctuated unpredictably, along with the region's economic fortunes. During hard times, these workers suffered more than any other labor group. Many migrated while others simply waited, collecting in the small rail towns or on the outskirts of Torreón and Gómez Palacio in hopes of finding work.

As centers of transportation and employment, the small free towns gathered information about work opportunities throughout the area from central Mexico to the United States. These towns became important mustering points for migrant labor and, attracing a diverse population, gained reputations as centers for drinking, gambling, prostitution, and the sale of stolen cotton and guayule. On the whole, while planters depended heavily upon temporary workers, they considered these towns the collecting points for *gente mala*—troublemakers. Significantly, it was in free towns that the political influence of the Mexican Liberal Party of Ricardo Flores Magón first gained strength in the region.[6]

By 1910 the cutting and processing of guayule provided work for eleven thousand laborers, whose employment and wages also fluctuated erratically with the general business climate and the price of rubber. Likewise, for the ten thousand industrial workes of Gómez

Palacio and Torreón, the close interrelationship between agricultural and industrial sectors meant that fluctuations in one influenced employment in the other. Since the majority of industrial workers originally came from the agricultural sector, they frequently returned to the countryside during periods of unemployment, further increasing the large pool of landless labor.[7]

The Evolution of Protest: Smallholders

To understand the social forces which transformed the Laguna into a major center of revolution after 1910, it is important to examine the tradition and form of protest which evolved among both smallholders and agricultural wage laborers.

A strong tradition of armed protest and rural violence is ingrained in the history of the region. From the seventeenth century, large hacendados and free pueblos relied upon arms to protect themselves against periodic Indian raids and to drive nomadic tribes from the zone. From the mid-nineteenth century, large landowners' claims to land and water conflicted with those of would-be colonists and Indian villagers. As a result, a frontier individualism developed in which armed conflict provided the means of expressing discontent, settling disputes, and obtaining justice.

The battles between large landowners and landless settlers constitute the earliest cases of rural groups taking up arms to defend their rights. Once rid of nomadic Indians, landowners actively attempted to prevent or remove any independent settlements within their vast domains. In 1862 the smallholders of Matamoros resisted an armed attempt by the local landowner to expel them, establishing a proud tradition of armed resistance to protect their lands. While stopping short of violence, in 1869 the settlers of San Pedro also threatened to resist by force any attempt by the landowner to drive them from their recently established colony. In short, to survive and to preserve their right to live on and work small plots of land, these early settlers fought not only against the elements and nomadic tribes, but also against the landowners.[8]

With the area's rapid development, in the late 1870s, these armed confrontations gained increased significance. Violence flared again in the countryside in 1880 and 1881, when colonists of San Pedro armed several hundred workers and raided the large cotton plantations in the upper river area around Lerdo, destroying their dams to protest the upper river planters' usurpation of water rights from residents of the lower river zone.[9] In 1888 settlers from San Pedro again threatened to attack the upper river zone of Durango. This time, however, Díaz intervened to prevent widespread violence by sending extra troops to the region and placing the issue of water distribution under federal control.[10] The president was not the only one concerned by intraregional warfare. By this time the range of rural violence had caused many landowners to have second thoughts about their private armies of peons. As the Laguna's population grew, the increased potential of rural violence and banditry became an important issue at both the local and national level. Therefore by 1890 private armies had disappeared, but both smallholders and large landowners threatened to revive their private forces whenever they felt wronged by one another or dissatisfied with the government's handling of their claims.

Whether in passive or active resistance, the smallholders of Matamoros posed an independent threat to the stranglehold which large plantations exerted over the region's economy and politics. Given the influence of cotton growers in the Porfirian political system, smallholders such as those at Matamoros had no power at the state or federal level. They therefore considered arms the only effective means of defending their land and water rights. With the growth of Torreón and neighboring plantations, Matamoros lost both water and prosperity. The Díaz government consistently ignored the complaints of the Matamoros colonists, and the area became a center of anti-Díaz sentiment. The hostility was mutual. The Laguna's planters resented Matamoros's existence and complained of the obstreperousness and independence of its population, charging that the town provided refuge for bandits and an exchange point for stolen cotton, guayule, and arms.

A similar situation existed in the upper river zone of Durango. Here smallholders and indigenous communities also established a tradition of protest and armed resistance against the expansion of large plantations. Unlike the lower river area, however, the upper zone contained a number of Indian *pueblos* that preserved their traditional rights to the land and continued to eke out an existence on the region's arid soil. As cotton and guayule interests expanded in the zone, conflicts developed between landowners and the Indian pueblos. From 1884 the free pueblos and smallholders of the upper river zone complained that Díaz's land policies favored large planters while ignoring the claims of legitimate landholders. Predictably the Porfirian authorities did nothing about these complaints. When smallholders took matters into their own hands and reoccupied disputed lands, they were forcibly expelled by federal troops.[11] In 1897 the municipal government of Nazas complained to the federal government of land seizures by the enormous Santa Catalina estate. With tensions building and an armed conflict in the making, the state governor again sent troops, which protected the Santa Catalina workers while they fenced the disputed land into the large hacienda.[12]

Just to the south, in the Cuencamé district, the Ocuilán Indians first complained to the government in 1890 about seizures of their traditional lands by the Hacienda de Sombreretillo. In the next ten years, conflict between the local population and the hacienda reached such a degree that in 1901 Governor Fernández, of Durango, intervened and appointed an arbitrator. To no one's surprise, the arbitrator supported the hacienda's claims, despite the fact that the pueblos held legal titles from the colonial era. Attempting to avoid further trouble, Governor Fernández also asked General Bernardo Reyes to station a garrison of troops in the Laguna to guard against future uprisings. But the disputes continued between smallholders and large landowners. In 1905 the pueblos around Cuencamé actively resisted further land grabs by the hacienda. Again the government sent in troops, broke the protest, and consigned its leader, Calixto Contreras, to the army.[13]

There are several significant aspects of these conflicts. First, such protests occurred consistently throughout the Porfiriato and contributed to a level of tension and hatred which divided the countryside and greatly fueled rural unrest. They represented a very clear dissatisfaction with Díaz's consistent support of the large landowners. The struggles between these two groups actively occupied the consciousness of the Laguna's population and underscored the situation of powerful versus powerless. But the issue was not simply rich against poor; it involved rights, traditional and acquired, which provided the ability to work and remain free. Smallholders and villagers who lost their lands had no alternative except to seek employment as part of the pool of landless wageworkers. As one hacienda administrator commented, "men such as these were persecuted viciously to the slow and brooding growth of vindictive hate that at last burst forth in the revolution."[14] By no coincidence, after 1905 the populations of Cuencamé, Nazas, Matamoros, and San Pedro supported the PLM and Anti-Reelectionist movements. These areas also became major centers of revolutionary activity and recruitment. Prominent among early leaders of the Revolution were Calixto Contreras, leading the Ocuilán Indians, and Sixto Ugalde, a smallholder who mobilized discontent in the Matamoros area.

The Evolution of Protest:
Landless Agricultural Wageworkers

Landless wageworkers provided the major source of popular discontent in the agricultural sector, generating the most widespread and consistent protest. Their complaints differed from those of the small landholders, which generally focused on a specific incident and remained isolated from the struggles of other free pueblos battling similar problems. The landless agricultural work force fought to gain a livelihood and improve its material circumstance, directing its protests toward a variety of demands concerning employment, wages, food costs, housing, working conditions, and eventually, the right to organize and strike.

Over time the discontent of landless agricultural workers expressed itself in everything from social banditry to food riots, organized strikes, and ultimately open revolt. All workers shared a common vulnerability to annual fluctuations in employment and food supply. After 1900 changes in migration and the availability of jobs in the southwestern United States also influenced the work situation for agricultural workers. Out of these fluctuations came the incidents of protest and social mobilization which punctuated the Laguna's history throughout the Porfiriato and which eventually coalesced in the political movement which overthrew Díaz and shaped the subsequent history of the region.

In the 1880s landowners became increasingly concerned with rural unrest and especially banditry. In the years between 1880 and

1884, low water, short crops, and high unemployment produced a dramatic increase in bandit activities. Planters realized the link between hard times and banditry, but they were unable to do anything about it, for a number of reasons. Given the general popular contempt for the federal army, *rurales,* and hacienda guards, banditry existed as a popularly legitimate, if dangerous, occupation. It took a variety of forms, ranging from small-scale theft of cotton and guayule by resident workers to organized bandit gangs operating in the countryside. Although the Laguna is flat and barren, surrounding mountains provided a nearby refuge for bandits. In addition, the size and isolation of the plantations made their stores and supplies an easy mark. Small bandit groups, operating from the hills on horseback, could arm and supply themselves, retreating into the hills before federal troops could mobilize. Given the size of the work force, agricultural workers could alternate employment as pickers in the fall with banditry in the winter. It was also possible to work in the upper river zone and raid in the lower. Moreover, hacienda guards, rurales, and the federal army proved reluctant to pursue bandits into the mountains. To reduce tensions and keep arms out of the hands of workers, planters adopted a policy of disbanding their private armies, limiting the amount of arms on hand, and relying on carefully chosen guards to protect property and keep order.

Despite the planters' efforts, major incidents of popular violence and protest occurred in eight of the twelve years between 1888 and 1900, again the product of scarce water, prolonged drought, and low cotton production. During such times the contradictions inherent in the region's development became so acute that the standard mechanisms of social control failed to maintain peace. Lacking work, money, food, organization, and a well-developed political consciousness, the landless agricultural workers simply endured or struck out violently. In the years 1888, 1890–1894 and 1898–1900, violence erupted repeatedly, bringing the countryside to the edge of social revolt and instilling the fear among the propertied class of a large and generalized popular uprising.[15]

The response of the landowners provides a clear indicator of the level of these tensions. In this period planters repeatedly complained of troublemakers agitating among the workers, stealing cotton and horses, slaughtering cattle and goats, and threatening administrators. Plantation owners responded to such outrages by increasing guards and spies on their properties, demanding tougher enforcement measures by local officials, and requesting additional federal troops. It was during the rise of bandit activity and unrest of 1888–90 that General Bernardo Reyes sent an extra squad of cavalry to the region to provide security for rural properties.[16] Nonetheless, planters complained that local officials could no longer guarantee their interests and had abandoned them to the mercy of the troublemakers.

The period between 1891 and 1893 was the worst for water in the region's history; the popular response to the agricultural crisis produced increasingly militant forms of unrest that threatened the region's entire social and political fabric. In the countryside, unemployment, popular unrest, banditry, and violence rose dramatically. Repressive measures by planters and government officials did not relieve the situation, as hungry mobs attacked grain shipments and warehouses in rural areas and began to move on the cities. In 1891, only three years after its founding, Torreón experienced a major food riot. As men, women, and children massed in the streets demanding food and work, local authorities placed guards around Torreón, Lerdo, and San Pedro to prevent more unemployed from entering. The specter of mass rebellion led local officials further to increase the military force, to crack down on so-called vagrants, and finally, to initiate a public works program to decrease popular distress. These measures only partly reduced tensions, and urban residents continued to live with the terrifying vision of unemployed mobs taking over the cities.[17]

The popular riots of 1891 frightened authorities and alerted them to the importance of a quick response to unemployment crises. When 1893 produced another year of short water, government forces immediately moved unemployed workers out of the region and clamped down on the countryside. Nevertheless, banditry again increased, and planters became aware of the suffering and smoldering resentment of the workers. Spies also reported secret meetings among workers, in which they insulted the landowners and sang songs glorifying the exploits of local bandits.[18]

In years of steady water supply and general prosperity, planters managed to recoup losses and pay off loans, but the situation of the region's agricultural workers did not improve. With no savings, dependent on a small daily wage, and employed by planters who rarely lent money, workers faced an additional problem: the supply and price of corn, their basic foodstuff. Given its monocrop economy, the Laguna never produced enough food to feed its population; planters depended largely on corn imports from the southwestern U.S. to avoid shortages and food riots. In years of drought, as Mexico's corn production declined further, corn imports assumed an even more critical importance. In addition, with Mexico's currency based on the silver standard, the decline in world silver prices and currency devaluations after 1893 drove up the price of all imports, including corn. This proved especially harmful for the working class. During this period, workers' salaries remained fixed or declined as planters took advantage of the labor surplus produced by the economic downturn to reduce wages. As a result, the shortage and high price of corn emerged as an additional source of protest for rural workers. Planters blamed corn shortages for increased protests and robberies in 1893, 1894, and 1895.[19] In an effort to ease the problem, in 1896 the federal government reduced the tariff on imported corn and planters purchased additional stores of corn from the U.S. to relieve popular discontent.[20] Still, corn prices continued to rise while the workers' prospect of purchasing sufficient food for winter continued to depend upon factors outside their control.

While 1897 proved to be a peaceful year, rural violence flared up again in 1898 and 1899. In 1899 there were major bandit uprisings in the lower river zone, with frequent attacks on plantations. One administrator blamed the increase in rural violence on the proliferation of arms among the troublemakers. "We are in the hands of so many bad people, and almost totally abandoned to our own resistance because the authorities do not respond as they should, in matters as important as giving security, not only to people but also to private interests. Here [in the Laguna], the most wretched peon carries his pistol without anyone saying even half a word, and it would be very suitable that the government issue orders that no one carry arms except those who can provide security for their behavior."[21]

The century closed with another major food shortage in 1899.

The next ten years would witness a further increase in the region's population and periodic crises contributing to a further deterioration of working-class living conditions, with unrest and discontent on the part of both smallholders and wage laborers increasing dramatically in frequency and intensity.

Fortunately for cotton planters and the Díaz government, sufficient water and above average cotton crops between 1901 and 1904 reduced unemployment and eased social tensions enough to reestablish the veneer of peace in the countryside. However, the availability of work in the region no longer depended solely upon water and climate. By this time the Laguna had become a major mustering point for Mexican labor, and the movement of migrant workers to and from the U.S. directly affected the employment situation in the countryside and contributed to the development of worker consciousness and political movements. In years of low water, planters either encouraged or actively moved workers northward to find jobs in the U.S. During times of labor shortages, of course, the same planters demanded that federal and state officials prevent workers from leaving the Laguna and banned outside agents from recruiting workers in the zone. In order to keep wages low, planters also reaffirmed their informal agreements not to compete among themselves for workers in times of high labor demand.[22]

Attitude posed another problem. By 1904 planters were complaining of laborers' belligerence, demands, and unwillingness to work, particularly among those with experience in the U.S. or along the border. Clearly the accumulated consciousness of fifteen years of hardship and protest combined with exposure to new experiences and ideas to make agricultural workes more aware of their condition. This mounting social awareness and their continued vulnerability to economic cycles proved to be the beginning of an increasingly political consciousness among workers.

Landowners sensed the workers' changing attitude. As one planter stated in 1905, "In the last five years everything has changed with regard to workers in the Laguna. Before then, the peon was content with his reed hut and with 32 centavos per day. Today he demands a house of adobe and a salary of two or three times more. All the haciendas are now forced to construct new housing for workers and if not, we will not be able to secure good working people."[23]

Even though 1906 brought a good flow of water and a healthy crop, sporadic uprisings of workers occurred on haciendas in the lower and middle river zones. A planter in the lower river area complained of growing unrest among the workers and increasing bandit raids. Although social tensions remained high, there were no reports of attempts to spark a general rebellion, and the planter concluded that while the situation was serious, it still had not reached "alarming proportions."[24]

Planters remained uneasy, nonetheless, and charged that local authorities were unable to enforce order and that workers were leaving their jobs without paying their debts. Landowners were also troubled by the activity of labor agitators among the work force, who were implanting radical ideas. A principal culprit was the Mexican Liberal Party (PLM) and its newspaper, *Regeneración*.[25] These tensions increased significantly after 1906 with PLM activity in the strikes in Cananea (Sonora), Río Blanco (Veracruz), and San Luis Potosí. In addition to these more prominent strikes, labor agitation and wildcat strikes occurred in various mining and industrial centers throughout the north during this period.

In September 1906, members of the PLM staged an uprising in the town of Jiménez, in eastern Coahuila, seizing the plaza, cutting the telephone lines, sacking the treasury, and opening the jail before retreating from federal troops. Other PLM raids occurred in eastern Coahuila. Although the Laguna experienced no serious uprisings, the Jiménez raid had significant psychological impact on the region's propertied classes. Armed troops patrolled the streets as the population of Torreón and other towns braced for a mass uprising from the countryside. On the plantations, administrators noted an "undercurrent of excitement" among the workers. Given the popular discontent of the previous spring, planters reacted in their usual manner by increasing spies among the workers and raising the number of guards on their properties.[26]

Then came the economic downturn provoked by the crisis of 1907. In early 1907 a financial panic struck Wall Street, bringing about a monetary crisis and an economic recession felt in commercial and financial circles throughout the U.S. and Europe. By July the crisis reached the Laguna as interest rates rose, money and credit tightened, and Mexican laborers deported from the U.S. flooded the region, searching for employment. In the midst of these problems, water failed to appear in the Río Nazas. Faced with a disastrous agricultural season, landowners had no access to credit; the majority of the population lacked work and could not feed itself. As wages dropped, work stopped, and prices soared, workers in the countryside suffered increasingly severe conditions and the Laguna entered another period of heightened social conflict. As one administrator reported, "corn prices have risen in an astonishing manner, and conditions are very bad; the lower class is resorting to violence for food."[27]

Although landowners initially welcomed the downturn as a chance to decrease wages and discipline an increasingly independent and recalcitrant working population, the crisis soon produced a situation too severe for discipline to be effective. As plantations reduced employment to a minimum and drove squatters or migrants from their lands, masses of unemployed and suffering workers collected in the towns, merging with large groups of unemployed mining and industrial workers. Overcrowding and drought worsened the already precarious situation in the towns and caused alarm among city residents. As the streets and parks filled with workers, authorities forcibly "encouraged" workers to migrate northward. In response to the recession, however, the U.S. increased the number of border guards, deported thousands of Mexican workers, and enforced its immigration laws more strictly.[28] Consequently workers arrived in the Laguna as quickly as they were shipped out. The severity of the crisis is reflected in the comment of a Torreón merchant who preferred deported workers over local unemployed, since "stranded peons have more money than Torreón's poor and appear much better off than the working people stationed here."[29] Confronted by a worsening situation, state and federal authorities stepped up the removal of both unemployed and newly repatriated workers to other areas in Mexico.

From mid-1907, as workers reacted to their situation, reports of violence increased dramatically. Newspaper headlines described riots of hacienda workers, fighting in the working-class sections of towns, and cases of police retaliation. As rural agitation increased, bandit groups became bold enough to openly engage local police forces in battle. Although authorities increased rural police, in January 1908 the newspapers reported that bandit activity remained serious.[30]

As the year progressed, attacks on hacienda authorities increased. Peons from the Hacienda de Nazareño assaulted its owner, who then requested soldiers from Torreón. Arriving on a special train, they suppressed the uprising while workers shouted "death to the Spaniards."[31] Commenting on the increase in regional warfare, the *Mexican Herald* explained that "for the last year there have always been hungry men in the states of Coahuila and Durango. From these hungry hordes are recruited the bandit gangs of Durango and once hearing the call of the wild they are bandit gangs in every sense, but most generally when they hear that call they are hungry."[32]

As the nearby hills provided an accessible refuge for bandits, Gómez Palacio suffered in particular from robberies. Together merchants and other residents financed a private mounted police force to patrol the city at night, hoping to "rid the city and neighborhood of the element that has caused the death of several men and looted a number of places in the last few weeks . . . civil authorities are giving special instructions to keep watch on this class of people."[33]

In contrast to lower-class discontent during the previous recession, the 1907 incidents assumed a distinctly political tone. The ensuing politicization and popular mobilization between 1907 and 1910 combined with the tradition of protest to accentuate the contradictions in the countryside. The Mexican Liberal Party helped politicize the workers, protesting the miserable situation of wage-workers in agriculture and mining, while denouncing the influence of foreign interests in Mexico. As in 1906, Laguna planters noted with alarm the PLM influence and complained about the circulation of *Regeneración* and the presence of so-called agitators in the camps of unemployed workers. In addition of PLM activity, experience in the U.S. heightened the social and political awareness of the working class, providing them with exposure to various forms of labor organization and agitation, as well as to anarchist and socialist ideas. This political consciousness and antielite feeling intensified with the insecure food and employment situation and Díaz's repression of strikes in 1907 and 1908. For many workers this repression confirmed PLM charges of the favored position which foreigners and monied interests occupied in Mexico and underscored the government's disregard for labor's demands.

Responding to this situation, the Mexican Liberal Party also appealed to the workers to rebel against their employers. In June 1908 a PLM editorial denounced peaceful strikes and Díaz's methods, ending with the following proclamation: "Passive resistance must be substituted by a revolutionary action. Arms, instead of being crossed, must handle a weapon. If any blood is to be shed, let it be in the struggle. Your masters need examples, by breaking their machinery to pieces, causing their mines to cave in, burning their plantations. Laborers, arm yourselves without delay as revolution will soon break out."[34] A week later reports circulated throughout northern Mexico that an armed group called the "Mexican Cotton Pickers" planned an attack in Coahuila from strongholds in Texas. On 24 June the *jefe político* of Viesca received a coded telegram from Coahuila's Governor Cárdenas, warning of a supposed imminent popular uprising in the Laguna. With vast numbers of unemployed workers in the countryside, authorities increased the police force and alerted federal soldiers.[35]

At dawn on 25 June, an armed band of between forty and eighty men attacked Viesca. Shouting "long live the Mexican Liberal Party," they robbed the branch office of the Banco de Nuevo León, the post office, and the express office, attacked police, broke open the jail, and released the prisoners. The battle with local police caused seven deaths. Before fleeing the raiders cut wires, leaving the town without outside communication, and burned railroad bridges to prevent pursuit by rail. They pillaged nearby ranches and then, reportedly, set out to attack Matamoros. However, pursuit by federal, state, and local forces from Torreón and San Pedro forced the group to split into two bands and retreat toward the mountains. Eventually they divided into twos and threes and made a "desperate break for safety in a country which lends iteself to all the ruses and tricks of irregular bands." Local troops failed to locate the rebels and within a week over ten thousand troops from Saltillo and Mexico City joined the chase. By that time, however, the raiders had reportedly slipped out of the mountains and "returned to their homes, again taking up their work as if nothing had happened."[36]

Stunned government officials initially said nothing, and newspapers maintained a significant silence. Eventually the government reported the raid, but insisted that it had no political significance and should be blamed on "hunger and crop failures." Officials claimed that the uprising began bacause "many men have been out of employment for months due to the shutting down of so many mines and industrial plants, and the widespread want caused by the shortage of beans and corn crops of last season."[37]

The reaction in Torreón to the Viesca raid indicates the degree of social tension generated by the crisis of 1907. At first city authorities feared that raiders planned to ransack Torreón and so called out armed volunteers to guard the city. Consular agents reported that "Torreón was turned into an armed city, being ready to resist attacks on banks and stores. The tops of many business houses and banks are veritable fortresses and bristling with rifles. Thirty-five Americans occupied the roofs of the banks and nearly every man on the street was armed."[38] Two days after the raid, a reporter from the *Mexican Herald* arrived in Torreón and found that "everything was in a state of great excitement. Even the most conservative men had temporarily lost their heads." According to rumors, a heavily armed force was ready to attack the city.[39] Two days later federal troops arrived in Torreón and "the city remained outwardly calm but there is an undercurrent of excitement such as the city has not known since the Jiménez uprising of September 1906." Most landowners left their plantations and moved to the city. Interestingly the two landowners whose properties bordered Matamoros and Cuencamé chartered a special train and fled to Mexico City.[40]

For the Laguna's residents, the Viesca raid provided a clear example of the expanding protest and social mobilization of the agricultural workers. According to the *Mexican Herald*, "the alarm of the people [was] founded upon the knowledge unexpressed in words or definite shape, of the distress among the lower classes." The newspaper also reported a general recognition among propertied interests that "the feeling of the lower classes of Coahuila was never stronger against law and order than at present," and that lower-class discontent had never before taken so coherent a form.[41]

Predictably each of the region's political factions had a different explanation for the Viesca raid. Evaristo Madero, Francisco's grandfather, attributed the motive of the raid to "hunger and poverty stemming from the present financial crisis," but stated that "the revolutionary political activities of the Flores Magón brothers clearly have contributed to this unrest." In contrast, the governor of Coahuila attributed the raid to "men occupying high social positions that head the movement," obviously a veiled reference to Francisco I. Madero's political activity.[42]

Despite the government's disclaimers, the Viesca raid had strong political implications, and the Mexican Liberal Party immediately took credit for it, as well as for an attack on Las Vacas, Coahuila. The government continued to deny the political nature of the outbreak, but popular opinion held with the PLM version. The American consul, Carothers, reported that "I am convinced the raid was of a political nature, had the sympathies of the common people, represents an attempt to precipitate a general disturbance, and was frustrated on account of the government being advised in time to stop it."[43] U.S. sources concluded that "it is evident that there is something more serious than a band of robbers at the bottom of it." The *Mexican Herald,* summing up the situation, expressed a similar opinion: "It is ironic that only a small body of men had frightened to its wits' end half the country."[44]

The Viesca raid clearly startled everyone in the Laguna, and the agricultural working class took note of a band of workers causing such a scare among the region's privileged classes. The PLM continued to claim credit for the raid, which demonstrated to workers their power to strike out against continued repression and exploitation.

Politicization and Revolution

While cotton production increased and incidents of protest decreased in late 1908 and early 1909, the political situation and interclass tensions continued to intensify. Not only did the PLM continue to agitate and recruit among rural workers, but the political campaign of native son Francisco I. Madero also helped politicize the rural sector. From 1904 Madero actively campaigned against the Díaz machine in Coahuila. While never appealing directly to the popular classes for support, he established a modest reputation as a man of the people, a popular and paternal figure among the workers of his own lower river plantation. However, neither his reputation for providing better housing, schooling, and medical care for his resident workers, nor his political activity pleased his fellow landowners. In 1905, in fact, the combination of political and popular unrest led several newspapers to dismiss Madero as "a nut who, with the support of his peasants, embolden[s himself] in a few of the small towns in the Laguna."[45] After the 1908 Viesca raid, Madero's increasing political activity led many people to warn him that he was tampering with a volatile situation. But this did not stop Madero. In mid-1909 the Anti-Reelectionist movement began actively to organize political clubs and to recruit in towns throughout the Laguna. Madero also directly subsidized several newspapers to further publicize his cause.[46]

Slowly Madero's campaign attracted popular attention. By July 1909, when he spoke to a rally in Torreón, over one thousand people attended.[47] While still addressing his campaign to urban groups, the stirring of popular support alerted many planters to the danger that Madero's campaign could ignite discontent in the countryside. Shortly after his tour through the Laguna, both Madero's father and grandfather urged him to "give up his political dabblings," stating that "you are far from knowing the country in which you live."[48] Disregarding such advice, Madero called a secret meeting of supporters in Torreón, in late 1909, in which he proposed that "we begin a general struggle, ready to repel arms with arms."[49]

Shortly thereafter, the Anti-Reelectionists took their campaign to the rural workers of the Laguna, taking advantage of potential support generated by rural discontent and the season of slack work. This was a new level of recruitment and organization for them. Madero's attempt to recruit support among rural workers enraged his fellow planters, as manifested in the following editorial: "Is Madero a saviour? No, Madero is a crazy millionaire, enriched through the sweat of various generations of workers who have given up their health and their lives, bent over the hot soil of the Laguna picking cotton."[50]

For most landowners in 1910, however, the real possibility of Madero gaining widespread support in the countryside seemed small. As Madero's campaign continued and the summer progressed, most landowners assumed that it would be a good year for cotton but a bad year for Madero. With everyone involved in the harvest, the circumstances of Madero's arrest, Díaz's reelection, and Madero's escape to the United States failed to spark any protest from rural workers. As work picked up in the fall, planters looked forward to an extended picking season and an end to the type of political and popular agitation which had constantly disturbed the region's peace since 1908. When Madero issued his call to revolt for 20 November, most planters considered the countryside at peace.

The events of the next six months proved the planters wrong. An appreciation of the interrelation of work, protest, and social mobilization is critical for an understanding of the popular revolt which engulfed the Laguna. The events are clear: on 20 November a group estimated at between forty and eighty men attacked Gómez Palacio in response to Madero's call for armed revolt. Led by a coalition of Anti-Reelectionist and PLM veterans, the rebels battled federal troops for several hours before fleeing into the Durango hills. The government declared the uprising a failure, even though it had neither defeated nor captured any of the raiders. But the planned rebellion had not succeeded; no popular uprisings followed the attack and no towns fell to the raiders.

While not an apparent success, the Gómez Palacio raid marked the official beginning of the Mexican Revolution in the Laguna and ultimately provided the spark which ignited popular discontent in the countryside. Six months later a popular army numbering between five thousand and seven thousand marched into Torreón, after defeating the federal army. The popular movement had triumphed, placing the Laguna in the hands of an armed coalition of agricultural workers, smallholders, miners, and Indians. Their revolt constituted the first mass uprising in the Laguna and an early vision of the course of events that would follow.[51]

The mobilization of the region's agricultural workers between November and May unified the different groups and forms of protest which had characterized popular discontent for the previous thirty-four years. Smallholder resentment flared in several areas. In addition to the Gómez Palacio raid, similar uprisings occurred in Cuencamé and Matamoros, and they became centers of rebel activity for the remainder of the Revolution. After each attack, the raiders retreated into the hills, broke into smaller groups to avoid federal pursuit, and adopted the familiar bandit tactics of the region. Throughout

December and January, rebel groups avoided battles with government troops, while attacking outlying ranches in small groups to steal arms and supplies, recruiting support among the work force, and retreating back into the hills.

The Gómez Palacio raid startled the Laguna's planters, and they noted a great deal of excitement among their workers. However, the landowners were accustomed to bandit activity and expected the federal army to suppress it. By early December planters considered the problem over and claimed that total tranquility reigned in the zone. In late December their reports noted that while the so-called bandits still remained active, "they posed no larger threat and only managed to keep the federal army occupied."[52] In early January an administrator stated that "complete tranquility reigns except for a reported group around Matamoros which are not revolutionaries but simple bandits who are taking advantage of the circumstances to rob."[53] In late January a planter acknowledged that the bandit activities in the upper river area were the work of "the same group which staged the Gómez Palacio raid."[54]

As unrest continued, however, planters realized the increasing complexity of the situation. From the beginning local accounts had pointed out the rebels' overwhelming support among the people in the countryside. Furthermore, in the tradition of social banditry, the more the rebels evaded and frustrated the government troops, the more support they gained. As the cotton pick ended and the plantations began to reduce their work forces, the rebellion offered an ever-larger number of workers an alternative source of activity and income for the winter. Consequently, as the revolt continued, new groups and popular leaders appeared, promising agricultural workers "certain hours of looting, future large increases in wages, apportionment of lands."[55] The federal army proved unable to counter the tactics of these various small groups and was unwilling to pursue the rebels into the hills. In short, by January the rural situation had deteriorated so much that the government censored reports of rebel attacks and began rounding up unemployed workers in the countryside and imprisoning them in camps in Torreón.[56]

Despite this repression, the rebels' strength continued to grow and their attacks grew bolder. In February between forty and fifty bands, composed of more than two thousand rebels, began a general offensive, raiding plantations and attacking small towns. With rebel activity disrupting rail communication, plantations began to shut down. As unemployment rose, rebel recruitment increased through March and April. Significantly rebel activity remained strongest in the Matamoros and Cuencamé areas, which, as the British consul noted, were rife with small bands that "controlled no territory and set up no governments." He also doubted "if more than 10% of the insurrectos have any definite object in view; they are simply having a good time at the expense of those who were formerly their masters." He concluded that "they are independent, and owing no central authority accounts for the very different way in which they have behaved."[57] Other reports noted the independence of the various groups, although they also reported that the rebels behaved well toward civilians and obeyed their leaders.

Operating independently these groups established virtual control of the countryside by early April, moving onto plantations in broad daylight to recruit from the resident work force and to seek out the administrators and local authorities. Such tactics quickly convinced the remaining plantation staffs and government officials to flee to the cities for protection.

Once in control of the rural areas, the insurgent groups began their march on the region's towns. By the end of April, they had captured Matamoros, Viesca, San Pedro, Lerdo, Mapimí, Nazas, and Cuencamé. In early May the Maderista leadership managed to unite the various groups for a drive on Torreón. On 12 May between five thousand and seven thousand *insurrectos* surrounded Torreón; they occupied the city two days later, after federal troops fled in the night. The countryside had triumphed over the city, and the incidents which followed the capture of Torreón dramatize the social and economic discontent contained within the region's popular movement. After the occupation, a riot broke out within the city. Joined by a city mob estimated at ten thousand, the rebel troops looted the town and massacred over two hundred of its Chinese inhabitants. The rampage stopped with the arrival of Emilio Madero, Francisco's brother, who took charge of the situation by declaring martial law, with the penalty of death for further looting and killing. He also ordered the return of stolen property within twenty-four hours. By evening armed peons patrolled the streets and the city remained quiet. The next day the return of stolen goods began. The Laguna was now in the hands of its rural work force; ten days later Díaz resigned. Six months earlier, neither event would have seemed possible.[58]

But even with a Madero victory, the problem of work, protest, and popular mobilization did not disappear. Emilio Madero immediately confronted the difficult problems of restoring rail traffic, obtaining food and fuel for the population, and returning planters and workers to the fields to generate employment and produce the crop. Unemployment and hunger, which had previously aided the Maderista cause, now threatened it. To put the rebels back to work, Madero faced yet another problem: in order to pacify the popular movement which had just brought victory, he had to confront the issues which had initially mobilized the workers.

None of these problems proved easy to solve. Planters were skeptical of the Maderistas' ability to control these armed peons, while the workers did not want to return to the same conditions that had previously existed in the countryside. Through promises and demobilization, Madero returned workers to the plantations, but planters complained of increased labor agitation, charging that many peons did not return to the fields to work but to spread discontent and agitate for increased pay and shorter hours.[59] By June the Maderistas' popular coalition began to disintegrate. A wave of strikes swept through the region as workers demanded higher wages, shorter hours, better housing, the right to strike, and distribution of land. Planters around Cuencamé complained of workers seizing land and protested that the Maderista military leader in the zone refused to prevent land occupations. That leader was Calixto Contreras.

To compound the rural problem, the Laguna again faced a water shortage. As the summer wore on and the drought continued, it became clear that unemployment, food shortages, and popular unrest would again pose major problems. As early as June, bandit activity once again appeared in the countryside, and reports stated that many of these men were recently discharged Maderistas. To counter this threat, Madero had to pit recent comrades-in-arms against one another in battle. Rather than *Viva Madero,* the cry to revolt was now *Viva Magón*. In Durango and Coahuila the Magonistas reportedly offered recruits five pesos per day and the promise of twenty acres of land to join in another revolt.[60]

In short, between May and November, popular protest agains swept through the region's rural sector. The workers' complaints seemed familiar: lack of work, low wages, food shortages, bad working conditions, no right to strike. Having united the Laguna's popular movement, Madero did not meet its demands. The tradition of protest continued; without solving the problems of the workers, the Maderistas themselves soon became the victims of a widespread social mobilization of smallholders and landless agricultural wageworkers. Their protest and struggle set the tone of the Revolution in the region. Having once united behind Madero, they now mobilized behind a number of leaders who made a variety of promises, from higher wages to land.

While the source and form of protest by the Laguna's smallholders and agricultural workers would remain the same for many years, their experiences and the Revolution had transformed their consciousness. That transformation and their protests eventually changed the land-tenure system of the entire region.

NOTES

1. For an overview of the debate concerning the nature of the popular movement after 1910 and the links between the so-called populist and revisionist interpretations of the origins and outcome of the Mexican Revolution, see Gilbert M. Joseph's "Mexico's 'Popular Revolution': Mobilization and Myth in Yucatan, 1910–1940," *Latin American Perspectives* 6 (Summer 1979): 46–50.

2. William K. Meyers, "Interest Group Conflict and Revolutionary Politics: A Social History of La Comarca Lagunera, Mexico, 1888–1911," Ph.D. diss. (University of Chicago, 1979), 144–79.

3. For a survey of the Laguna's development, see José Onésimo Castro Alanis, *La Comarca Lagunera como región ejidal: Realidades, posibilidades y problemas* (México, 1965); Eduardo Guerra, *Historia de La Laguna* (México, 1953) and *Historia de Torreón* (México, 1957). See also Meyers, "Interest Group Conflict," chapters 1–3. Statistics on the yearly volume of the Nazas are listed in Enrique Najera, Manuel López Portillo, and Estanislao

Peña, *Informe general acerca de La Comarca Lagunera* (Mexico City, 1930), 167–68.

4. José Santos Valdés, *Matamoros: Ciudad Lagunera* (México, 1973), chapters 2, 3, 8, and 9; Guerra, *Historia de Torreón*, 44–48; Guerra, *Historia de La Laguna*, 280–90; and Pastor Rouaix, *Diccionario geográfico, histórico y biográfico del estado de Durango* (México, 1946), 165–75.

5. Concerning the cultivation of cotton and the organization of agriculture in the Laguna, see Najera, *Informe general de la Comisión de Estudios de La Comarca Lagunera*, 198–261; Archivo de la Suprema Corte de Justicia de la Nación (hereafter cited ASCJ), Juicio ordinario de la Companía Agrícola, Industrial, Colonizadora de Tlahualilo contra el Gobierno Federal, libro 12, leg. 6, 70–104; Interrogatorio no. 3, 1 Jan. 1910; Meyers, "Interest Group Conflict," 148.

6. Meyers, "Interest Group Conflict," 147–73; James D. Cockcroft, *Intellectual Precursors of the Mexican Revolution, 1900–1913* (Austin, 1968), 152–53, 180; *El Nuevo Mundo* (Torreón), 12 July 1908, 2.

7. Meyers, "Interest Group Conflict," 173–84.

8. Guerra, *Historia de Torreón*, 44–48; Guerra, *Historia de La Laguna*, 280–90.

9. Emiliano G. Saravia and Francisco Viesca y Lobatón, *Breves apuntes sobre la naturaleza jurídica del Río Nazas* (México, 1909), pp. 40–41; ASCJ, libro 16, leg. 8, arch. 19, 1–2.

10. Miguel Othón de Mendizábal, "El problema agrario de La Laguna," in *Obras completas de Miguel Othón de Mendizábal* (México, 1946), 4: 237–38; Clifton B. Kroeber, "La cuestión del Nazas hasta 1913," *Historia Mexicana* 79 (enero–marzo 1971): 428–56.

11. Alan Knight, "The Dynamic of Revolution in Mexico: 1910–1917," paper presented at the Latin American Studies Conference, Leeds, 1972, p. 11; see also British Foreign Office, (hereafter cited as FO), Public Records Office, London, Report of British Vice-Consul, Durango, FO 371-1147, File 1573/17946, 19 April 1911.

12. FO 371-1147, File 1573/17946, 19 April 1911; Rouaix, *Diccionario geográfico*, 89, 111–12, 136, 155–56.

13. Patrick O'Hea, *Reminiscences of the Mexican Revolution* (Mexico, 1966), 31.

14. Santos Valdés, *Matamoros*, 149–50, 312–22.

15. Castro Alanis, *La Comarca Lagunera*, 35. Reports of rural unrest come from three major sources: the Archive of the Mexican Cotton Estates of Tlahualilo, Ltd. (hereafter cited as ACET), the Lawn, Speen, Newbury, U.K.; the Archivo de la Casa Guillermo Purcell, 1888–1911 (hereafter

cited as ACP), San Pedro de las Colonias, Coahuila, Mexico; and newspapers. For an analysis of banditry as a form of social and economic protest, see Eric Hobsbawm, *Primitive Rebels* (Manchester, 1959), and *Bandits* (Middlesex, 1969).

16. ACET, 14 Aug. 1891, Informe de los Ranchos; ACP, 17 Oct. 1899, Correspondencia General, 274.

17. Clarence Senior, *Land Reform and Democracy* (Gainsville, 1959), 48–56; ACP, 2 Oct. 1891, G. A. Lynch to F. Holschneider; 4 Jan. 1892, p. 283, F. Holschneider, San Pedro, to Sres. Lamberto Reynaud & Cía., México; *La Idea* (Villa Lerdo), 15 June 1893, #32, 1 diciembre 1892, 1.

18. ACP, 21 Jan. 1894, A. Ramírez to F. Holschneider, p. 268; ACET, 13 Dec. 1893, Informe de los Ranchos.

19. ACP, 28 Sept. 1891, A. Ramírez to F. Holschneider, p. 353; 6 June 1892, C. Olck to G. Purcell; 18 July 1894, Correspondencia General, J. L. S. Hunt to G. Purcell; 19 April 1895, p. 31, Correspondencia General, Juan Salcedo to G. Purcell. See also Paul Eiser-Viafora, "Durango and the Mexican Revolution," *New Mexico Historical Review* 49 (1974): 225, on the socioeconomic impact of the decline in the price of silver.

20. ACP, 6 Aug. 1896, G. Lynch, Saltillo, to F. Holschneider, San Pedro.

21. ACP, 17 Oct. 1899, A. Ramírez to G. Purcell, p. 274; "Correspondencia del 28 de Nov. de 1898 al 26 de Agosto 1900"; "Rural Violence in Lerdo," *Mexican Herald,* 20 May 1898, 5.

22. ACP, 11 July 1908, F. Holschneider, San Pedro, to S. Don Jesús Saracho, Concordia.

23. ACP, 9 Nov. 1905, p. 398, Asuntos de las Haciendas de San Pedro, A. Ramírez to G. Purcell.

24. ACP, 17 May 1906, p. 153, Correspondencia General de las Haciendas de San Pedro to F. Holschneider, Saltillo.

25. "Revolutionary and Anti-Foreign Labor Movements," FO 368-32-2770, 1 Aug. 1906, no. 24, Commercial, Confidential, Max Mueller to Grey; ACP, 15 Aug. 1906, p. 48, Herculando Cerda to F. Holschneider.

26. ACP, 5 Oct. 1906, p. 438, Correspondencia General, F. García to H. Cerda.

27. ACP, 15 Nov. 1907, p. 211, D. Francisco Martínez Solís, Hacienda San Marcos, to F. Holschneider, Saltillo; *Mexican Herald,* 27 Sept. 1907, 11; and 19 Aug. 1908, 5.

28. FO 371-479-13571, April 21, 1908; *El Nuevo Mundo,* 26 enero 1908, p. 7.

29. *Mexican Herald,* 18 June 1908, 5.

30. *El Nuevo Mundo,* 1 July 1907, 2; 12 July 1907, 2; 4 Aug. 1907, 1; 26 Jan. 1908, 7.
31. *Mexican Herald,* 18 Sept. 1908, 1; 1 Oct. 1908, 5.
32. Ibid., 5 July 1908.
33. *El Nuevo Mundo,* 2 Feb. 1908, 8.
34. United States' Records of the Department of State Relating to the Internal Affairs of Mexico, Record Group 59, 812 file (hereafter cited as RDS), "Reforma, Libertad y Justicia," 15 June 1908, Enclosure number 4 in no. 1150, numerical file 549, 1906–1910, cases 8173–8183/180.
35. 486d., no. 40, 29 June 1908, G. Carothers to Charles Freeman.
36. *Mexican Herald,* 28 June 1908, 1. Government troops combed the region, made wide-scale arrests among the agricultural workers, and eventually sentenced eight men to death and twenty-three men to prison for the Viesca raid; FO 371-480-25096, 8 July 1908.
37. FO 371-480-24855, 18 July 1908; Howard to Grey, FO 371-480-25096, 8 July 1908; *El Nuevo Mundo,* 29 June 1908, 1.
38. RDS, numerical file (hereafter cited as NF) 549, 1906–1910, Carothers to Freeman, 29 June 1908, Cases 8173–8183/180.
39. *Mexican Herald,* 2 July 1908, 1.
40. Ibid.
41. Ibid., 28 June 1908, 1.
42. Ibid.; *El Nuevo Mundo,* 12 July 1908, 2.
43. RDS, NF 594, 1906–1910, Carothers to Freeman, 29 June 1908, Cases 8173–8183/180.
44. *Mexican Herald,* 5 July 1908, 1; RDS, NF 594, 1906–1910, Carothers to Freeman, 29 June 1908, Cases 8173–8183/180.
45. Ildefonso Villarello Vélez, *Historia de la revolución mexicana en Coahuila* (México, 1970), 64–70.
46. Santos Valdés, *Matamoros,* 150.
47. Villarello Vélez, *Historia de la revolución,* 165.
48. Charles C. Cumberland, *Mexican Revolution: Genesis under Madero* (Austin, 1974), 88.
49. Villarello Vélez, *Historia de la revolución,* 163.
50. Ibid., 166–67.
51. Miguel A. Sánchez Llamego, *Historia militar de la revolución mexicana en la época maderista* (México, 1976), 133–34; Guerra, *Historia de La Laguna,* 136–44.
52. ACP, 27 Dec. 1910, 214, G. Friedrich to F. Holschneider.
53. ACP, 14 Jan. 1911, Correspondencia General, San Pedro, to F. Holschneider, Alemania.

54. ACP, 30 Jan. 1911, Correspondencia de las Haciendas de San Pedro to F. Holschneider, Alemania.

55. FO 204-392-20, C. Cummins to Holher, enclosure in Mr. Hohler's dispatch no. 166 of 17 July, "Report by Mr. Vice Consul Cummins on the recent and present political situation in the Laguna district," 2–3.

56. RDS, 812.00/689, 27 January 1911, unsigned to Department of State.

57. FO 371-17946, Graham to Hohler, enclosure no. 1., 12 May 1911.

58. RDS, 812.00/2026, May 15, 1911; C. A. Heberlein to Dept. of State; 812.00/2005, May 23, 1911, letter from J. B. Potter quoted in G. C. Carothers to Dept. of State.

59. FO 204-39220, C. Cummins to Hohler, 17 July 1911, "Report by Mr. Vice Consul Cummins," p. 5.

60. "Magonistas in Durango," *Mexican Herald,* 17 July 1911, 2.

10
Conclusion: Opportunities for Further Regional Study

William H. Beezley

The Children of González

Professor Luis González, with the publication of his prize-winning *San José de Gracia: Mexican Village in Transition* and his collection of essays, *Invitación a la microhistoria,* has become the outstanding spokesman for regional and local studies of Mexico.[1] His example and his suggestions have spawned a rich and significant group of studies during the past ten years. The authors of the essays in this collection are but the most recent to abandon the capital city for the provinces and to adopt a region as a test for the generalizations of the Porfirian era. González recommended this change of focus for the course of Mexican history; other scholars in 1973 pointed out the particular need for microhistories of the Porfiriato. Anthony Bryan, Robert Potash, and Paul Vanderwood identified opportunities for regional investigation of this enduring dictatorship.[2]

Responding to the call of González and others, the studies in this volume demonstrate three facets of regional study: state politics, regional economics, and local life and labor. All of these themes need further elaboration in other sections to reveal the local characteristics of Porfirian Mexico.

The greatest triumph of the Porfirian years was the political and economic consolidation of the country. This process was uneven in nature and the work of different hands: in some regions the dictator pressed for political centralization; in others, entrepreneurs, with the national government's legal and military backing, broke down provincialism; in still others, ambitious strongmen used national assistance to defeat local rivals by incorporating their region into authoritarian, capitalistic Mexico. The nature of this centralization and its varying quality changed over time. After all, even though the dictator survived for thirty-five years in office, this period represents two generations of Mexicans—a long time and an even longer period of administration when compared to the life span of previous Mexican regimes. The Díaz-potism changed to survive. The nature of this regime's centralization as it changed offers explicit motives for the men and women who took up arms after the turn of the century against the Díaz administration, first with the Mexican Liberal Party and later with the series of revolutionary outbreaks loosely under the direction of Francisco I. Madero.

The Opportunities

Examination of state government and local politics will enable us to evaluate the character of Porfirio's authoritarian paternalism, based on the actions and personalities of the governors. Both the institution of the governorship and the individual governors have been overlooked by historians. The study of this institution must draw on the major source for the period, the Colección General Porfirio Díaz. Most of the documents in this extensive archive are incoming letters from state officials, reporting political affairs to the president.[3] The governorship should be examined, looking at the relationships between the office and the central government, the regulation of local elections, manipulation of the local economy, relations with businessmen (especially foreign entrepreneurs), and the influence on the judicial system. In some instances governors served nearly the same term that Porfirio sat in the presidential chair. Others left the office for positions in the federal government; some for obscurity. Why and when they left office needs consideration.

The Porfirian governors also offer some excellent subjects for political biographies, none better than Miguel Ahumada. This longtime bureaucrat served as governor of Jalisco and went as the Porfirian troubleshooter to Chihuahua, when the Terrazas family failed to maintain its working relationship with the dictator and its control of the factions in the state. Ahumada served in the customs service, fought against the French during the intervention, was elected to local offices and the legislature of Jalisco, and ended his career as a member of the state chamber during the Huerta years, then went into exile in El Paso, Texas.[4]

In some states, as in Chihuahua, an extended family rather than an individual dominated state politics. Mark Wasserman's examination of the Terrazas family followed the direction first indicated by Charles Harris, in his studies of Coahuila's "overmighty" family, the Sánchez Navarros.[5] Other family clans that might be investigated include the Valenzuelas of Tabasco and the Maderos of Coahuila.

Whether an individual or an extended family dominated state affairs, the governors were the delegates of the president throughout Mexico. And the position carried greater or lesser authority depending on its distance from the capital (only in the late 1880s did the telegraph and the railroad begin to reduce somewhat the isolation that allowed autonomous action). The governors should be examined as independent agents, operating freely within the framework created by the dictator. These state executives, even after the turn of the century, saw themselves as officials with sufficient authority to make their own decisions as long as they did not violate the general guidelines established by Porfirio. This sense of autonomy resulted in the formation of the Círculo de los Gobernadores, led by Ramón Corral and Enrique Creel. Relations between governors, as well as with the national government, should also be explored.

The governor as elector needs most study. Common wisdom makes the governor the executor of the president's wishes in elections and the balloting little more than an opportunity for the voters to affirm support for the Porfirian regime. Yet we know little about how and how well this system of controlled elections operated. Miguel Ahumada traveled to Mexico City on at least one occasion to receive orders directly from Díaz on the elections in Jalisco. But Ahumada made it clear that he wanted these instructions several weeks in advance, so that he could prepare public opinion for the eventual winner.[6] Ahumada's behavior demonstrates an awareness of public opinion and a greater concern than simply falsifying election returns. Moreover, we know that some genuine election campaigns took place, although the president eventually intervened to impose his choice. These campaign struggles reveal differences of opinion on personalities and policies. Francisco Madero first campaigned in the 1905 gubernatorial race in Coahuila against Venustiano Carranza's candidate.[7] This period of electioneering before the voting allowed for some discussion of issues and permitted some expressions of dissent; historians can profit from a study of elections even though the results were manipulated at the will of the dictator. The dynamics of the electoral process generally need evaluation; this can only be accomplished at the local and state levels.

Examination should also focus on the relationships between the governor and the other branches of administration within the state. Bernardo Reyes, governor of Nuevo León, for example, restructured the administration so that he directed the elections of municipal presidents, who became responsible to him. The result of this program was the elimination of the institution of the *jefe político* by 1905 in the state.[8] Was this an example of Reyes's efforts to build his own political apparatus, or was this a cautious response to the well-known demand in the northern states for the *municipio libre?*

It is also necessary to assess the relations among the branches of state government. The legislature and judiciary have been ignored so far by studies of the Porfiriato. Yet these elite organizations were centers of economic opportunity and social status, whether or not their political self-sufficiency was curtailed or contained by the governor. The Chihuahua legislature, for example, decided the legislation, including tax exemptions, that furthered the Terrazas's commercial and banking empire. For this to happen, the Terrazas family had to defeat their rivals within the state chamber.[9]

We need to know something about the relative bargaining power of different governors on the national scene, and how they obtained the president's favor. The governors played for high stakes—access to federal assistance, development programs, railroad routes, and federal troops. How did Díaz respond to them? To his favorites first, to the strongest, or to those in the most difficult situations?

Few studies examine the dictatorship's authoritarian nature on the local level. The jefe político, as the agent of the central government, superceded the munícipio government and became the instrument of the dictator's authority. This delegate came armed with the power to call for the support of the *rurales* and the army, with authorization to license economic ventures, conscript local men for military service, and report directly to Mexico City. These prefects represented the national government and the outside world; as such, they upset the local political and economic hierarchy. As crucial as these men were as agents of centralization, we know little about them or their reception in the hinterland. By 1910 some three hundred people held this position in Mexico.[10]

An investigation of the jefe político offers historians the opportunity to use the methodology of social history. The number is large enough to utilize the latest techniques of quantification developed for prosopographical studies, yet small enough to be manageable for in-depth biographical treatment. This study should do more than simply chart averages of prior career, military service, residence before appointment, etc., as interesting as this would be. Besides the obvious need to compile information on the background and the careers of these men, it is crucial to examine the timing of the appointments in different areas. Here the demands on the historian extend beyond the scope of prosopography; the chronology of these appointments must be correlated with local political and economic developments. John Coatsworth has demonstrated the critical relationship of chronology in his study of projected railroad expansion, land accumulation, and agrarian revolts.[11] Local crises may well have predicated the appointment of jefes. Examples that spring to mind immediately include local economic development, threatening situations such as hostile Indians and messianic revivals, and labor shortages created when peons fled the haciendas and debts for better opportunities. On the other hand, some appointments may reflect Porfirio Díaz's planned centralization rather than a response to challenges to his authority.

How repressive was this regime? One indicator may be freedom of the press. Certainly this was no more than a constitutional statement in Díaz's Mexico. Yet newspaper critics of the regime as virulent as the Flores Magón brothers were arrested, sentenced, and released, then arrested, sentenced, and released again, all within five years. Their arrests demonstrate a repressive government, but these journalists did not simply disappear into the night (as they would have under certain regimes in contemporary Chile or Argentina). Their prison terms were rather short and the conditions, while deplorable, did not cause the death of either Ricardo or Enrique. Other journalists experienced the same fate. Silvestre Terrazas, José María Pino Suárez, and others served terms in prison, but lived to challenge the dictatorship in the revolution. This topic deserves careful investigation.

Beyond the questions of government repression, political consolidation, and economic modernization, religious patterns also need to be explored. There remained many committed Liberals, including veterans of the Reform era, who deplored the Porfirian arrangement with Church leaders; others argued that the time of religious troubles had ended and the Church could safely be allowed to return to some of its traditional activities. Meanwhile, in the 1890s, so-called new prelates, taking positions throughout the country, brought renewed commitment to Church intervention in secular life inspired by the papal encyclical *Rerum Novarum*.[12]

Rededication to Catholicism climaxed in the crowning of the Virgin of Guadalupe in 1895. We know little about this event and its acceptance throughout the country. The crowning required the authorization of Pope Leo XIII and the permission of President Díaz for the public ceremony. This episode, attracting an international delegation that included the archbishops of New York, New Orleans, and Santa Fe, symbolically sealed the working arrangement between Church and state for the Porfirian years. Although Díaz did not attend the crowning, many of his cabinet and administration did. The jefe político of Guadalupe Hidalgo hosted a banquet for Church leaders, government officials, and prominent citizens attending the celebration. The following day foreign Church fathers visited the president before embarking on a government-arranged tour of Mexico. Several delegations from Indian communities were denied admission to the church during the crowning ceremony, in yet another example of the Porfirian anti-Indian policy.[13]

We need investigations of the regional dimensions of religion. An indication of local religious fervor, or at least of a charismatic priest, was the pilgrimage. These tours took the devoted to the shrine of the Virgin of Guadalupe, Our Lord of Chalma, or Our Lady of Ocotlán. The pilgrimages and their places of origin were regularly reported in the newspapers; the study of these tours offers a first step toward identifying centers of religious enthusiasm. They also provide a window on the culture of ordinary Mexicans. As the anthropologist Victor Turner has demonstrated, it is "necessary to take into account the contemporaneous structure of Mexican society and culture" in order to understand this religious phenomenon. Turner's preliminary research found that the annual visit to Tepeyac that began in 1890 has continued without interruption for the parishioners of Querétaro. These popular pilgrimages, which he suggests are comparable to labor migration, await historical investigation.[14]

An inspired portrait of local Mexico, including its fanatic religious devotion, during the Porfirian years is Agustín Yáñez's famous novel, *The Edge of the Storm*.[15] This novel offers a dozen themes that beckon historians. Yáñez, for example, describes the social network of a rural community. Colonial historians have identified similar networks in the records of local parishes, in court cases, and in probate information. These sources are available for the Porfirian era as well and could provide a test for Yáñez's fictional society. The author also explores the disruption of the community that resulted when several young men who had gone north, even crossing the border to become wage-earners, returned home. They arrived with changed attitudes, new experiences, and exciting stories that must have rivaled those of Marco Polo in the ears of the villagers. Paul Friedrich has completed a case study of one such adventurer and his disruptive effect on his community when he returned to Michoacán.[16] Other such studies will give historical depth to the statistics of internal and international migration compiled by El Colegio de México and of growth in the cities of the north by Richard Wilkie.[17] Case studies of Mexicans who stayed in town or returned to their native villages seem especially promising. Taken together these topics suggest the kind of ethnographic community study written by Luis González. As his *El pueblo en vilo* shows, this approach yields fascinating results.

We know little about what might be called the Porfirian Persuasion—the customs and currents of thought and interest that prevailed in the nation. The principal axis was formed by developmental capitalism, positivism, and Mexican liberalism, hardened in the Wars of the Reform and the French Intervention. Liberalism, anarchism, and positivism have been the subject of graceful, thought-provoking analyses by scholars for the national level, but the intellectual history of the regions remains a mystery.[18] The intellectual life in cities as prominent and provincial as Guadalajara or Puebla seems particularly attractive as a topic. Another promising subject would be the intellectual and political life of Veracruz, the port connecting Mexico to world commerce and foreign customs.

An important aspect of the Porfirian Persuasion was the attitude toward the indigenous population and culture. Beyond the anti-Indian policies of the government, there seems to have been a kind of romantic view of the Aztec as Noble Savage. This romance comes across in newspaper references to the capital as Old Tenochtitlán and reports of Aztec culture that included important historical studies of the pre-Columbian and colonial past.[19] In its most fanciful form, this attitude led to the celebration of the Aztec Flowery War. Mexico City's high society decorated its coaches and carriages with elaborate and expensive floral arrangements. Drivers paraded these floats, precursors of the Rose Parade, before the residence of don Porfirio and on to the reviewing stand, where judges awarded prizes.[20] Is this interest in the noble Aztec a seedbed for the later, revolutionary promotion of Mexico's Indian culture? Or is this attitude so romantic and idealized as to represent no more than victorian escapism? Or is it further evidence of the Porfirian denigration of Indians by holding up the greatness of their ancestors?

Porfirian society in the capital city emulated Western culture. The ladies who rode floats in the Flowery War celebration wore the latest Paris frocks as they held their parasols. Porfirian gentlemen adopted fashionable European and North American recreations and amusements. These should be examined. In fact, two arresting theories contend that the rise of organized sports can reveal as well as any other indicator the existence of modern society. Allen Guttmann argued persuasively that sports will attract interest only in those communities harnessed to the clock, to bureaucratic record-keeping, to secular control and the tyranny of production (the drive for record-breaking performances in sports), and so forth.[21] We can test this cross-cultural theory with studies of Mexico. The sociologists Norbert Elias and Eric Dunning have examined the rise of sports and tied its organization to what they describe as the quest for "excitement in unexciting societies."[22] Certainly bullfighting, *charriadas,* and informal horse racing existed before the latter Porfiriato. But bullfighting was a ritual celebration of Spanish culture, the charriada existed as a work-related recreation, and horse racing displayed important, although unorganized proof of wealth and position (stud books were not kept for Mexican horses until the last years of the Porfiriato). Ritual, recreation, and display are part, but not all or even the most important of the constellation of attributes describing modern sports. Elias and Dunning argue that the craving for excitement does not surface in frontier communities, boom towns, or lawless societies. The excitement of constant *golpes del estado,* foreign intervention, and religious controversy made Mexico an unlikely location for the rise or practice of sports until the time of Porfirio.

Did the Porfirian peace reduce the struggle for survival and success to the point that Mexicans sought the thrill of excitement in the risks of sports? Certainly high-society Mexicans arrived in crowds for the horse races at the Indianilla track (opened in 1895) and wheeled to Popocátepetl on the ordinary (high-wheeled) bicycle or later whisked to Acapulco on a safety (modern) version of the vehicle. Did the Porfirians restore interest in their dull lives of peace and prosperity (at least among their class) by circling on roller skates the wooden rink, complete with wintry scenes, constructed in the Alemada, or by joining the Lakeside Sailing Club that held regular regattas on Lakes Chalco and Xochimilco and traveling to Veracruz to sail with that city's yacht club?[23] Did adrenaline rush through the blood of Porfirian gentlemen at the prize fights sponsored by the Mexican Athletic Club, or at the tennis matches held by the

Reforma Athletic Club, or at bat for either the Mexico City Baseball Club or the Mexican National (Railroad) Baseball Club, or on horseback in the Christmas polo matches?[24]

Perhaps this rise of organized sporting activities represented nothing more than the growing influence of the foreign community in Mexico. Certainly foreigners made themselves at home, indicating the security they felt in the dictator's country. Germans in Puebla quickly began brewing Vogel beer, and sales became so successful that the owners ordered a team of Clydesdales from St. Louis to pull the wagonloads of beer to customers. This brewery opened a Tívoli garden, with regular Sunday afternoon concerts and entertainment for Puebla's society. Spaniards in Mexico City wanted to enjoy old-country recreation, so they built Mexico's first jai alai *frontón*. The building had the necessary playing area, lounge, restaurant, restrooms, and, of course, a betting room, where the patrons could use the latest Paris mutual method to win or lose money. The Spanish champions came to Mexico to inaugurate the frontón in December 1895, before an appreciative audience that included the presidential cabinet. In Pachuca, Cornish miners organized Cornish wrestling for their pleasure, while their English cousins played in an English football (soccer) league in town. In Monterrey, North Americans wasted little time in forming a baseball team and opening the Monterrey Gymnastic Club, with membership open to any city resident.[25]

The foreigners and their foreign enclaves need fuller investigation. To this point two aspects of their activity have received attention: their investments and observations. The coming of foreign capital and technology to Mexico has been a major theme in historical studies; the impact of foreign entrepreneurs has yet to be examined in local communities. Foreign travelers, although there is no study of them as a group, have been the source of colorful descriptions and caustic remarks about the nation. Mrs. Tweetie, Charles Flandrau, and others offer the enterprising scholar materials for an analysis of the clash of customs that occurred in different regions.[26] Other activities of the foreign community should be investigated as well.

Many foreigners maintained an interest in world affairs, especially in the politics of their native lands. Mexico's Spaniards held a succession of benefits to raise money to support the Spanish military efforts in Cuba. North Americans campaigned in Mexican newspapers against the practice of lynching in the United States. Foreigners also attacked Mexican practices they opposed. The anti-lynch-law foreigners used the same arguments in their efforts to end bullfighting in the federal district of Mexico. Protestants proposed demonstrations to disrupt the crowning of the Virgin of Guadalupe, although these plans were canceled. Those who supported the Oriental exclusion laws in the United States called for similar statutes to stop the immigration of Asians to Mexico.[27]

The least known of the foreign groups remain the Japanese and Chinese, despite excellent work by Evelyn Hu-DeHart. Asians had first come to Mexico during the colonial period (including the *China poblana*), but the great influx of Chinese took place during the Porfiriato. These immigrants went to all parts of the country, but concentrated in large numbers in Sonora, Chihuahua, and around Torreón. We need a study of their activities in the north. Some of the sources on the history of these unpopular immigrants may be located in United States consular and court records. The federal district court records contains a wealth of material on the societies on both sides of the border. W. Dirk Raat, Louis R. Sadler, and Charles Harris have demonstrated the possibilities of using these court records to locate the activities of rebels, smugglers, German spies, and outcasts.[28] Because Orientals were excluded from the United States, a flourishing smuggling business developed along the border, with regular shipments of Chinese workers going north across the Rio Grande. Many of these undocumented workers ran into legal problems, and their cases can be found in the federal court records.

The Japanese had both a commercial and military interest in Mexico. Yet we know next to nothing about Japanese activity in the country and the question of their interest and activities in Baja California, especially around Magdalena Bay. The Japanese were not subject to the same xenophobic reaction as met the Chinese, and during the years of the depression of the 1930s, when the Chinese were barred from immigrating to Mexico, the Japanese could still enter the country.[29]

The comment known to every first-year student of Mexican history, "Mexico, mother of foreigners, stepmother of Mexicans," certainly was not true for the Chinese and should be tested for other alien groups as well. The legal treatment of foreigners, in fact, constitutes the biggest gap in our knowledge of their activities in Mexico. Prevailing wisdom favors a judicial system geared to the service of foreigners, of justice dispensed in favor of the outsider over the native. Was this the case? The answer requires an examination of the law codes and court records. The definition of the law offers a necessary and fascinating first step. Certainly the rise of the modern economy led to the introduction of new laws. Boys enjoyed placing rocks on train rails, sometimes with unfortunate results. Soon derailing a train carried a twenty-year prison sentence. The editors of the *Mexican Herald* applauded the conviction of several ten- and twelve-year-old boys and suggested that the seriousness of the crime might logically demand the death penalty. An intellectual history could trace the economic, political, and social paradigm that justified the legal code and its enforcement. The passage of laws in the federal district calling for the assignment of pickpockets to hard labor in the tobacco fields resulted in the consignment of from sixty to eighty prisoners a month in 1895.[30] This and other laws that created forced labor should be examined to discover the society's view of work and justice. Scholars have only made a start in their investigation of the legal code and the operation of law enforcement that will enrich the available crime statistics.

Crime and justice in general need study. State archives in Coahuila and Chihuahua have stacks of wanted posters for peons who had jumped their debts and fled to greater oppotunities.[31] These posters, the localities where they were issued, and their increasing frequency give added information on the population shift toward the northern border. Laws and their enforcement against vagrants offer a revealing portrait of Porfirian society, especially as these laws were most often applied to such groups as migrants to the city and to immigrants such as the Chinese.

Criminal studies will open a window on the Mexican masses in the different regions of Mexico. The definition of lower class, the masses, or the dangerous elements differed across the country. Flandrau claimed that in the capital city, "by the masses . . . although the distinction is a loose one, is meant persons who still wear native costume." He continued that social mobility required no more than the purchase of "a cheap, ill-fitting suit of American cut . . . ."[32] These Mexicans are the essence of the parochial regions called the *patrias chicas* of this patchwork nation. Foreign travelers offer some expression of this attitude and its diversity, but they did not go everywhere nor did they comment on all groups in society. Statistics of migration, urbanization, population growth, and crime—all the categories of the census, in fact—offer clues about these regional residents. It is not enough. We need further expressions of these people to appreciate them and their activities. Two lines of investigation have been too little utilized.

Mexican oral tradition has come increasingly under investigation, but the results of these studies remain almost confidential because historians have not searched out this source. Other historians have reconstructed the African past, the immigrant experience, the slave's life, and the industrial worker's world; they have used oral traditions, folk art, and handicrafts to recreate the lives of these people. Mexican historians have only skimmed these materials, most often turning only to the *corrido* for a short piece of doggerel to use as an epigraph or quotation to enliven their essays or lectures. However, Merle Simmons has offered directions in the use of the corrido for the study of the Revolution. This kind of study should be pursued in a larger sweep, including the Porfiriato. Folk life, a generic term for tradition, not simply the quaint epigrams and superstitions, provides a key to village life, ethnic subcultures, occupational groups, and the residents of the same *barrio* of large cities. Studies of folk life blend into evaluations of folk art, and these analyses should be expanded to the study of the art of Porfirian Mexico.

Examining art, historians should be prepared to use their own methodology. Questions of who painted whom or what, when, and why allow us to take portraits, landscape paintings, and newspaper etchings and draw plausible conclusions about the society.[33] Above all, since we are searching for the people, not the ideals of high culture, we should seek out examples of pictorial descriptions of society. Wanted posters have specific, not idealized, descriptions and sketches that offer a catalog of information on the population. As accurately as possible these posters give physical characteristics, including evidence of disease (pockmarks, scars), clothing (that often determines social stratification), and frequently occupation. These are all indicators of social class. The graphic art of José Guadalupe Posada and others who served as pictorial reporters for the cheap newspapers of the day give us clues about the clothes, stature, behavior, leisure, interests, and beliefs of everyday Mexicans during the Porfirian years. Posada's work is the most available and demands the analysis that Ronnie Tyler suggested in the catalog of the Posada exhibition in Washington, D.C.[34]

For years historians have neglected the fact that photography reached Mexico before Porfirio Díaz first claimed the presidency, in 1876. Yet photographs are used as little more than filler for monographs. Casasola's volumes of the *Historia gráfica de la revolución mexicana* have been consigned to the coffee tables of historians and tourists.[35] These volumes should be carefully analyzed. No hocus-pocus is required here; no need to master statistics or purchase a home computer. Only the methodology of historical analysis needs to be used, but it must be used as carefully as with manuscripts.[36] With photographs at hand, we can see the modernization or lack of it in Porfirian towns and villages. We can see the store fronts, indicating *ofertas* of imported goods, ownership by natives or foreigners. We can see store-bought clothes and shoes or campesino costumes and sandals. The tools so proudly grasped by workers tell us about working conditions, levels of technology, and ultimately levels of modernization. Pictures of women reveal their status in the community. The choice of what should be included in a photograph reveals what has meaning to the subject and the photographer. A favorite dog or horse, a new hat, a gleaming machete, or a complete family portrait offer tantalizing hints about everyday life that otherwise escape notice, even on the tax rolls.[37]

The essays in this volume have used imaginative and skillful techniques to obtain information on the people of Porfirian Mexico. This remains the most elusive aspect of the Porfirian society to uncover. People of the lower classes and the masses, the outcasts, give a living demonstration of Lesley Byrd Simpson's description of the country as *Many Mexicos*. One way of capturing these regional distinctions was suggested by James Wilkie's volume on the Revolution. Wilkie carved the nation into seven geosocial regions, based on levels of poverty. Since these regions do not cut across state lines, the unit of investigation can be an entire region or a representative state within it.[38] These regions, described as geosocial units, probably represent cultural regions as well. They might be examined as a cultural anthropologist would approach them.

Of all the cultural manifestations ignored by historians, the outstanding one is the artifact. Rare indeed are studies of material culture. Only a few have appeared, but excellent examples that offer Mexican historians a demonstration of the possibilities include the study of Texas gravestones, an examination of the sod house in the Great Plains, and the recreation of settlers' lives by evaluating the log cabin.[39] Material culture swings a wide net, capturing all sorts of evidence that historians should become accustomed to using. *Metates* and *petates,* grinding stones and sleeping mats, hacienda quarters (the *casco*) and the peons' adobes, and agricultural implements—these are only the first in a list of things that should reveal the cultural attributes of the geosocial regions. These things are also the staples of state and local museums, therefore accessible in such places as the museum at the Ateneo Fuente, in Saltillo, Coahuila.[40]

Food and clothing offer an important starting place for a study of everyday Mexicans in different regions. The Spanish began the effort to replace the tortilla with bread; it is a dietary campaign that continues today. Of course diet reflects the available foodstuffs, income, and personal choice. But this food item allows evaluation of the masses. The Díaz regime gave even more attention to clothing. It was during this regime that the town council of Guanajuato adopted a so-called trousers law that required all men to wear trousers rather than the traditional peasant drawers or indigenous breechcloths. A flourishing business soon developed at the edge of town, renting trousers to men without their own.[41] But the costumes of Mexicans reflect more than a western, modern split from the traditional, *campesino* or Indian dress. Etchings and photographs show occupational stratification in the clothing worn by different workers; hacendados, herdsmen, and overseers dressed differently from field hands because they rode horses; shopkeepers and craftsmen often dressed in coat and cravat rather than the simple, buttonless, pullover shirts and breeches of domestics and hack drivers. A regional difference appears as well. In the north the common clothes seem to be store-bought, ready-made pants and shirts, worn with sandals or boots, when possible. This may be the influence of the western United States or the emulation of men in the cattle industry, or it may reflect the fact that many in the north had become rootless wage earners, incorporated into the modern money economy.

Tools and agricultural implements suggest the nature of the work in different parts of Mexico. Forced laborers, who had only a machete as a tool, were part of the same Mexican work force as were farm workers on large haciendas in the Bajío, who were learning how to use the plow imported from the United States. Villagers hacking mule paths through the *selva* had an entirely different relationship to their tools and their world than did the migrant gandy dancers at the railhead, using company-owned shovels, picks, and sledgehammers.

We may also find people at the lower end of society by examining their celebrations. Births and deaths far surpass marriages and school graduations as the passages of life most important in Mexico's traditional society. Religious holidays extend beyond those of the civic calendar, even Cinco de Mayo and Quince de Septiembre. Births, deaths, and holidays should be examined through newspapers, oral traditions, and photographs.[42]

New techniques, new sources of information, and new appreciation of the techniques of other disciplines should not obscure the fact that traditional history, if focused on the states and localities during the Porfirian years, will yield valuable results. Such traditional studies as the examination of the elite, for example, will offer a greater perspective on the rulers of Mexico. In most cases these Porfirian henchmen are pasteboard figures, not because the information on them does not exist, but because of a lack of monographs examining them. Biographies of regional strongmen and collective biographies of regional elites need to be completed. Studies, done in the standard way, of state and local politics, including political campaigns and efforts to challenge incumbents, are missing; such studies, I suspect, will reveal that the dictator was primarily interested in establishing the boundaries of political activity. The dictatorship was authoritarian, not tyrannical. Local studies should reveal the range of politics permissible during the Díaz years. We will also find, I believe, that the intrusion of foreign capital and rising profits provided for shifting the political balance not between parties, but between families and towns. Stuart Voss has found these shifting town elites in Sonora. In Chihuahua, the Terrazas family, who controlled Chihuahua City, soon smothered the ambitions of the politicians from Guerrero City, leaving a desire for revenge that surfaced in 1906 and 1910. These town rivalries appeared also in Chiapas. Thomas Benjamin has traced in detail the controversy that still exists today between Tuxtla Gutiérrez and San Cristóbal Las Casas.[43] These are expressions of the political dynamism of the Porfirian years.

For many, especially the triumphant Liberals, Porfirio's ascendance created a time of opportunity. Historians need to determine the nature of this sense of opportunity, which included a strong sense of optimism that life could be more than simply protecting the property one owned.[44] Increasingly this notion of political and economic opportunities narrowed because of the full car, as the continuation of Díaz's favorites in office was called, and the foreigners who increasingly controlled the economy. But the topic remains a rich one, especially in its regional manifestations, as different states suddenly appeared during the Díaz period as places where a man could make his mark.

Studies of national institutions should be expanded to include the regional expressions and variations of these national organizations. Paul Vanderwood's study of the rurales provides a wealth of information on both this agency of law enforcement and the bandits it supressed.[45] It offers suggestive information on the regions of recruitment of rurales and areas where they were often active. These are clues that should be pursued.

Moreover a study should be done on the Porfirian army as well. The operation of the *leva* and origins of the rank and file would be as valuable as Vanderwood's study. A similar portrait needs to be provided on the officer class, not just the socioeconomic background of those who attended the Colegio Militar, but also geographic origins, promotion patterns, retirement, and political involvement. Was there a shift in the residential origins of these cadets that reflects the rise and fall of the demographic, political, and economic importance of different sections of Mexico? Studies of the army should include internal social organization, its military campaigns against the Yaquis in the north and the rebellious Maya in Quintana

Roo, and questions of professionalism, the fostering of esprit de corps, career patterns, and recruitment policies among the officers.

Other government institutions remain to be placed in regional perspective: the postal system, the Ministry of Finance (including its granting of permission to establish banks of emission), and the customs service.

We also know little about the powerful corporations that operated in Mexico during these years. The work of Wells, Joseph, and Benjamin has revealed a great deal about the activities of International Harvester in Yucatán and Meyers has done valuable work on the Tlahualilo Company in the Laguna, but we have only hints about Anasco and its mining operations, little about the Grace and Company operations in Sonora and Baja California del Norte, and the various German brewing and land companies in the center and the south.[46] Business history has yet to establish itself in Mexico, and certainly not for the Porfirian years.

The Porfirian regime's critics and sympathizers alike have generally agreed that one of the outstanding individuals during these years was the minister of education, Justo Sierra, who encouraged the national education program and supported programs in the states. Despite the recognition of Sierra's importance in the regime, the separate federal and state educational systems have been ignored. Except for the highly visible National University (established in 1910), the elite salon Ateneo de la Juventud, and studies of educational ideology, we have little but scraps of evidence that include the general expansion of the educational system as both national and state levels of government attempted to provide primary education across the nation.[47] This program created new teaching positions, with the prestige of carrying out an important government policy with reasonable salaries and reasonable support funds.

Apparently the program collapsed in the last decade of the Porfiriato. In Coahuila the state budget reduced funds for the public education system, left teachers' salaries unchanged despite higher prices for food and rent, and reduced money for building maintenance, equipment and books. The social position of teachers eroded as well. There should be little surprise that James Cockcroft discovered numerous teachers in the ranks of the Mexican Liberal Party, many of whom continued their revolutionary activities in the decade from 1910 to 1920. Opportunities for social mobility may have declined as well when state and federal scholarship programs were reduced. Scholarships for students to attend the National University were funded for Coahuilan students by both the national government and the state legislature. But the depression of 1905 undercut these programs, leaving scholarship students stranded without help; no further students were named to receive this opportunity to study in the national capital.[48]

Beyond this, we need a study of the nature of the education offered in Mexican schools, including the Church-operated institutions. What kind of world did the Mexican student discover during the two or three years most of them spent in school? The kind of intellectual study done for the Baroque period by Irving Leonard could be accomplished for the states as well as the nation.[49]

In addition to regional studies of the Porfirian education program, an excellent study would be a general evaluation of the transportation system in Mexico that pulled the nation closer together. We have some excellent studies of the expansion of railroads during these years, especially Coatsworth's study of the railroad and economic development, but a map locating the railroad lines reveals how much of the nation remained beyond this transportation system. We have no studies of the road system, stage lines, and mule trains. Yet these were the interstices of economic growth. The improvement of the transportation and communications networks brought new political importance to some towns, while others lost political influence if they were not tied into the transportation system. These towns should be examined. The Porfirian government also spent money on the improvements of ports—not just Veracruz, but also Tampico, Acapulco, Mazatlán, and Ensenada as well. What economic and political consequences followed these developments?

Traditional history, especially political and biographical, should be focused on the last decade of the Porfirian regime. We know little about these years, the crisis era, when the dictator's grasp on the country weakened to the point that in 1911 revolutionaries who had captured only an isolated bordertown could force his resignation. The rivalries, aspirations, and fears of the Porfirian ruling clique need to be examined, by studying among other topics, the shifting importance of regional leaders and the rise of political parties that remained loyal to Porfirio but with different opinions about who should succeed him. The Reyistas, of course, are a major example, but the Church-organized political groups should be included here as well. The nature of the Reyes-Limantour rivalry would make an excellent theme; the opposition, or even better the hatred, of Ramón Corral offers another side of the Porfirian political situation. Porfirian neglect of such traditionally important states as his native Oaxaca may also have played a part in the increased splintering of the Díaz coterie in the last decade.

The number of hacienda studies has increased greatly in recent years, giving historians an invaluable source of information on the economic character of the regions. There are several major haciendas that have not been studied, such as Barbicoa, one of the most notorious foreign-owned properties, and the Palomas Land and Cattle Company, which straddles the border.[50] The archive of ranching and stock raising at the University of Wyoming holds clues to the properties in northern Mexico.

For the northern and southern borders, we need a study of smuggling. Traditionally this activity has been lumped into general studies of foreign relations either between Mexico and the United States or Mexico and Guatemala, but the topic should be the subject of detailed analysis. In the north it is certain that smuggling made fortunes and bestowed political power. The Guadarrama family, stretching across the New Mexico–Chihuahua border, moved cattle and Chinese north and took guns and merchandise south, to build a powerful family fortune.[51] Studies also need to examine the operation of the so-called free zone along the border and the impact of the cycles of boom and bust in the southwestern United States. These cycles may have sparked related changes in smuggling activities.

The greatest needs for the Porfirian years remain a perceptive biography of the general-president (1830–1915) and a one-volume synthesis of his regime (1876–1911). Both of these projects will be made possible by studies such as those in this volume and by the monographs of other children of González who venture into the provinces. In the hinterland, whether one wears the sombrero of González or the beret of Braudel is a choice of emphasis. The latter makes explicit statements on the limits of traditional and local societies; the former, who describes himself as "nearsighted and pedestrian by nature," understates conclusions that are just as perceptive and certain as Braudel's.[52] Following either scholar, or both, will lead historians into the other Mexicos.

NOTES

1. *Pueblo en vilo* (México, 1968) received the American Historical Association's Clarence H. Haring Prize in 1973 and was published in translation as *San José de Gracia: Mexican Village in Transition* (Austin, 1974); *Invitación a la microhistoria* (México, 1973).
2. See Anthony T. Bryan, "Bibliographical Essay: A Research Review," from *The Politics of the Porfiriato: A Research Review* (Bloomington, 1973), reprinted in *The Age of Porfirio Díaz*, ed. Carlos B. Gil (Albuquerque, 1977), 165–88; Robert A. Potash, "Topics in Need of Study: Modern Mexico," and Paul Vanderwood and Anthony T. Bryan, "Research Materials for the Porfiriato," in *Research in Mexican History*, ed. Richard E. Greenleaf and Michael C. Meyer (Lincoln, 1973), 21–23, 159–62. For a recent statement, see W. Dirk Raat, *The Mexican Revolution: An Annotated Guide to Recent Scholarship* (Boston, 1982), xxxiii, 143–62.
3. Vanderwood and Bryan, "Porfiriato," 159. See also Laurens B. Perry, *Inventario y guía de la Colección General Porfirio Díaz* (México, 1969).
4. *Diccionario Porrúa*, 3rd. ed. (México: Editorial Porrúa, 1970), 1: 45.
5. See Charles Harris, "The 'Overmighty Family': The Case of the Sánchez Navarros," in *Contemporary Mexico*, ed. James W. Wilkie, Michael C. Meyer, and Edna Monzón de Wilkie (Berkeley, 1976), 47–61.
6. Ahumada to Ramón Corral, 9 Dec. 1909, Archivo de Ramón Corral, carpeta 2, documento 1239, Centro de Estudios de Historia de México, Fundación Cultural de Condumex, México.
7. Minutario Francisco I. Madero, carpeta 1, documentos 67–83; carpeta 2, documentos 84–165, Centro de Estudios de Historia de México, Fundación Cultural de Condumex, México, contain Madero's correspondence concerning the 1905 gubernatorial election in Coahuila.
8. Bryan, "Bibliographical Essay," 172.
9. William H. Beezley, *Insurgent Governor: Abraham González and the Mexican Revolution in Chihuahua* (Lincoln, 1973), 1–12; Mark Wasserman, "Oligarchy and Foreign Enterprise in Porfirian Chihuahua, Mexico, 1876–1911," Ph.D. diss. (University of Chicago, 1975).
10. Dudley Charles Ankerson, "Saturnino Cedillo and the Mexican Revolution in San Luis Potosí, 1890–1940," Ph.D. diss. (University of Cambridge, 1981), 4.

11. John H. Coatsworth, *Growth against Development: The Economic Impact of Railroads in Porfirian Mexico* (De Kalb, 1981).

12. Robert E. Quirk, *The Mexican Revolution and the Catholic Church, 1910–1929* (Bloomington, 1973), 3–20.

13. *Mexican Herald,* 14 Oct. 1895.

14. Victor Turner, *Dramas, Fields, and Metaphors: Symbolic Action in Human Society* (Ithaca, 1974), 208; see chapter 5, "Pilgrimages as Social Processes," 166–203. Victor Turner and Edith Turner, *Image and Pilgrimage in Christian Culture: Anthropological Perspectives* (New York, 1978), chapter 2, "Mexican Pilgrimages: Myth and History," 40–103.

15. Agustín Yáñez, *Al filo del agua,* translated as *The Edge of the Storm* by Ethel Brinton (Austin, 1963).

16. Paul Friedrich, *Agrarian Revolt in a Mexican Village* (Englewood Cliffs, 1970).

17. Moisés González Navarro, *Estadísticas sociales del Porfiriato, 1877–1910* (México, 1956); Richard W. Wilkie, "Urban Growth and the Transformation of the Settlement Landscape of Mexico, 1910–1970," in *Contemporary Mexico,* ed. Wilkie, Meyer, and de Wilkie, 99–134.

18. Leopoldo Zea, *Positivism in Mexico* (Austin, 1974); W. Dirk Raat, *El positivism durante el Porfiriato: 1876–1910* (México, 1975); John M. Hart, *Anarchism and the Mexican Working Class, 1860–1931* (Austin, 1978); Charles Hale, "'Scientific Politics,' and the Continuity of Liberalism in Mexico, 1876–1910, *Dos revoluciones, México y los Estados Unidos* (México, 1976), 138–54.

19. *Mexican Herald,* 13 Sept. 1895.

20. Ibid., 14 Sept. 1895.

21. Allen Guttmann, *From Ritual to Record: The Nature of Modern Sports* (New York, 1978), 57–90.

22. Norbert Elias and Eric Dunning, "The Quest for Excitement in Unexciting Societies," in *The Cross Cultural Analysis of Sports and Games,* ed. Gunther Luschen (Champaign, 1978), 31–51.

23. *Mexican Herald,* 16, 29 Sept. 4 Nov., and 27 Dec. 1895; Arthur Inkersley, "A Winter Regatta in Aztec Land," *Outing Magazine* 23, no. 4 (January 1894): 302–8; T. Philip Terry, "In Aztec Land Awheel," *Outing Magazine* 23, no. 6 (March 1894): 461–63, "My Ride to Acapulco: A Cycling Adventure in Mexico," *Outing Magazine* 29, no. 6 (March 1897): 593–96.

24. *Mexican Herald,* 25 Nov., 12, 15, 21, 26, 30 Dec. 1895; J. B. Macmahan, "Polo in the West," *Outing Magazine* 26, no. 5 (August 1895): 385.

25. Jai alai at this time was called Eler Jai; *Mexican Herald,* 10, 12

Nov., 9, 15 Dec. 1895. See also Moisés González Navarro, "The Hours of Leisure," in *The Age of Porfirio Díaz*, ed. Gil, 129–38; Louis A. Zurcher, Jr., and Arnold Meadow, "On Bullfights and Baseball: An Example of Interaction," in *Sport in the Sociocultural Process*, ed. Marie Hart and Susan Birrell (Dubuque, 1981), 654–75.

26. Garold L. Cole, *American Travelers to Mexico, 1821–1972: A Descriptive Bibliography of Criticism* (Troy, 1978).

27. *Mexican Herald*, 19 Sept., 14 Nov., and 3 Dec. 1895.

28. W. Dirk Raat, *Revoltosos: Mexico's Rebels in the United States, 1903–1923* (College Station, 1981); Louis R. Sadler and Charles Harris, "The Witzke Affair: German Intrigue on the Mexican Border," *Military Review* 59, no. 2 (February 1979): 36–50; "The 1911 Reyes Conspiracy," *Southwestern Historical Quarterly* 83, no. 4 (April 1980): 325–48, "The 'Underside' of the Mexican Revolution: El Paso, 1912," *The Americas* 39, no. 1 (July 1982): 69–84.

29. Leo M. Jacques, "Have Quick More Money Than Mandarins: The Chinese in Sonora," *Journal of Arizona History* 17 (1976): 217.

30. *Mexican Herald*, 22 Sept., 9, 30 Oct., 3, 31 Dec. 1895.

31. David C. Bailey and William H. Beezley, *A Guide to Historical Sources in Saltillo, Coahuila* (East Lansing, 1975), 59–61.

32. Charles Macomb Flandrau, *Viva Mexico* (Urbana, 1964), 288.

33. James West Davidson and Mark Hamilton Lytle, *After the Fact: The Art of Historical Detection* (New York, 1982), 113–38.

34. Jas Reuter, "The Popular Traditions," in *Posada's Mexico*, ed. Ron Tyler (Washington, 1979), 67–68; Hugh Hiriart, *El universo de Posada: Estética de la obsolescencia*, vol. 8 of *Memoria y olvido: Imágenes de México* (México, 1982).

35. Gustavo Casasola, *Historia gráfica de la revolución mexicana, 1900–1970*, 5 vols. (México, 1965–71). See also Casasola, *Biografía ilustrada del general Porfirio Díaz, 1830–1915* (México, 1970).

36. For historical analysis of photographs, see Davidson and Lytle, *After the Fact*, 205–31; Steven E. Schoenherr, "Hull-House through Photographs," *Newberry Papers in Family and Community History* (Chicago, 1978), 1–35; for the history of photography in Mexico, see Judith Hancock de Sandoval, "Cien años de fotografía en México (Norteamericanos, Europeos y Japoneses)," *Artes Visuales: Revista Trimestral: Museo de Arte Moderno* 12 (Oct. 1976): i–xvi; Emma Cecilia García, "Possible Outline for a Future Historiography of Photography in Mexico," *Ibid.*, 33–34; Keith McElroy, "Foreing [*sic;* Foreign] Photographers before the Revolution," *Ibid.*, 35–36.

37. These remarks are based on an examination of the Colección C.

B. Waite, expedientes "Vida Cotidiana," "Retratos Étnicos," "Trabajo y Tecnológico," "Fiestas y Diversiones," and "Communicaciones y Transportes," Centro de Información Gráfica del Archivo General de la Nación, México. Waite photographed Mexico during the last decade of the Porfiriato.

38. James W. Wilkie, *The Mexican Revolution: Federal Expenditure and Social Change Since 1910* (Berkeley, 1967), 243–45.

39. See, for example, Terry G. Jordan, *Texas Graveyards: A Cultural Legacy* (Austin, 1982); Everett Dick, *Sod-House Frontier 1854–1890* (New York, 1937); and Henry Glassie, "The Types of the Southern Mountain Cabin," appendix C in *The Study of American Folklore*, Jan Harold Brunvand (New York, 1968), 338–70.

40. Bailey and Beezley, *Guide*, 68–69; Brunvand, *Folklore*, chapter 18, "Folk Architecture, Handicrafts, and Art," 268–86.

41. Flandrau, *Viva Mexico*, 69–70.

42. See Fernand Braudel, *The Structures of Everyday Life: The Limits of the Possible*, trans Siân Reynolds (New York, 1981). Braudel refers to the lives of these people as material life, or material culture; he recreated it by studying what he calls "parahistoric" topics such as "demography, food, costume, lodging, technology, money, towns" (p. 27). Another important historiographic starting point is Carlo Ginzburg, *The Cheese and the Worms: The Cosmos of a Sixteenth-Century Miller*, trans. John and Anne Tedeschi (New York, 1982).

43. Stuart Voss, "Towns and Enterprises in Sonora and Sinaloa, 1876–1910," Ph.D. diss. (Harvard University, 1971); Mark Wasserman, "Foreign Investment in Mexico, 1876–1910: A Case Study of the Role of Regional Elites," *The Americas* 36 (July 1979): 3–21; Thomas Benjamin, "Passages to Leviathan: Chiapas and the Mexican State, 1891–1947," Ph.D. diss. (Michigan State University, 1981).

44. For an effort to examine this opportunity in one region, see William H. Beezley, "Opportunity in Porfirian Mexico," *North Dakota Quarterly* 40 (Spring 1972): 30–40.

45. Paul J. Vanderwood, *Disorder and Progress: Bandits, Police, and Mexican Development* (Lincoln, 1981).

46. Allen Wells, "Henequén and Yucatán: An Analysis in Regional Economic Development, 1876–1915," Ph.D. diss. (State University of New York at Stoney Brook, 1979); G. M. Joseph, *Revolution from Without: Yucatán, Mexico, and the United States, 1880–1924* (Cambridge, 1982), 1–92; Thomas Benjamin, "International Harvester and the Henequén Marketing System in Yucatán, 1898–1915: A New Perspective," *Inter-American Economic Affairs* 31 (Winter 1977): 3–19; William K. Meyers, "Politics, Vested Rights, and Economic Growth in Porfirian Mexico: The

Company Tlahualilo in the Comarca Lagunera, 1885–1911," *Hispanic American Historical Review* 57 (August 1977): 425–54.

47. James A. Starkweather, Jr., "The Ateneo de la Juventud: The Formulation of a Quest," *North Dakota Quarterly* 40 (Spring 1972): 41–50; Josefina Zoraida Vázquez, *Nacionalismo y la educación* (México, 1970); Mary Kay Vaughan, *The State, Education, and Social Class in Mexico, 1880–1928* (De Kalb, 1982).

48. James D. Cockcroft, "El maestro de primaria en la Revolución Mexicana," *Historia Mexicana* 16 (April 1967): 565–87; Archivo General del Estado de Coahuila, legajo 311, expediente Congreso: legajo 306, expediente Saltillo.

49. Irving Leonard, *Baroque Times in Old Mexico* (Ann Arbor, 1959).

50. Abraham González, father of Chihuahua's revolutionary governor, denounced vacant lands in Temosachic, 7 July 1879, and three years later ceded them to Celso Gonzalez, who later sold them to William Randolph Hearst. These lands were the basis for the Barbicoa holding. See title search in behalf of Phebe Hearst and the Barbicoa Company, Archivo de la Secretaría de la Reforma Agraria, Ramo: Tierras Nacionales, Baldíos, legato 1.21(06), expediente 628. (My thanks to Paul Vanderwood for bringing this information to my attention.)

51. See the Guadarrama Collection, University Archives, New Mexico State University, Las Cruces. See also Haldeen Braddy, *Mexico and the Old Southwest: People, Palaver, and Places* (Port Washington, 1971), chapters entitled "The Underworld of Pablote and La Nacha," 74–79, and "Smugglers' Argot in the Southwest," 95–101.

52. González, *San José de Gracia*, xxv.

Suggestions for Additional Reading: Still Other Mexicos

The secondary literature on Porfirian Mexico is vast. Over two thousand books, pamphlets, and articles pertaining entirely or in large part to the Porfiriato have been published over the last one hundred years. While it is true that a large portion of this historiography has little enduring value, it is difficult to know where to begin. There is no substitute, of course, for plunging ahead and reading as much as possible. Beginning students and even old hands, however, could benefit from consulting several excellent historiographical essays that discuss the classic works and give some organization to interpretative trends, past and present, within the field.

Historiographical Essays

The only essay that analyzes the history of Porfirian historiography is Thomas Benjamin and Marcial Ocasio, "Organizing the Memory of Modern Mexico: Mexico's Porfirian Historiography in Perspective,

1880s–1980s," *Hispanic American Historical Review* 64 (May, 1984). Daniel Cosío Villegas has briefly sketched the political and diplomatic historiography and compiled extensive bibliographies in "El Porfiriato: Su historiografía o arte histórico," which is in his book *Extremos de América* (México, 1949), 113–82; and in such articles as "La historiografía política del México moderno," *Memoria de El Colegio Nacional* 2 (1952): 36–111; "México-Guatemala, 1867–1911: Una bibliografía para el estudio de sus relaciones," *Memoria de El Colegio Nacional* 3 (1959), 55–120; "Nueva historiografía política del México moderno," *Memoria de El Colegio Nacional* 5 (1965): 11–176; and "Última bibliografía política de la historia moderna de México," *Memoria de El Colegio Nacional* 7 (1970): 41–222. An excellent analysis of some of the revolutionary-period views of the Porfiriato is provided by Alvaro Matute, "La revolución mexicana y la escritura de su historia," *Revista de la Universidad de México* 36 (Jan. 1982): 2–6. Also of interest in this regard is Robert A. Potash, "Historiography of Mexico since 1821," *Hispanic American Historical Review* 40 (Aug. 1960): 383–424. The more recent contributions are discussed by Laurens B. Perry, "Political Historiography of the Porfirian Period of Mexican History," in *Investigaciones contemporaneas sobre historia de México: Memorias de la Tercera Reunion de Historiadores Mexicanos y Norteamericanos, Oaxtepec, Morelos, 4–7 de Noviember de 1969* (México, 1969), 458–77; Anthony T. Bryan, "Political Power in Porfirio Díaz's Mexico: A Review and Commentary," *The Historian* 38 (Nov. 1975): 648–68; and Stephen R. Niblo and Laurens B. Perry, "Recent Additions to Nineteenth-Century Mexican Historiography," *Latin American Research Review* 8, no. 3 (1978): 3–45.

General Porfirian Histories

One of the most impressive works in all of Mexican historiography is the ten-volume *Historia moderna de México* (México, 1955–72), organized, edited, and partly written by Daniel Cosío Villegas. The *Historia moderna* covers the period 1867–1911; six volumes are devoted exclusively to the Porfiriato. This is an encyclopedic work that contains considerable political, social, and economic information on the various states and important regions. Still, as several reviewers have noted, there is a definite emphasis on events in the capital city and dependence upon Mexico City newspapers as source material. The same reservation applies to the classic histories of the period: Justo Sierra, coord., *México, su evolución social,* 3 vols. (México, 1900–1902); Francisco Bulnes, *El verdadero Díaz y la revolución* (México, 1920); Emilio Rabasa, *La evolución histórica de México* (México, 1920); José López-Portillo y Rojas, *Elevación y caída de Porfirio Díaz* (México, 1921); and Ricardo García Granados, *Historia de México desde la restauración de la república en 1867 hasta la caída de Huerta,* 4 vols. (México, 1923–28). The best modern works of synthesis, which also betray a metropolitan bias, however, are José C. Valadés, *El Porfirismo: Historia de un régimen,* 3 vols. (México, 1941–48); Jorge Fernando Iturribarria, *Porfirio Díaz ante la historia* (México, 1967); and Ralph Roeder, *Hacia el México moderno: Porfirio Díaz,* 2 vols. (México, 1973). Two general works in English— Wilfred Hardy Callcott, *Liberalism in Mexico, 1857–1929* (Stanford, 1931); and Carleton Beals, *Porfirio Díaz, Dictator of Mexico* (New York, 1932)—have long been out of date. A useful anthology of readings on this period is edited by Carlos B. Gil, *The Age of Porfirio Díaz: Selected Readings* (Albuquerque, 1977). See also W. Dirk Raat, ed., *Mexico: From Independence to Revolution, 1810–1910* (Lincoln, 1982).

Regional History: Where to Begin

Most local, regional, and state histories of the Porfirian period were written by contemporary local historians. Luis González y González provides the best bibliography of these little-known histories published in Mexico between 1871 and 1970 in *Invitación a la microhistoria* (México, 1973), 98–183. Each of Cosío Villegas's bibliographies, furthermore, has a section entitled "Historias Particulares" that includes local, regional, and state histories. One often overlooked source of regional Porfirian history is travel accounts by foreigners. A bibliography of 394 titles is provided by C. Harvy Gardiner, "Foreign Travelers' Accounts of Mexico, 1810–1910," *The Americas* 8 (Jan. 1952): 321–51. Of even greater interest and value is Garold L. Cole's *American Travelers to Mexico, 1821–1972: A*

Descriptive Bibliography of Criticism (Troy, N.Y., 1978). Two journals which regularly publish articles on regional Mexican history are *Historia Mexicana* (published by El Colegio de México) and *Relaciones: Estudios de Historia y Sociedad* (published by El Colegio de Michoacán). There are also several excellent regional historical journals, such as the *Revista de la Universidad de Yucatán*.

Themes in regional Mexican history are discussed in Harry Bernstein, "Regionalism in the National History of Mexico," in *Latin American History: Essays on Its Study and Teaching, 1898–1965*, edited by Howard Cline, 2 vols. (Austin, 1967), 1: 389–94; Lydia Espinosa, "Historia regional: El rincón de la fatalidad," *Nexos: Sociedad, Ciencia, Literatura* 1, no. 7 (July 1978) 11–13; Barry Carr, "Recent Regional Studies of the Mexican Revolution," *Latin American Research Review* 15, no. 1 (1980): 3–14; and Luis González y González, *Invitación;* and *Nueva invitación a la microhistoria* (México, 1982), chapter 7, "Guía para monógrafos de las provincias de México."

A few studies have synthesized earlier regional findings and demonstrate the kind of imaginative work that can and should be applied to other topics and broad regions. See Daniel Cosío Villegas, "El norte de Porfirio Díaz," *Anuario de Historia* 1 (1961): 13–57; Barry Carr, "Las particularidades del norte mexicano, 1880–1927: Ensayo de interpretación," *Historia Mexicana* 22 (Jan.–March 1973): 320–46; Ronald Waterbury, "Non-Revolutionary Peasants: Oaxaca Compared to Morelos in the Mexican Revolution," *Comparative Studies in Society and History* 17 (1973): 410–42; Friedrich Katz, "Labor Conditions on Haciendas in Porfirian Mexico: Some Trends and Tendencies," *Hispanic American Historical Review* 54 (Feb. 1974): 1–47; Jean Meyer, *Problemas campesinos y revueltos agrarios (1821–1910)* (México, 1975); and Moisés González Navarro, "El trabajo forzoso en México, 1821–1917," *Historia Mexicana* 27 (April–June 1978): 588–615.

Regional History: Social and Economic Topics

The growth industry within recent historiography is social and economic history. Rural labor and the history of the *campesinado* during the Porfiriato is almost entirely a new field, in no small way due to: Moisés González Navarro, *Raza y tierra: La guerra de castas y el henequén* (México, 1970); Raymond Th. Buve, "Protesta de obreros y campesinos durante el Porfiriato: Unas consideraciones sobre su desarrollo e interrelaciones en el este de México central," *Boletín de Estudios Latinoamericanos* 13 (Dec. 1972): 1–20; Jan Bazant, "Peones, arrendatarios y aparceros: 1868–1904," *Historia Mexicana* 24 (July–Sept. 1974): 94–121; and "El trabajo y los trabajadores en la Hacienda de Atlacomulco," in *El trabajo y los trabajadores en la historia de México,* ed. Else C. Frost, Michael C. Meyer, and Josefina Vázquez (México, 1979), 378–90; and Thomas Benjamin, "El trabajo en las monterías de Chiapas y Tabasco, 1870–1946," *Historia Mexicana* 30 (April–June 1981): 506–29. Rural unrest in regional settings is documented in Leticia Reina, *Las rebeliones campesinas en México, 1819–1906* (México, 1980); and analyzed in Arturo Warman, *Y venimos a contradecir: Los campesinos de Morelos y el estado nacional* (México, 1976); John M. Hart, *Anarchism and the Mexican Working Class, 1860–1931* (Austin, 1978); Paul J. Vanderwood, *Disorder and Progress: Bandits, Police, and Mexican Development* (Lincoln, 1981); Elena Azaola Garrido, *Rebelión y derrota del magonismo agrario* (México, 1982); and Donald Fithian Stevens, "Agrarian Policy and Instability in Porfirian Mexico," *The Americas* 39 (Oct. 1982): 153–66.

Economic institutions and development in regional settings is examined in Edith Couturier, "Modernización y tradición en una hacienda: San Juan Hueyapan, 1902–1911," *Historia Mexicana* 18 (July–Sept. 1968): 35–55; Jan Bazant, *Cinco haciendas mexicanas: Tres siglos de vida rural en San Luis Potosí (1600–1910)* (México, 1975); Frederic Mauro, "El desarrollo industrial de Monterrey (1890–1960)," in *Los beneficiarios del desarrollo regional,* ed. David Barkin (México, 1972), 96–124; William K. Meyers, "Politics, Vested Interests, and Economic Growth in Porfirian Mexico: The Company Tlahualilo in the Comarca Lagunera, 1885–1911," *Hispanic American Historical Review* 57 (Aug. 1977): 425–55; Allen Wells, "Economic Growth and Regional Disparity in Porfirian Mexico: The Case of the Southeastern Railway Company," *South Eastern Latin Americanist* 22 (Sept. 1978): 1–16; Frans J Schryer, "A Ranchero Economy in Northwestern Hidalgo, 1880–1920," *Hispanic American Historical Review* 59 (Aug. 1979): 418–43; Leo E. Zonn, "The Railroads of Sonora and Sinaloa, Mexico: A Historical Survey," *Social Science Jour-*

nal 15 (April 1978): 1–15; and Bernardo García Díaz, *Un pueblo fabril del Porfiriato: Santa Rosa, Veracruz* (México, 1982). The role of foreign investment during the Porfiriato upon economic growth, social structures, and politics is most thoroughly examined in regional studies. See Mark Wasserman, "Oligarquía e intereses extranjeros en Chihuahua durante el Porfiriato," *Historia Mexicana* 22 (Jan.–March 1973): 279–319; and "Foreign Investment in Mexico, 1876–1911: A Case Study of the Role of Regional Elites," *The Americas* 36 (July 1979): 3–21; Gilbert M. Joseph and Allen Wells, "Corporate Control of a Monocrop Economy: International Harvester and Yucatán's Henequén Industry during the Porfiriato," *Latin American Research Review* 17, no. 1 (1982): 69–113; Allen Wells, "Family Elites in a Boom-and-Bust Economy: The Molinas and Peóns of Porfirian Yucatán," *Hispanic American Historical Review* 62 (May 1982): 224–53; and G. M. Joseph, *Revolution from Without: Yucatán, Mexico, and the United States, 1880–1924* (Cambridge, 1982).

Regional History: Political and Church-State Topics

Political history no longer monopolizes the output of Porfirian studies. Research on state and regional politics has tended to concentrate on the north, and specifically the state of Chihuahua. Anthony T. Bryan has examined Nuevo León in "El papel del General Bernardo Reyes en la política nacional y regional de México," *Humanitas* 13 (1972): 331–40. San Luis Potosí and Morelos are discussed by James D. Cockcroft, *Intellectual Precursors of the Mexican Revolution* (Austin, 1968); and John Womack, Jr., *Zapata and the Mexican Revolution* (New York, 1969). For Chihuahua we have Harold D. Sims, "Espejo de caciques: Los Terrazas de Chihuahua," *Historia Mexicana* 18 (1969): 379–99; Robert Sandels, "Silvestre Terrazas and the Old Regime in Chihuahua," *The Americas* 28 (1971): 191–205; William H. Beezley, "Chihuahua in the Díaz Era," in *Mexico: From Independence to Revolution*, ed. Raat, 219–31; Sandels, "Antecedentes de la revolución en Chihuahua," *Historia Mexicana* 24 (1975): 390–402; and Mark Wasserman, "The Social Origins of the 1910 Revolution in Chihuahua," *Latin American Research Review* 15, no. 1 (1980): 15–38.

Issues pertaining to the Church-state relationship outside of Mexico City are examined in José Roberto Juárez, "The Use of Counter-Oaths in the Archdiocese of Guadalajara, Mexico, 1876–1911," *Journal of Church and State* 12 (1970): 79–87; and Karl M. Schmitt, "The Díaz Conciliation Policy on State and Local Levels, 1876–1911," *Hispanic American Historical Review* 40 (1960): 513–32.

Community Studies

There are several outstanding community studies which treat the Porfiriato, at least in passing. At the top of every list is Luis González's prize-winning *Pueblo en vilo: Microhistoria de San José de Gracia* (México, 1968), translated by John Upton and published in English as *San José de Gracia: Mexican Village in Transition* (Austin, 1974). Paul Friedrich examines the village of Naranja, in the state of Michoacán, in *Agrarian Revolt in a Mexican Village* (Englewood Cliffs, N.J., 1970); Henri Favre examines the Indian municipios of the highlands of the state of Chiapas in *Cambio y continuidad entre los mayas de México* (México, 1973); Mario T. García examines the Mexican immigrants of El Paso, Texas, in *Desert Immigrants: The Mexicans of El Paso, 1880–1920* (New Haven, 1981); Oscar J. Martínez examines El Paso's sister city, *Border Boom Town: Ciudad Juárez since 1848* (Austin, 1978); and Bernardo García Díaz examines a Veracruz mill town in *Un pueblo fabril del Porfiriato: Santa Rosa, Veracruz* (México, 1982).

Research Guides

The preceding list of titles is suggestive, not exhaustive. For those interested in pursuing original research, the single most important documentary source is the Colección General Porfirio Díaz. Thousands of letters from states, regions, and localities describe, often in great detail, political events, social and economic problems and developments, and local-state and state-federal relations. The original documents are open to researchers at the Universidad Iberoamericana in Mexico City, and a microfilm copy is located at the Universidad de las Americas in Cholula, Puebla. Laurens B. Perry has published a nondescriptive inventory of the microfilm collection in *Inventario y guía de la Colección General Porfirio Díaz* (México, 1969). Useful guides to other important documentary collections are J. Jesús García y García, *Guía de archivos contienen material de interés para el estudio del desarrollo socioeconómico de México* (México, 1972); Richard E. Greenleaf and Michael C. Meyer, eds., *Research in Mexican History: Topics, Methodology, Sources, and a Practical Guide to Field Research* (Lincoln, 1973); Michael Grow, *Scholars' Guide to Washington D.C. for Latin American and Caribbean Studies* (Wash., D.C., 1979); and Enrique Arriola Woog, coord., *Guía general de los fondos que contiene El Archivo General de la Nación* (México, 1981). One particularly useful guide to Mexican archives with regional materials is John Hart, "The Advancement of Mexican Historical Studies: An Assessment of the Archivo Histórico del Tribunal Superior del Distrito y Territorios Federales and the Archivo Seis de Enero de 1915 of the Comisión Nacional Agraria," *The Americas* (July 1980), 101–10.

Archival guides to state and local manuscript collections vary widely in quality and quantity. Researchers should first direct their attention to Manuel Carrera Stampa, *Archivalia Mexicana* (México, 1952); and C. Alan Hutchinson, "Bibliographical Guide to Archival Collections in the Mexican States," in *Research in Mexican History*, ed. Greenleaf and Meyer, 193–96. A few historical journals—*The Americas, Historia Mexicana, Relaciones,* and the *Boletín del Archivo General de la Nación*—occasionally publish short guides to state and local archives. The Instituto Nacional de Antropología e Historia (INAH) in Mexico City has microfilmed considerable portions of many state archives. See Antonio Pompa y Pompa, "Contribución del Instituto Nacional de Antropología e Historia para la conservación de los archivos mexicanos fuera de la capital," in *Memoria del Primer Congreso de Historiadores de México y los Estados Unidos* (México, 1950), 71–81. The Departamento de Investigaciones Históricas of INAH, in collaboration with the Archivo General de la Nación, is currently preparing and publishing catalogs of regional and local archives. This project is discussed by Sergio Ortega Noriega, "Archivos históricos regionales y locales: Un proyecto de catálogo," *Boletín del Archivo General de la Nación* (July–Sept. 1977): 33–34. Two excellent guides that are models for further such efforts are David C. Bailey and William H. Beezley, *A Guide to Historical Sources in Saltillo, Coahuila* (East Lansing, 1975); and Maria del Pilar

Sánchez Gómez, *Catálogo de fuentes de la historia de Tamaulipas*, 2 vols. (Ciudad Victoria, 1976).

In the final analysis, investigators of regional Mexican history have to blaze their own trails. Published guides only scratch the surface. The difficulties and thrills of discovering other Mexicos go hand in hand. For those who want to investigate regional Mexico, topics and documents exist in abundance.

The Editors

Thomas Benjamin is Assistant Professor of History at Central Michigan University. He received his Ph.D. at Michigan State University in 1981 and held a Doherty Fellowship for Advanced Study in Latin America in 1980–1981. He has published articles in *Historia Mexicana, The Americas, New Mexico Historical Review,* and *Inter-American Economic Affairs.*

William McNellie is a Foreign Political Analyst at the Central Intelligence Agency in Washington, D.C. He received his Ph.D. from Michigan State University in 1981 and was a Fulbright-Hayes Research Fellow in Mexico in 1978–1979. He has published articles in *The Red River Valley Historical Journal, The Americas,* and *Latin American Digest.*

The Contributors

Stanley Langston is a Policy Analyst at the Department of Defense in Washington, D.C. He received his Ph.D. from Tulane University in 1980 and has published an article in *The Red River Valley Historical Journal.*

Mark Wasserman is Assistant Professor of History at Douglass College, Rutgers University. He received his Ph.D. from the University of Chicago in 1975. He co-authored, with Benjamin Keen, *A Short History of Latin America* published in 1980 and has published articles in *Historia Mexicana, The Americas,* and *Latin American Research Review.*

Evelyn Hu-DeHart is Associate Professor of History at Washington University, St. Louis. She received her Ph.D. from the University of Texas at Austin in 1976. Her book *Missionaries, Miners, and Indians* was published in 1981. She currently holds a Social Science Research Council Grant to study Chinese immigrants in Mexico.

Frans J. Schryer is Associate Professor of Sociology and Anthropology at the University of Guelp, Ontario. His book *The Rancheros of Pisaflores* was published in 1980.

Allen Wells is Assistant Professor of History at Appalachian State University. He received his Ph.D. from the State University of New York at Stony Brook in 1979 and held an Organization of American States Dissertation Fellowship in 1976–1977. He has published articles in *Latin American Research Review, South Eastern Latin Americanist,* and *Revista de la Universidad de Yucatán.*

Daniela Spenser is a Research Fellow at the Centro de Investigaciones y Estudios, Escuela Superior de Antropología e Historia in Mexico City. She is a graduate of the University of London and formerly a professor of Mexican history at the Universidad Autónoma de Chiapas, San Cristóbal Las Casas.

Index

age of dominance, the, 61
agriculture, commercial, 15, 16, 120, 145, 290; Hidalgo, 153; Soconusco, 126, 127; Sonora, 178, 182, 200
Ahumada, Miguel, 42, 49, 277, 278
Alba, Victor, 4
Almada, Adolfo, 183
Alvarado, Evaristo, 158, 160–62, 163
Alvarado family, the, 160–61, 163
amendments, 10, 11, 59
Anti-Reelectionists, 45, 47, 48, 83, 265
Arellano family, the, 43
Arizpe y Ramos, Francisco, 64, 65
army, the federal, 7, 8, 10, 42, 81, 93, 163, 222, 253, 266, 291

Arnold, Channing, 214, 234
art, 287–88
authoritarianism, 55
autonomy, 277
ayuntamiento, 34
Aztec, the, 4, 124, 148, 282

Bailyn, Bernard, 19
banditry, 255, 267
Barbarous Mexico, 189
Barrios, Justo Rufino, 126, 127, 128
Baz, Enrique, 60
Benítez, Fernando, 228
Benjamin, Thomas, 291
Bonilla, Pomposo M., 87

Braudel, Fernand, 294
Brazil, 139
Bryan, Anthony, 275

Cacho Alonzo, Francisco, 226
Cahuantzi, Próspero, 80
Cajeme, José Mará Leyva, 184
Calderón de la Barca, Fanny, 7
Calles, Plutarco, Elías, 178, 180
Calzada, Gabriel, 68
Cámara Peón, José Encarnación, 224
camarillas, 56
campesinos, 174, 233
Cañete, Rafael P., 91
capitalism, dependent, 123, 139 n 1
Carascosa, Manuel, 131
Cárdenas, Lázaro, 178
Cárdenas, Miguel, 58, 60–69
Cárdenistas, 56, 63
Carranza, Venustiano, 166, 278
Carranza brothers, the, 58, 62
Carrasco, Juan B., 78, 97
Carrillo, Lauro, 39, 41
Carson, W. E., 173
Casares, Eulalio, 226
Casas Grandes, 49
Casasola, Gustavo, 288
Casavantes, Jesús José, 37, 38, 39
centralists, 7, 8
centralization, 55, 276
Cepeda, Victoriano, 56
Cervantes, Julio, 58, 59, 61
Chiapas, 124, 131
Chihuahua, 28, 33
Chinese, the, 181, 192, 196, 285
Church, the, 7, 8, 148, 180, 280
científicos, 13, 42, 58, 66, 67, 68
Círculo de los Gobernadores, 277
clothing, 146, 289
Club Democratico Benito Juárez, 68, 69
Club Unión Liberal, 67
Coahuila, 29, 55
Coatsworth, John, 279, 293
Cockcroft, James, 292
coffee, 124, 129, 134, 137, 154

Colección General Porfirio Díaz, 276
communication, 81, 96, 150. *See also* railroads, transportation
Conservatives, the, 36, 37, 178
Contreras, Calixto, 253, 254, 269
Corral, Ramón, 69, 183, 189, 193, 277, 294
Cosío Villegas, Daniel, 13
Cravioto family, the, 161
Creel, Enrique C., 40, 41, 42, 45, 46, 277
Creelman, James, 12
Cuamatzi, Juan, 85

Dávila, Encarnación, 59
del Pozo, Agustín, 93, 97
Díaz, Felix, 96
Díaz, Porfirio, 3, 9, 293, 294; Chinese policy of, 192, 203, 205; Coahuila and, 59, 61, 65, 69, 70, 71; Escobar and, 127; first term of, 9; Hidalgo and, 151, 159; immigrant policy of, 194; Laguna and, 247, 252, 261, 266; Puebla and, 79, 82, 85, 89; resignation of, 29, 49, 89, 269; second term of, 10; Soconusco and, 135; Sonora and, 183; Yaqui policy of, 174, 188, 189, 204
diet, 231, 289
Dunning, Eric, 283
Durán, Juan N., 225

economics: Chiapas, 124; Chihuahua, 40, 42; Chinese business, 196–98, 200; coffee, 124, 129, 134, 137, 154; cotton, 246, 247, 250; deportation and Yaqui, 191; development of ranchero, 150; henequen, 213, 219, 228, 233; Hidalgo, 150, 154; Laguna, 246, 247, 250; modernization, 140 n 2; partnerships, 43, 134; regional specialization, 123; rural growth, 119; Sonora, 184; sugar, 150; Terrazas, 40, 42
Edge of the Storm, The, 281

education, 158, 292
elections, 80, 277; Coahuila and, 63, 66; Puebla and, 94, 95, 96, 97
Elguezabal family, the, 56
Elias, Norbert, 283
Escobar, Sebastián, 127, 132

Falcón, Cayetano Ramos, 58
family power, 277, 294; Coahuila and, 56, 58, 67; Hidalgo and, 149, 161; Puebla and, 87; Sonora and, 182; the Terrazas, 33, 36, 43
Farrera, Agustín, 132
federalists, 7, 8
Figuerro, Manuel, 132
Filisola, Vicente, 124
Flandrau, Charles, 284, 286
Flores Magón, Ricardo, 250; Magonistas, 270
Flores Magón brothers, the, 45. See also Partido Liberal Mexicano
Flores, Nicolás, 162, 163, 166
foreign enterprise, 11, 19, 284, 290, 292; Chihuahua and, 36, 41, 44; Coahuila and, 60; Sonora and, 178, 190
French Intervention, the, 6, 8, 33, 34, 37, 61, 150, 159, 178
Friedrich, Paul, 281
Frost, Frederick J. Tabor, 214, 234
Fuentes, Frumencio, 58, 62, 69, 70

Galán family, the, 56
Gálvez, José, 68
García, Fructuoso, 69
García Peña, Ángel, 182
Garza, Catarino E., 41
Garza Galán, José María, 56, 59
Garza Galanistas, 56, 64, 65, 68, 69
Genovese, Eugene, 233
González, Abraham, 49, 299 n 50
González, Carlos, 58
González, Celso, 39, 40
González, Luis, 275, 282
González, Manuel, 10, 15, 39

governorship, the, 276–79
Guatemala, 124, 126–29, 135
guerrerenses, 39–41
Gutman, Herbert G., 173
Guttmann, Allen, 283

haciendas, 294
Hacienda de Encinillas, 36
Hacienda San José Kuché, 229
Harris, Charles, 277, 285
Hearst, William Randolph, 299 n 50
henequen, 213, 219, 228, 233
Henkel, Guillermo, 133
Herrera, Cástulo, 48, 49
Herrera, Jesús, 62
Herrera, Manuel de, 39
Hidalgo, 145. See also Sierra de Jacala
Hipólito, Charles, 56, 59
Hubbe de Molina, Luisa, 235
Hu-DeHart, Evelyn, 176, 285
Huerta, Adolfo de la, 178
Huerta, Victoriano, 78, 98, 163
Huller, Luis, 128

immigrants, 6, 285; Chihuahua and, 36; Chinese, 181, 192, 196; German, 36, 133–35, 137; Hidalgo and, 150, 153; Laguna and, 248; Soconusco and, 129, 131, 133–35, 137; Sonora and, 181, 192, 193, 196; Yucatán and, 226, 227
indebtedness, 131, 153, 220, 231
Indians: Chihuahua and, 34; Díaz policy on, 281; Hidalgo and, 146, 148, 149; Laguna and, 251, 252; Mayan, 214; Soconusco and, 131, 132; Sonora and, 173, 180, 184, 187; Yaqui, 180, 184, 227; Yucatán and, 214, 227
industrialization, 12
insurrection, 18, 34, 93. See also rebellion, revolts
Isunza, José Rafael, 86
Izábel, Rafael, 183, 186–88

Japanese, the, 285
jefes políticos, 11, 279; Chihuahua and,

47; Coahuila and, 59, 70; Hidalgo and, 152; Nueva León and, 278; Puebla and, 80, 82, 87; Soconusco and, 127, 132; Yucatán and, 222, 225, 234
Joseph, Gilbert M., 30
journalists, 280
Juárez, Benito, 8, 9, 36, 38, 126, 146, 152, 158

Katz, Friedrich, 17, 19, 231
Ki, 228

LaFrance, David, 30
Laguna, the, 247
Lajous, Luis, 58
land: codueñazgo, 168 n 16; desamortización, 152; expropriation of, 15, 17, 22 n 22, 48, 120, 131, 182, 221; Hidalgo rancheros, 145, 156, 161, 163, 164; Laguna smallholders, 251; Soconusco development, 128, 129, 137
Langston, William Stanley, 30
laws, 286
Ledezma, Dolores, 161
Leonard, Irving, 293
León de la Barra, Francisco, 91, 92
Lerdo de Tejada, Sebastián, 8, 9, 38, 127, 152
Leytón, Guillermo, 197, 202
Liberals, the, 8, 9, 34, 158, 221, 276
Limantour, José Y., 13, 42, 56, 66, 294
Llevera, Armando, 81
Logan, Walter, 185
Lucas, Juan Francisco, 81, 88

Maas, Joaquín, 98
Maceyra, Félix Francisco, 39
Madero, Emilio, 268, 269
Madero, Evaristo, 56, 59, 68, 263
Madero family, the, 42, 277
Maderistas, 56, 60, 66, 67, 69, 82, 85, 88, 89, 90
Madero, Francisco I., 29, 45, 48, 49, 78, 276, 278; Coahuila and, 68, 79; Laguna and, 264; Meléndez and, 90, 92, 93, 94, 95; Puebla and, 83; Sonora and, 192
Magonistas, 270. *See also* Flores Magón brothers, the
Maldonado, José E., 225
Maldonado, Juan, Tetabiate, 185
Martínez, Joaquín, 159
Martínez, Mucio P., 78, 94
Mata, Margarito, 159, 162
material culture, 289
Maytorena, José María, Sr., 182, 183
Maytorena family, the, 192
Meléndez, Nicolás, 94
Méndez, Santiago, 234
Mendoza, Camerino Z., 91
Merodio, Telesforo, 127
Mexican American War, the, 7, 8
Mexican Liberal Party, 250, 259, 261, 262, 264. *See also* Partido Liberal Mexicano
Mexico City, 4, 6, 12, 13, 17, 182, 247; Chihuahua and, 46, 48; Coahuila and, 61, 70; Puebla and, 92, 94; rancheros and, 146, 162; Yucatán and, 226
Meyers, William K., 176
Michoacán, 14
migration, 281. *See also* immigration
militia, 80, 95, 222. *See also* army, the federal; rurales
mining, 44, 59, 182, 206
Molina, Olegario, 16, 189, 226
Montejo, Demetrio, 223
Montes, Avelino, 235
Municipal Land Laws, 45, 48
Muñoz, José Eligio, 37
Múzquiz, José María, 63, 64
Múzquiz family, the, 56

Naranjo, Francisco, 56, 59
nationalism, 6–8, 180, 201
New Spain, 6
Nuevo León, 58, 60, 66, 278

Oaxaca, 16
Obregón, Álvaro, 178
Ochoa, Antonio, 38
Olvera, Rafael, 159
oral tradition, 287
Orozco, Pascual, Jr., 48, 49, 96
Ortega, Toribio, 48, 49
Ortega y Gasset, José, 61
Ortiz Peace, the, 185

Pacheco, Carlos, 39, 41
Partido Liberal Mexicano, (PLM), 45, 48, 203, 205, 250, 259, 261, 262, 264
paternalism, 233
Patoni, José María, 37
patria chica, 4, 287
Peón Casares family, the, 233
Peón y Maldonado, Manuel José, 218
people, the, 173, 288
Pérez, Ceferino, 48
personalism, 71
photography, 288
pilgrimage, the, 281
Pimental, Rafael, 132
Pino Suárez, José María, 224
Pisaflores, 148, 150, 155
politics: boundaries of, 290; Coahuila intraelite, 55; concessions, 59, 60, 80; Díaz rivals, 10, 11, 27–29; federal assistance, 9, 65; intraregional, 160; Martínez and Puebla rivals, 81, 83, 84; ranchero, 158; reform, 66, 69, 71, 91; Restored Republic, 8; style, 6; Terrazas rivals, 36, 43. *See also* state government
popular mobilization, 176, 264
population, 282, 284, 286, 290
Posada, José Guadalupe, 288
Potash, Robert, 275
presidios, 48
press, the, 10, 47, 81, 202, 224, 235, 261, 263, 264, 265, 280
Puebla, 15, 29, 77
Purcell, William, 60

Quintana Roo, 16
Quon Yui Sen, Luis, 199

Raat, W. Dirk, 285
Rabasa, Emilio, 131, 132
railroads, 11, 12, 15, 17, 293; Chihuahua and, 39, 48; Coahuila and, 59; Hidalgo and, 154; Laguna and, 247, 249; Soconusco and, 136; Sonora and, 181; Yucatán and, 220
rebellion: Díaz first term and, 10; Mayan Caste War, 219; rural Laguna, 246, 256, 259, 266; Tehuitzingo, 82; Terrazas inspired, 41; Yaqui, 184, 204. *See also* insurrection, revolts
recession, 10, 13, 45, 132, 190, 231, 259
regionalism, 4–9, 18, 276; central, 14; northern, 16, 44; southern, 15
religion, 281; the Church, 7, 8, 148, 180, 280
revolts, 176; Chihuahua and, 45, 48; Coahuila and, 58; early independence and, 7; economic j-curve and, 54 n 41; Laguna worker, 255–57, 262, 266; Liberal, 34; Puebla and, 84, 96; Yucatán worker, 234, 235, 236. *See also* insurrection, rebellion
Revolution, the Mexican, 244; Laguna and, 254, 266; Sierra de Jacala and, 164; Sonora and, 184, 191; Yucatán and, 234
Revolutionary Institutional Party, 30
Reyes, Bernardo, 278, 294; Coahuila and, 59, 62–68; Laguna and, 253, 256; Puebla and, 82, 94
Rivas, Francisco, 68
Rodríguez, José María, 68
Rodríguez, Mauricio, 58
Rodríguez, Pedro, 163
Romero, Matías, 126, 128
Romero Rubio, Manuel, 58, 59
Roosevelt, Theodore, 12
Rosas, Manuel, 58
Rubio, Joseph Joaquín, 149

Rubio family, the, 149, 157, 160–65
rurales, 15, 16, 17, 291

Sadler, Louis R., 285
Saltillo, 60, 65
Samaniego, Mariano, 38
San Andrés, 47, 48
Sánchez Navarros, the, 277
Santa Anna, Antonio López de, 34, 126
Schryer, Frans J., 121
Seargeant, Helen, 129
Serdán, Aquiles, 82, 84, 91
Sierra de Jacala: class structure in, 155; description of, 148; early history of, 148; emergence of ranchero in, 150; local politics in, 158; Mexican Revolution and, 164
Sierra, Justo, 292
Simmons, Merle, 287
Simpson, Lesley Byrd, 7, 288
Sinaloa, 9
smuggling, 294
society, 281–83, 290; Chihuahua and, 44, 47, 48; Chinese threat to, 202, 206; Coahuila elite, 56; folk life, 287; geosocial units, 289; Hidalgo and, 146, 151, 155, 166; Laguna and, 247, 264; plantation, 216, 232; protest mobilization, 244, 246, 251, 254, 264; Puebla and, 86, 89; ranchero, 146, 151, 166
Soconusco, 124, 127, 132
Sonora, 9
Southworth, John R., 197
Spenser, Daniela, 121
sports, 283
state government, 278; Hidalgo rancheros and, 158; modernization, 140 n 2; replacing officials in, 47, 59, 87, 92, 159, 166, 183; Soconusco oligarchy, 132
sugar, 150

Talamantes, Porfirio, 48
Tampochocho, 149, 151, 160, 163
Tannenbaum, Frank, 12
taxation, 47, 60, 83, 132, 156
Tenochtitlán, 6
Terrazas, Luis, 28, 33, 36, 37, 183
Terrazas family, the, 33, 36, 42, 46, 48, 277, 278, 291
Terrazas, Silvestre, 47, 49
Torres, Luis, 183, 185, 189
trade, 6, 135, 154, 197; tiendas de raya, 38, 199, 221
transportation, 135, 223, 293. See also communication, railroads
Treaty of Ciudad Juárez, 89
Treviño, Francisco, 62
Treviño, Gerónimo, 67
Trías, Angel, Sr., 34, 37
Trías, Angel, Jr., 38
Turner, John Kenneth, 189, 214, 225
Turner, Victor, 281
tuxtepecanos, 38
Tweetie, Mrs., 284
Tyler, Ronnie, 288

Ugalde, Sixto, 254
United States, the, 8, 17; Chihuahua and, 40 44; Chinese and, 193, 199, 201; Laguna and, 257, 258, 260, 264, 266; social unrest and, 173; Soconusco and, 126, 128, 136, 137, 139; Sonora and, 177, 181; Yaqui problem and, 188, 190; Yucatán and, 214, 231, 232

Valdéz family, the, 58
Valenzuelas, the, 277
Valle, Luis G., 80, 85, 86
Vanderwood, Paul J., 10, 275, 291
Vázquez Gómez, Emilio, 93, 96
Vázquez Gómez, Francisco, 93
Vazquistas, 94
Viesca y Arizpe, Mariano, 68
Villa, Pancho, 48, 49
Virgin of Guadalupe, the, 280
Voss, Stuart F., 9, 291

Wallace, Dillon, 174

wanted posters, 287
War of Reform, the, 8, 33, 34, 150
Wasserman, Mark, 3, 30
Wells, Allen, 176
Wilkie, James, 288
Wilkie, Richard, 281
Willard, A., 193
workers: Chihuahua and, 43; Chinese, 194–96, 199; henequen, 214, 217, 221, 228; Hidalgo and, 154, 164; Laguna and, 248, 250, 251, 254, 262; mobilization of, 176, 264; protest by, 235, 251, 254; Soconusco and, 127, 131, 138; United States/Yucatán contrast, 232; Yaqui, 186, 227; Yucatán and, 214, 217–19, 221, 224, 228

Yáñez, Agustín, 281
Yucatán, 16, 188

Zapata, Emiliano, 93, 146
Zapatistas, 95

www.ingramcontent.com/pod-product-compliance
Lightning Source LLC
Chambersburg PA
CBHW021832220426
43663CB00005B/216